D0875451

IMPROBABLE PATRIOT

IMPROBABLE PATRIOT

The Secret History of Monsieur de Beaumarchais,
the French Playwright Who Saved
the American Revolution

HARLOW GILES UNGER

UNIVERSITY PRESS OF NEW ENGLAND

HANOVER AND LONDON

University Press of New England
www.upne.com
© 2011 Harlow Giles Unger
All rights reserved

Manufactured in the United States of America
Designed by April Leidig-Higgins

Typeset in Garamond Premier Pro by Copperline Book Services, Inc.

University Press of New England is a member of the
Green Press Initiative. The paper used in this book meets
their minimum requirement for recycled paper.

Library of Congress Cataloging-in-Publication Data
appear on the last printed page of this book.

5 4 3 2 1

IN MEMORY OF MY FRIEND

Edward W. Knappman

Gold, by God! It's the fuel of life. I shall by my wiles
put vigilance to sleep, awaken love, seduce with songs —
mislead, intrigue, and overcome all obstacles.

FIGARO

CONTENTS

Contents

ILLUSTRATIONS

IN 1853, Professor Louis de Loménie of the Collège de France on the Left Bank in Paris described following one of Beaumarchais's grandsons up to the attic of a house on the rue du Pas-de-la-Mule, which runs into the boulevard Beaumarchais. Indeed, the corner of rue du Pas-de-la-Mule and the boulevard Beaumarchais marks the corner of what had been the sumptuous one-acre Paris estate and home of Beaumarchais. The French government appropriated the entire property in 1818 and leveled it to make room for the big boulevard that now bears the Beaumarchais name and runs into the place de la Bastille.

What Loménie says he found in that "uninhabited and silent cell—beneath a thick layer of dust—were . . . all the papers left fifty-four years ago by the author of *Le Mariage de Figaro.*" When the government razed the Beaumarchais property, Loménie explained, "his papers were removed to a neighboring house and stored in the room where I found them." After the death of his wife and daughter, his son-in-law and grandchildren decided to leave the remaining Beaumarchais papers untouched—and so they did, for twenty years, until they granted Loménie access. Admitting that he felt "as if I was performing an exhumation," Loménie spent the next four years studying the Beaumarchais papers and writing what remains the definitive biography of Pierre-Augustin Caron de Beaumarchais. The Loménie biography runs two volumes in French (one volume in the English translation) and is a vital resource for all Beaumarchais biographers. Loménie was the only person to have had access to all the Beaumarchais papers during the fifty years after Beaumarchais's death.

Although a trove of papers still exists, many of the papers that Loménie examined and cited have disappeared—either into private collections or into dust. No subsequent biographer (including me) has had access to as many original Beaumarchais papers as Loménie—which is the reason he is cited so often in the notes to this work. I have also drawn substantially from the work of Elizabeth S. Kite, an American studying in Paris at the dawn of the twentieth century. Deeply interested in rectifying the failure of Americans to recognize the role of Beaumarchais in securing our independence from England, she wrote a two-volume biography, drawing almost entirely from her translations of the Loménie papers at a time when more of them were intact than now.

Since then, two world wars have dispersed innumerable collections of French manuscripts, and today's biographers and historians are heavily reliant on the work of these earlier researchers. What makes the ensuing work different from previous works on the subject has been my reliance on previously unpublished manuscripts and documents in the archives of the French Foreign Ministry in Paris and various collections in the United States, including those of the Library of Congress. In addition, my translations may vary considerably from previously published biographies of Beaumarchais, because I have tried to reflect the sense and intent of French quotations rather than simply providing a literal translation. This is especially important in translating the many double entendres—the *jeux de mots*—that are still such a basic element of everyday spoken French, and were especially so at the time of Beaumarchais. In addition, I have modernized spellings and syntax of French, English, and American manuscripts and documents to make reading easier and more pleasant.

Finally, a word of thanks to Pamela Madsen, at Harvard University's Harvard Theatre Collection, and to Micah Hoggatt, at Harvard's Houghton Library, for their assistance in finding and reproducing scenes from *The Barber of Seville*. My thanks as well to the many freelancers and staffers at the University Press of New England who worked long and hard behind the scenes to produce this work, including Peter Fong, production editor, and Christi Stanforth, copyeditor. And lastly, my deepest thanks to my editor, Stephen P. Hull of UPNE, for his support in this project, and to my late literary agent, Edward W. Knappman, whose dogged persistence and boundless faith gave Figaro new life.

IMPROBABLE PATRIOT

1

We Must Help the Americans

AS 1776 NEARED ITS END, the news from America sent British King George III into paroxysms of joy. His army had routed the heralded George Washington and his so-called Continental Army. The American Revolution was all but over. Once numbering more than 30,000, Washington's ragtag rebels had turned tail and run after crack British and Hessian troops landed on the eastern shore of Manhattan Island in New York. Even Washington galloped away to safety, as British buglers sounded the fox-hunting call instead of the standard military charge. As Redcoats roared with laughter, Pennsylvania General Joseph Reed confessed, "I never felt such a sensation before. It seemed to crown our disgrace."[1]

Reduced by desertions to a pathetic band of 5,200, Washington's Americans dragged their collective heels from New York across New Jersey and over the Delaware River into Pennsylvania, where they lay shivering on the ground, without tents, wrapped in rags, leaves, twigs—anything—their feet bleeding, fingers frozen, out of rum to keep them warm, their bodies thrust against each other for warmth, with no ammunition, awaiting the inevitable.

Annihilation.

"We are all of the opinion," Reed confided to Washington, "that something must be attempted to revive our expiring credit. Our affairs are hastening fast to ruin if we do not retrieve them by some happy event."[2]

To the north, British gunboats had sent "Admiral" Benedict Arnold's fleet of comic "gundalows"—rowboats rigged with a single mounted gun on each—to the bottom of Lake Champlain. Meanwhile, three British forces on land prepared to converge on Albany and crush the American Northern Army, then sweep across the Northeast to extinguish the last embers of opposition to British rule.

"The Americans can no longer hold their ground," wrote the French *chargé d'affaires* in London to French foreign minister Charles Gravier, comte de Vergennes, at the palace in Versailles. "They have no choice but surrender."[3]

In Philadelphia, America's "Continental Congress," the pitiful prattlers who had pompously proclaimed themselves "free and independent" the previous July, all but confirmed the dire French evaluation. Without authority to raise taxes, buy arms, or levy troops, Congress fled the national capital at Philadelphia and debated capitulation as it reached a temporary safe haven in Baltimore on December 12, only five months after its arrogant declaration of independence. To their astonishment, they—and the 30,000 volunteer "citizen-soldiers" who had rallied around Washington in New York—quickly discovered that all men were not created equal—that on the battlefield high-spirited untrained farmers and hunters with rusty flint-lock pistols and muzzle-loading muskets were no equal to mean-spirited, well-trained, and well-equipped professional British and Hessian troops.

The American disaster had started in early August, when an armada of 150 British ships bounded over the horizon into New York Bay and disgorged more than 30,000 troops, including 9,000 merciless German mercenaries, onto Staten Island. On August 22—less than fifty days after Congress had issued the provocative Declaration of Independence—20,000 English Redcoats and their German hirelings stormed ashore in Brooklyn, where Washington had mustered a mere 5,000 "men"—mostly wide-eyed farm boys without battlefield experience. Within a week, the British and Hessians had slaughtered 1,500 Americans and captured 1,000 more, including their two commanding generals. The British commanders—the brothers Admiral Lord Richard Howe and Major General Sir William Howe—sent one of the American generals back across the lines with a peace proposal, and Congress sent three signers of the Declaration of Independence—John Adams of Massachusetts, Benjamin Franklin of Pennsylvania, and Edward Rutledge of South Carolina—to Staten Island to meet the Howes. When the British insisted on revocation of the Declaration of Independence as a precondition for peace talks, the Americans stomped off, and the Howe brothers ordered their troops to resume the slaughter.

On September 15, the British and Hessians crossed the East River from Brooklyn to Manhattan, where Washington had posted 8,000 Connecticut militiamen to repel British attempts to land. As British ships methodically pounded the amateurishly built American emplacements, British and Hessian troops streamed ashore, and, within hours, 6,000 of the Connecticut troops had fled. In disbelief, Washington galloped toward the front line to rally the troops, but found none. The slaughter on Long Island had so terrified them that officers and soldiers alike were sprinting to the rear—without firing a shot—when Washington and his aides arrived.

"Good God," Washington cried out. "Are these the men with which I am to defend America?"[4] It was then that British buglers had sounded the humiliating calls to the fox hunt, and Washington galloped back to Harlem Heights in northern Manhattan, with the enemy "within stone's throw of us."

"If I were to wish the bitterest curse to an enemy," he wrote in despair to his cousin Lund Washington, "I should put him in my stead. . . . I do not know what plan of conduct to pursue. . . . In confidence I tell you that I never was in such an unhappy, divided state since I was born."[5]

Worse was to follow.

British ships sailed up the Hudson and East Rivers on either side of Manhattan Island, expecting to encircle the northern tip, trap Washington's force, and end the war by compelling him to surrender or face useless slaughter with his remaining troops. Alerted by lookouts, however, Washington ordered his army to evacuate Manhattan and regroup at White Plains, on the Westchester mainland to the north. He foolishly yielded to the bravado of several officers who insisted on remaining with a few thousand men at Fort Washington, which stood on what seemed an impregnable bluff in northern Manhattan overlooking the Hudson River.

Too late to trap the Americans on Manhattan, the British landed in Westchester and marched to White Plains, where Washington—his army

George Washington, commander in chief of the
American Continental Army, received a mysterious
letter from "A Friend to America," offering
secret French military aid.

now half its former strength—fought the British to a stalemate, with neither side suffering many casualties. Just as Washington began to hope that
his Americans might be able to stand their ground against the British, a
messenger galloped into camp with word that the British had overrun Fort
Washington, capturing more than 2,600 American soldiers and 230 officers, together with a huge store of weapons, artillery, ammunition, and
other military supplies. Three days later, 4,000 British troops crossed the
Hudson and captured Fort Lee, directly opposite Fort Washington, thus
gaining control of the lower Hudson River valley, as well as Manhattan.
Threatened with attack from the east, south, and west, Washington sent
two-thirds of his army northward to establish a defense line in the Hudson

Highlands. He then led the remaining troops westward across the Hudson River and began a month-long forced march through sleet and freezing rain across northern New Jersey toward the Delaware River. On December 11, the remnants of his American army—a mere 5,200—one-third of them too sick or too hungry to serve—barely escaped capture by crossing the Delaware into Pennsylvania. Washington had had the foresight to send an advance guard to commandeer all the boats along a thirty-mile stretch on the east bank to carry the men across the river's swift currents and deprive the pursuing enemy of any means of following.

With southern New York and most of New Jersey in British hands, however, British marines prepared to storm ashore to seize the rebel capital of Philadelphia, and on December 12, Congress fled to Baltimore to resume the incessant, often infantile backbiting that they euphemistically called congressional debate. Many members seemed more at odds with each other than with their British overlords. South and North argued over the presidency of Congress, over command of the army, and over the status of slaves. Virginia and Connecticut each claimed lands in the Ohio Valley; Massachusetts claimed all of New York's western territory along Lakes Ontario and Erie; and New York, Massachusetts, and New Hampshire all claimed Vermont. Adding to the conflicts were bitter confrontations within each region between radicals favoring independence and moderates who sought only political autonomy from Parliament—without renouncing their loyalty to the king or their status as British subjects.

"Congress is divided," a French army officer reported back to French foreign minister Vergennes, "in spite of the watchwords . . . England, Country, Liberty, with which members cover up their mutual animosities. . . . The secret motive of their cabals, intrigues and everlasting bark is hatred between individuals or between states." The Frenchman said he found Pennsylvania "infested with Royalists" and Maryland refusing to join the Revolution "in order to preserve its territorial rights." He described North Carolina as "feeble" and South Carolina as having "neither moral nor physical energy."[6]

In stark contrast, another letter from a most unlikely source lay on

Comte de Vergennes, Louis XVI's minister of foreign affairs,
with whom Beaumarchais plotted to provide surreptitious
French financial and military aid during the first
years of the American Revolution.

the French foreign minister's desk and held his noble eyes in thrall: "The
Americans will triumph, but they must be assisted in their struggle. We
must . . . send secret assistance in a prudent manner to the Americans."[7]

Its author was, of all people, a French music master and playwright—
Pierre-Augustin Caron de Beaumarchais, a man so gifted in plotting and
scheming on the stage that the French government had enlisted his skills
offstage as a master spy. Vergennes had *no* reason—and yet *every* reason—
to doubt Beaumarchais's words.

To most at the palace at Versailles, Beaumarchais was pure rogue—the most impudent, unscrupulous, outrageous intriguer; a double-dealing commoner and adventurer who stopped at nothing to advance his fame and fortune, singing defiantly in the face of those he exploited. But to thousands of others outside the confines of the French palace—across France, England, and Europe—he was a dashing hero: a towering intellect who thumbed his nose at arrogant aristocrats and stood ready to risk his all for the downtrodden, the needy, and the helpless.

In fact, he was all of the above . . . and more. He was also a brilliant inventor, musician, composer, lyricist, singer, actor, poet, publisher, man of fashion, courtier, swordsman, spy, diplomat, adviser to kings, arms dealer, canny investor, financier, shipping magnate, philanthropist, irresistible lover, devoted husband, doting father, loyal friend, champion of the poor and persecuted, advocate of individual liberty and equal rights, and staunch friend of the American Revolution . . .

. . . *and* he was unquestionably the most brilliant French playwright of his and perhaps any era, all but universally recognized from London to St. Petersburg for his revolutionary stage productions.

At once charming and infuriating, Beaumarchais had earned the love and devotion of the powerless and the scorn and rancor of the powerful, with the king banning his greatest artistic achievements from public view. The public prosecutor had stripped him of his civil rights and citizenship for not being a lawyer and trying to defend himself without hiring one—an act that powerful French judges deemed insolent and worthy of indefinite imprisonment, loss of citizenship, and public silence. Condemnation to public silence left him forbidden to appeal his punishments, either in court or before the public or in any publication. He simply was not allowed to speak in public. If he did, police would jail him—condemn him to indefinite solitary confinement. In the eyes of the state, Beaumarchais was a *nonperson*—a condition that left the comte de Vergennes shaking his head in disbelief as he read Beaumarchais's insolent letter to the king of France. A commoner, writing to the king of France, who ruled by divine right! It was unheard of—until Beaumarchais . . .

"The preservation of our possessions in America and the peace which your majesty seems to want so much," Beaumarchais warned the king, "depend entirely on this one proposition: *we must help the Americans.*"[8]

Despite Beaumarchais's past—or more likely *because* of it—Vergennes reread the letter several times. Beaumarchais was offering the king nothing less than a scheme to restore French power over her ancient English enemy. A strident nationalist, Vergennes could not, by his very nature, dismiss Beaumarchais's suggestion. After all, France and England had been warring for centuries—since the glorious conquest of England in 1066 by Normandy's Guillaume le Conquérant, William the Conqueror. England eventually retaliated during the Hundred Years' War of the fourteenth and fifteenth centuries, overrunning Normandy, Brittany, and most of northern France, but Louis XIV—the Sun King—restored the French Empire to its former glory in the seventeenth century, all but enveloping the globe in the Bourbon flag. Louis the Great, as he was also called, extended French hegemony across Europe and beyond—over the Mediterranean Sea and into Africa, eastward to India and the South Pacific and westward across North America. La Nouvelle France encompassed most of Canada, from the Arctic and Atlantic shores, across the Great Lakes, westward to the Rocky Mountains and southward along the western slopes of the Appalachian Mountains to the Gulf of Mexico and into the Caribbean. Louis outlived both his son and grandson, and when he died, his five-year-old great-grandson ascended the throne as Louis XV.

"The French king is master and arbiter of Europe," the boy-king's mentor Cardinal Fleury explained. "Our neighbors have everything to fear from us—we nothing from them. . . . The diplomatic object of this Crown has been and will always be to enjoy in Europe that role of leadership which accords with antiquity, its worth and its greatness—to abase every power which shall attempt to become superior to it."[9] A regent governed the empire until Louis reached the age of majority, at which time he found that royal responsibilities were a royal bore compared to the raptures that awaited in his royal bedroom.

In the interests of sovereign succession and French territorial expansion, the regent arranged a territorially advantageous marriage of the French boy-king to Marie Leszczynska, the ugly twenty-one-year-old daughter of the Polish king. Only fifteen at the time, Louis couldn't stomach the sight of his wife and limited his contacts with her to brief, infrequent encounters that kept her pregnant most of the time and confined to her bedchamber. While the queen labored in her apartment to produce a procession of ugly little princesses, Louis labored in his apartment to possess a procession of pretty little mistresses, who collectively earned him the often misinterpreted sobriquet of "Louis le Bien-Aimé"—Louis the well-loved.

The motives for women's love of Louis varied. Some offered themselves to win noble titles for their families; others went to the king's bed by order of their husbands or sons seeking profitable land grants, government contracts, or other favors; still others—believing themselves inheritors of Jeanne d'Arc's mantle—swore they heard the voice of God command them into the arms of the king who had been "crowned by God." But *their* motives were secondary. When a woman or girl caught the king's eye, neither she, her parents, nor her husband dared reject the blessing of a royal command, and off she went to the king's bedchamber, where her pleas, tears, or shrieks of pain only excited the king's lust.

He was "a mindless man without a soul, without feeling," said Étienne-François, duc de Choiseul, Louis XV's prime minister for twelve years. "He loved hurting people the way children love to make animals suffer. . . . He enjoyed making them suffer whenever he could; I don't think anyone who ever knew him ever saw him show any benevolence since the day he was born."[10]

"If she's pretty and I like her looks," the king salivated, "I say that I want her, and that ends it."[11]

During his first years on the throne, Louis XV left administrative duties to his mentor and surrogate father, Cardinal Fleury. Fleury died in

Louis XV, the French monarch from 1715 to 1774, was first to use Beaumarchais as a secret agent. More interested in pursuing palace pleasures than governing, Louis lost most of the great French empire of his forebear Louis XIV to the British.

Madame de Pompadour, daughter of a bourgeois financier and
wife of a wealthy merchant, so enraptured King Louis XV that
he snatched her from her husband, entitled her a marquise,
and placed her in his bedchamber as official Royal Mistress.
Her title refers to the estate the king gave her, not her hairdo.

RÉUNION DES MUSÉES NATIONAUX

1743, just as the beautiful twenty-two-year-old Madame Jeanne-Antoinette
Poisson Lenormant d'Étioles, daughter of a minor bourgeois financier, captured the king's heart, mind, and body. A star of influential Paris social
salons, she had married Charles Lenormant d'Étioles, a wealthy merchant
who made the mistake of presenting her at Versailles. Louis snatched her
from her husband, led her to the royal bedchamber, and, two years later,
emerged long enough to ennoble her as marquise de Pompadour—the
name of a manor he bought for her. Her distraught husband had no choice

but to skulk out of the palace and retire by himself to his own Château d'Étioles—too humiliated to set foot in the palace at Versailles except when protocol required. His wife, meanwhile, so enthralled the king that he created a new title for her, appointing her *maitresse en titre* (official royal mistress) at a formal court presentation, and giving her a standing and power never before accorded to royal mistresses. Choiseul called it "a scandalous presentation . . . that violated every rule of dignity and morality. Sovereign princes by nature almost always represent a lower form of life than the rest of mankind, but of all European princes, the French Bourbons rank as the lowest and most despicable."[12]

Apart from sex, Louis enjoyed nothing more than riding to hunt at Marly, a palatial hunting lodge between Versailles and Paris. His weeks-long hunting excursions left Pompadour the de facto prime minister to manage palace politics in the king's absence. She set about reshaping life at Versailles, ruthlessly disgracing anyone—especially any woman—she suspected of coveting the king's social, political, financial, or sexual favors and elevating to power men who submitted to her own social, political, financial, and sexual demands. Neither she nor the king noticed the fissures forming in the structure of the great empire that stretched beyond the palace gates. Louis and Madame de Pompadour assumed that the same God who had placed him and his forebears on the French throne would preserve his empire forever. The French military machine at the time held most of continental Europe in thrall; powerful French armies secured the wealth of India and West Africa's lucrative slave and ivory trades. And in North America, French troops—and their savage Indian allies—had confined British settlers to a pathetically small strip of land—about 1,000 miles long and 100 miles wide—that hugged the Atlantic coast.

Although some of Britain's thirteen colonies claimed lands as far west as the Mississippi River and the Great Lakes, they did not come into conflict with the French until the British population expanded and spilled over the western reaches of the Appalachians. Indian warriors were there to greet

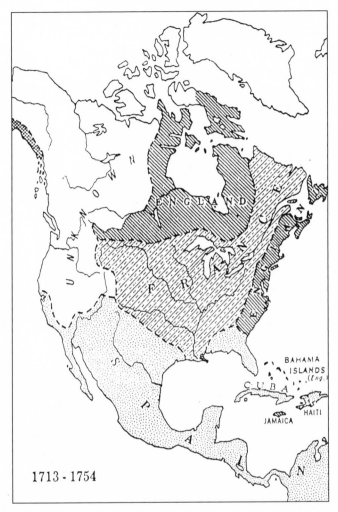

North America before the outbreak of the French and Indian
War in North America and the Seven Years' War in Europe.

them. Armed and spurred by their French allies, they massacred hundreds
of men, women, and children who settled on what the Indians claimed as
their ancient hunting grounds in western Pennsylvania and Ohio.

After French troops and Indians leveled a British trading post in western Pennsylvania in 1752, British governor Robert Dinwiddie, of Virginia,
dispatched twenty-year-old militia major George Washington to warn the

French to leave or face military retaliation. Met with a brusque rejection by the French military commander, Washington reported back to Dinwiddie, who promoted the young man to lieutenant colonel and ordered him to lead a company of volunteers "to the Fork of the Ohio . . . to make prisoners of or kill and destroy . . . any persons who . . . obstruct our settlements. . . . Pray God preserve you and grant success to our just designs."[13]

Washington rounded up seventy-five volunteers and hiked to the banks of the Youghiogheny River, sixty miles south of Fort Duquesne (now Pittsburgh), the primary French outpost at the fork of the Ohio. On May 27, one of Washington's scouts reported fifty French troops camped only six miles away, and Washington set out to attack the enemy. "We were advanced pretty near to them when they discovered us," he reported, "whereupon I ordered my company to fire. . . . We received the whole fire of the French, during the greatest part of the action, which only lasted a quarter of an hour, before the enemy was routed. We killed . . . the commander of the party, as also nine others. . . . The Indians scalped the dead and took away part of their arms."[14]

With his order to fire, the naive young Washington ignited the planet's first true "world war," a seven-year struggle between England, France, Austria, Prussia, Russia, and a kaleidoscope of allies and enemies for control of colonies in North America, Africa, and Asia and the sea lanes in between. Often called the "Great War for Empire," the Seven Years' War changed the map of the world, shifting national borders beyond recognition, leveling thousands of towns and villages, killing or maiming more than a million soldiers and civilians, and bankrupting a dozen nations, including England and France. The war not only bankrupted France, however, it humiliated her—stripped her of all her territories around the world, save a few malaria-infested islands in the Caribbean. The French lost all of Canada and Louisiana in North America and all her most vital colonies in Africa, India, and the South Pacific. Her once-powerful navy and merchant fleet lay either in British ports or at the bottom of the seas, and the British destroyed the fortifications at the strategically critical French channel port of Dunkerque and put the port and city under the command of a British commissioner.

As the ink was drying on the treaty that ended the war in 1763, Pompadour died and Louis XV forwent the pleasures of his bedchamber long enough to order Prime Minister Choiseul to avenge the French defeat and recapture at least some of the lost empire. As Louis returned to his bed to feast on newer, younger playthings, Choiseul set out to rebuild the nation's army and navy. To keep abreast of intrigues at home and abroad, he assumed authority over the post office and the mail flowing in and out of the palace. To cull secrets from foreign courts, he expanded a small espionage group into what he called the "Bureau of Interpreters," which sent a flock of agents in the guise of interpreters to every French embassy and consulate overseas. He ordered interpreters to accompany every French diplomat and important figure who went abroad, and he often assigned them dual roles as both diplomats and spies. It was easy to recruit agents among former army and navy officers eager to avenge their disgrace in the Seven Years' War—and among the unjustly condemned, whose only option for overturning their convictions was to serve the king in whatever way he wished.

In 1765, two years after the war, Choiseul sent a naval-officer-turned-spy—sieur Pontleroy—to evaluate colonist dissatisfaction in America and determine whether French arms and money might help incite rebellion and weaken the British enough to permit France to reclaim Canada without a costly war with England. The Seven Years' War had also left Britain bankrupt—victorious, but nonetheless as bankrupt as France. With King George III unwilling to reduce his lavish way of life and Parliament spending £300,000 a year to maintain its military garrisons in America, Chancellor of the Exchequer George Grenville raised duties on American imports and extended England's Stamp Act to the colonies to force Americans to pay for their own military protection. It was the first time Parliament had taxed the colonies directly, having previously relied exclusively on hidden, indirect taxes such as import duties, thus allowing colonial legislatures to raise their own local taxes. After Boston's James Otis responded to the Stamp Act by threatening to "set the province in flames," Choiseul sent

Duc de Choiseul, Louis XV's foreign minister,
envisioned French recapture of Canada by aiding
the American rebellion against the British.

RÉUNION DES MUSÉES NATIONAUX

Pontleroy in the guise of a French tobacco merchant to determine the true
extent and depth of the revolutionary fervor expressed by Otis. Traveling
the length and breadth of the thirteen American colonies, Pontleroy stood
at the door of the House of Burgesses in Williamsburg, Virginia, when
Patrick Henry raged that Virginians were not bound "to any law other
than the laws or ordinances of the general assembly of Virginia."[15]

As anti-tax rioting spread across America, representatives of eight colonies approved a "Declaration of Rights and Grievances of the Colonists in
America"—the first such joint action in colonial history. To Pontleroy's
astonishment, however, those same representatives expressed "glory in
being subjects of the best of kings" and called their connection with Great
Britain "secure" and, indeed, "one of their great blessings." Although vig-

orously opposed to the Stamp Act, they rejected outright rebellion—and Pontleroy advised Choiseul to abandon thoughts of encouraging colonist disaffection with the mother country. It was sound advice. Less than five months later, in February 1766, Parliament repealed the Stamp Act and temporarily quelled revolutionary fervor in America.[16]

The following year, however, the bankrupt English government tried to replenish its treasury with a wave of tax increases that swept 40,000 Englishmen into debtors' prisons and provoked anti-tax riots across England. Fearing the riots might swell into full-scale rebellion, Parliament reduced the tax increases at home, but compensated by imposing new taxes on the American colonies, where the cost of military garrisons had soared to £700,000 a year. The ensuing protests convinced Choiseul that colonial America might at last be ready to break from the mother country and weaken Britain enough to permit France to recapture French Canada without another costly war with England.

"Before six months have elapsed," he exulted to the king, "America will be on fire at every point. The question then is whether the colonists have the means of feeding it without the aid of a foreign [power]."[17]

Step by step, arrogant leaders in the English parliament seemed determined to turn Choiseul's prediction into a reality. In a series of legislative and military blunders aimed at crushing colonist willfulness, Parliament imposed trading regulations that prevented the colonies from trading with any nation other than the mother country. It imposed unbearably heavy import duties on essentials ranging from paper to tea—all of it necessarily imported from England under the new trading regulations. As costs of living soared, colonist protests resumed in Massachusetts and, at the end of 1767, Choiseul sent a second agent to America—the "Baron" Johann de Kalb, a gallant Prussian officer and mercenary in the French army during the Seven Years' War.

Born a peasant in Bavaria, Kalb was a bear of a man—brilliant, exceptionally learned but, like most commoners, self-educated. He invented his baronetcy to bypass French army rules that limited officers' ranks to noblemen. As a "baron," he rose to the highest ranks of the French army and Office of Foreign Affairs, acquiring diplomatic skills and fluency in several foreign languages, including English. His success in negotiating the return of French properties to their former owners after the Seven Years' War earned him fees that made him independently wealthy, and he married the daughter of a minor French nobleman, who added a big dowry to Kalb's fortune along with some legitimate luster—and land—to authenticate his fictional baronetcy.

Choiseul instructed Kalb to "learn the intentions of the inhabitants . . . ascertain whether they are in need of good engineers and artillery officers . . . find out what quantities of munitions of war and provisions they are able to procure . . . examine their resources in troops, fortified places, and forts . . . discover their plan of revolt, and the leaders who are expected to direct and control it . . . and determine the strength of their purpose to withdraw from the English government."[18]

A few months later, Kalb sent back an even more discouraging report than Pontleroy's, saying he found Americans "little inclined to shake off English supremacy with the aid of foreign powers. Such an alliance would appear to them to be fraught with dangers to their liberties." Although resentment against British rule was rising, he said, too many Americans remembered the savagery of French and Indian raiders during the Seven Years' War and despised the French more than the British. "In spite of their restive spirit," he concluded, "they all seem to be imbued with a heart-felt love of the mother country, from the leaders on down to the humblest citizen."[19]

Kalb predicted, however, that the colonies were "growing too power-ful to remain governed from so far away much longer" and that "an inde-pendent state will *certainly come forth in time.* . . . the opening of actual hostilities . . . cannot be far distant."[20]

2

Gold by God! The Fuel of Life!

MA JEUNESSE ÉTAIT si gaie, si folle, si heureuse, Beaumarchais recalled, describing his youth as a mixture of gaiety, craziness, and happiness.[1] Born a genius, he easily transformed his natural gifts into wealth, becoming one of France's youngest men of money—and certainly its happiest. A respected merchant and judge—and the nation's most celebrated playwright—he lived in a palatial mansion on the Left Bank of Paris, surrounded by a large family of adoring relatives and countless friends, who filled his house with music, song, dance, gaiety, and—France being France—exquisite foods and fine wines.

Beaumarchais had been born in a Paris clockmaker's shop forty-two years earlier, on January 24, 1732—a month before George Washington's birth in Virginia. Like Washington, Beaumarchais was a commoner—the son of decidedly uncommon parents who had planted the seeds of genius in their son at the moment of his conception. The future savior of the American Revolution was their only surviving boy—four others had died in infancy—and he grew up at the center of the family's collective attentions and affections in a household that resounded with the music, singing, and laughter of ever-joyful women—his two older sisters, three younger ones, and his mother. His mother was a talented musician who taught all the children to sing, compose music and lyrics, and play a variety of instruments. Together, she and the children wrote scores of poems, playlets, musical skits, and chamber works, which they performed for each other and the throngs of friends and relatives who regularly filled their salon.

Madame Caron and her husband enrolled their son in a local school, but grew dissatisfied with its stagnant pace and schooled him at home, where he read and studied eighteen books a month and mastered violin, cello, flute, piano, and harp by the time he was twelve. Adept at focusing on several activities at once, he learned to dismantle, repair, and rebuild clocks—while composing and singing melodies or reciting his own poetry. His smile, humor, and lightning wit left others, including his family, gasping to keep up with him. His deft hands, quick tongue, and even quicker mind turned him into a consummate performer, whose acting, singing, dancing, clowning, and juggling seldom failed to evoke a storm of laughter or tears, along with occasional awe at his precocity:

> Que souvent il me prend envie
> D'aller au bout de l'univers;
> Passer le reste de ma vie
> Eloigné des hommes pervers[2]

> How I wish I could spend my life
> in the far reaches of the universe,
> far from man's deceit.

With a boy of so many evident talents, the Carons taught young Pierre as many skills as they could. Caron *père* was a gifted clockmaker who had extended his knowledge of mechanics into a variety of other fields. Descended from Swiss Huguenot clockmakers, he abjured Calvinism and embraced Catholicism to bypass the religious discrimination that blocked entry by Protestants into the Watchmakers' Guild of Paris as a master craftsman. He set up shop on the rue de la Ferronnerie, near the right bank of the Seine River, just off the rue St. Denis, the teeming north–south axis of Paris along the ancient Roman road. The number of clockmakers, however, was greater than the demand for their services, and few could boast incomes large enough to support a family of nine. André-Charles Caron, therefore, pored over engineering texts and honed other mechanical skills to earn renown as a master engineer and attract commissions in fields un-related to clocks. From far-off Spain, for example, the governor of Madrid commissioned Caron to design machinery for dredging harbors and rivers.

His son Pierre-Augustin proved even more gifted, and his entry into his father's shop dramatically increased the productivity of the family business—until the boy reached adolescence. He fell in with a group of youths who followed him about the neighborhood looking for—and finding—mischief, sometimes singing young Caron's lewd lyrics *con brio* into the night to taunt sleeping neighbors. Unsatisfied with the allowance his father gave him, young Beaumarchais pocketed some of the money he received from customers for repairs he had made to their timepieces —money that should have gone into the store's general receipts. After an outburst of noisy recriminations, his father ordered the boy out of the house—into the streets to live with his loutish friends.

After a few days amid the terrifying dregs of humanity that slept on Paris streets at night, young Pierre sought refuge with relatives and family friends. Instructed in advance by his father, the friends offered the boy safe harbor—"one night or two, but no more"—and warned him he had best make amends with his father or face a life in the gutters. The boy wrote begging his father for forgiveness. After waiting for what he thought was a long enough time to frighten the boy to his core, Père Caron relented and invited the boy back into the family household—but under strict new rules:

> You shall make nothing, sell nothing, and cause nothing to be made or sold . . . except on my account. . . . You must get up at six in summertime and seven in winter; you must work until supper . . . at whatever I give you to do and at anything I give you to do, without showing any distaste for your work, using the talents which heaven has bestowed on you to become celebrated in your profession. . . .
>
> You must no longer go out at night, except on Saturdays and holidays, when you may dine with your friends, but must be home by nine. You must give up your party music and the company of young men. They have been your ruin. In view of your weakness for music, however, I will let you play

the violin and flute on condition that you only play them on working days after supper. . . . I will allow you your room and board and eighteen francs [about $60 today] a month pocket money. . . . If you devote yourself, as you ought, to the interests of my business, and you manage to obtain any orders independently, I will give you a one-quarter share of the profits of whatever work you bring in.[3]

Desperately lonely for the love and gaiety of his home—and determined to accept his father's challenge to become "celebrated in your profession" —he replied in the humblest terms:

Monsieur and honored father,
I agree to all your conditions with every intention of meeting them, with the help of the Lord; I am sorry I had to learn to fulfill my family obligations in so unfortunate a way. I deserve the humiliation you have imposed. I can only hope that my future good conduct will induce you to restore your love and kindness on your son,

A. Caron, *fils.*[4]

Beaumarchais returned home, and, choked by his own tears—and his adoring mother's embraces—immediately went to work in his father's shop with newfound determination. With the help of his ever-ebullient sisters, he set the Caron house ablaze again with song and laughter but, in accordance with his father's new rules, only after supper and only with proper folk songs and airs. He abandoned thoughts of street life and devoted himself to learning his father's craft. By the time he was nineteen, he had not only joined his father as a master craftsman, he had made several startling improvements in watch and clock mechanisms, learning advanced watch mechanics and design from books he borrowed from the king's own celebrated watchmaker—Monsieur Lepaute. Encouraged by Lepaute, the boy invented a revolutionary new inner mechanism—an "escapement"—that allowed him to make the first watch small enough and light enough to wear on the wrist and replace the bulky watches that men carried in their pockets and women wore attached to brooches.

Grateful to Lepaute for his tutelage, the boy rushed to show his invention to the great clockmaker, who pledged utter secrecy—but proceeded to incorporate it into a clock he was making for the king. Two weeks later, Caron sat in shock as he read the September 1753 issue of *Le Mercure de France*, the leading scientific periodical of the day. In it was an extensive report on the new Système Lepaute, which described in detail Caron's own invention.

As he raged about the house in tears, his father tried to calm the boy, explaining, "C'est normal" for the upper classes to step on those beneath them—"C'est comme ça," he said. "That's life."

But the boy was having none of it. Infuriated by his first confrontation with injustice, he sent his original designs to the Royal Academy of Sciences asking it to prevent the rival clockmaker from "taking from me the honor of a discovery which the Academy would have crowned with recognition!"[5] He then wrote to the editor of *Le Mercure*: "I have read with the greatest astonishment that Monsieur Lepaute announces as his invention a new escapement for watches and clocks."

> It is too important to me and my reputation to permit him to claim this invention by remaining silent about his breach of faith.... In the joy of my discovery last July 23, 1753, I had the weakness to confide this escapement to Monsieur Lepaute ... under the promise of secrecy, but how could I imagine he would appropriate it.... In congratulating himself about his discovery of my invention, he neglected to mention the letter he sent to my father—and signed—admitting that I had shared the details of my new escapement with him two months earlier.... I earnestly beg that no additional credence be given to Monsieur Lepaute's claim until the Royal Academy decides who is the author of the new escapement ... to expose the plagiarism.[6]

Three months later, the academy concluded that it would "regard Monsieur Caron as the true inventor of the new escapement and that Monsieur

Lepaute has only imitated the invention." The academy called Caron's invention "the most perfect yet invented . . . for watches"[7] and set off a wave of publicity that reached the Palace of Versailles, where King Louis XV translated his passion for unusual timepieces into orders for Caron's miniature watches for himself, his daughters, and Madame de Pompadour. Four months later, Caron wrote to his cousin, a watchmaker in London:

> I have at last delivered the watch to the king, who gave me the joy of immediately recognizing me and calling me by name. His Majesty ordered me to show the watch to all the noblemen. . . . His Majesty wanted to know the minutest details of my invention. The watch in a ring for Madame de Pompadour is . . . very much admired although it is not entirely finished. The king asked me to make another for him. . . . Each of the noblemen followed the king's example. . . . I have also made a curious little clock the king wants to give Mademoiselle Victoire [one of the king's daughters]. It has two dials so the time can be read on either side.[8]

Caron gasped as he walked through the palace for the first time, choked by aromas of perfume and talc, blinded by kaleidoscopic flashes of gold, silver, and crystal, and marble walls, ceilings, and floors. When he left, he all but floated across the Marble Courtyard beneath the royal apartments, exhilarated by faeried visions of ermine, silk, and velvet robes that few commoners ever saw, let alone wore or even touched. But it was the gold that captured his heart—the leaves of gold that lapped the cornices, frames, and furnishings. He tried to make sense of it all—that such a palace could be one man's house—a king's house.

Back in Paris, amid the smothering smells of slop and street sewerage, he applied his improving skills for swaying public opinion by writing to newspapers to proclaim himself "a young artist" whose new invention "the Academy has crowned with its approbation":

The main gate of the Palace of Versailles, which Louis XIV transformed
into the seat of government. It was here that Beaumarchais, then a young
Paris clockmaker, showed his amazing new miniature watches to
King Louis XV and began the climb to fame and fortune.

RÉUNION DES MUSÉES NATIONAUX

With this invention I can make watches as thin and small as may be desired,
thinner than any ever made before, without the slightest modification of
their fine quality. The first of these is already in the hands of the king; his
majesty has worn it a year, and is very pleased with it. I had the honor to
present to Madame de Pompadour . . . a watch built into a ring, only four
and one-half lines in diameter [three-quarters of an inch] and two-thirds of
a line thick [about one-tenth of an inch] . . . the smallest watch ever made.[9]

Caron signed his press notices *Caron, fils, Horloger du Roi*—Caron, the
Younger, Clockmaker to the King.

Demand for Caron's revolutionary watches brought a torrent of orders
to his and his father's shop and took him with increasing frequency to Ver-

sailles to deliver them to his noble customers. One of them—the beautiful Madeleine-Catherine Francquet—had married a palace sinecure twenty years her elder, whose work as Controller of the Pantry bored him as much as he bored his twenty-eight-year-old wife. Both, therefore, drew enormous pleasure from the sudden appearance of the ingenuously charming, handsome, and entertaining twenty-two-year-old Caron, who illuminated their gloomy salon with witty chatter and cheerful serenades of his own composition on the guitar, viola, flute, or harpsichord:

> Donne au plaisir le printemps de ta vie:
> Un âge vient où l'ont se sent vieillir;
> La fleur d'amour alors peut faire envie,
> Les sens glacés ne peuvent la ceuillir.

> Surrender to joy in the springtime of life
> Before you're too old and start to tire;
> Love's flower may still arouse desire,
> But frozen senses can't thaw in its fire.[10]

While Monsieur dozed, Madame slipped over to sit by Caron at the instrument, drawing ever closer, fingers glancing, meeting, caressing...

Within a few weeks, Madeleine convinced her husband to transfer his sinecure to Caron, and in November 1755, two years after Caron had invented his watch mechanism, a royal warrant appointed him *contrôleur clerc d'Office de la Maison du Roi*—a position that opened the palace gates and allowed him to begin a new life as a courtier.

> Great Stewards of France, high stewards and ordinary stewards of our household, masters and controllers of our pantry and account room, greetings! Upon good and praiseworthy report to us of Monsieur Pierre-August Caron and his zeal in our service, we have this day appointed him ... one of our *clerc-contrôleurs* of our household ... that he may have and exercise, enjoy and use, the honors, authorities, prerogatives, privileges, liberties, salary, rights, et cet.
>
> Given at Versailles under the seal of our trust, November 9, 1755.
>
> Louis[11]

The young Pierre-Augustin Caron de Beaumarchais, only twenty-three, was already a famed
watchmaker and on his way to becoming the
greatest playwright of his time, while pursuing a
second career as a government secret agent. Portrait
and engraving by Jean-Marc Nattier, 1865.

Two months later, old Francquet died, and, after an appropriate mourning period, Madeleine-Catherine married her handsome young lover and
gave him the new, aristocratic name of her small country estate—De
Boismarché—which he quickly corrupted into the more mellifluous de
Beaumarchais.

Although his striking good looks drew sighs from women at court, his
new veneer of nobility did little to disguise his commoner origins, which
drew nothing but sneers and snubs when he insinuated himself into clus-
ters of courtiers along the gilded halls and mirrored rooms of the palace.
His mechanical inventiveness had won grudging admiration, but his com-

mon clothes, manners, and bearing—and his swift insinuation into palace society—provoked only scorn. Over the ensuing months, Madeleine taught him court demeanor and helped him purchase an appropriate wardrobe, but after only nine months, she died without registering her will and left him without friends at court, a home, or any of her other assets to call his own. The manoir de Boismarché and the rest of her fortune reverted to her blood relatives—except for her beloved old harp, which he secreted from the house. To add to his grief—for he did, indeed, love his wife—he suffered the loss of his mother soon after.

Although his sinecure took him to the palace regularly, almost everyone he met rebuffed his social overtures. There were, of course, hundreds of courtiers with similar low-level sinecures clustered along the interminable palace corridors. Exchanging witty inanities, they gorged themselves at the king's tables in the innumerable reception rooms, where palace functionaries held endless receptions for a parade of visiting dignitaries, whose rank and importance determined the size and splendor of their receptions. Most courtiers at Versailles had backgrounds as ignoble as that of Beaumarchais, but they repeated their claims to noble blood so often that they came to believe their own inventions. As a result, they routinely snubbed newly arrived interlopers like Beaumarchais who tried to intrude into their midst. Regardless of how he embellished his dress or polished his manners, he only managed to infuriate them. In comparison to their often slovenly demeanor, he was tall, handsome, fit, and straight as a soldier, and he quickly learned to display the manners of a peer of the realm. When combined with his quick wit, brilliant conversation, and gift for repartee, his demeanor set all the king's courtiers agog—the ladies with love and the men with hatred born of envy and fear.

Discouraged by his failure to integrate into day-to-day palace life, but unwilling to return to the tedium of watch repairs, he moved in with a friend in Paris and frequented the city's literary haunts, meeting journalists, poets, writers, and philosophers. Within a few days, their erudition, eloquence, and wit—and snide responses to his comments—made him feel as inferior intellectually as palace courtiers had made him feel socially. Motivated by both anger and ardor, he devoured books by the bundle—literature, grammar, geography, history, mathematics, geometry, and philosophy. He all but absorbed in his soul Jean-Jacques Rousseau's *Discours sur l'origin et les fondements de l'inégalité parmi les hommes* (Discourse on the Origin and Foundations of Inequality among Men), which condemned the state as the cause of inequality and oppression.

"The first man who, having enclosed a plot of land, took it into his head to say *this is mine* and found people simple enough to believe him, was the true founder of class society," Rousseau declared in *Discours*.[12] Like Beaumarchais's father, Rousseau had converted to Catholicism to avoid state and institutional discrimination against Protestants. During the writing of *Discours*, he returned to his birthplace in Geneva to become a Protestant again before returning to Paris to resume his writing. In 1762, his *Le contrat social* (The Social Contract) stunned French thinkers with its opening proposal: "Man is born free, and everywhere he is in chains. He who believes himself the master of others does not escape being more of a slave than they."[13]

Le contrat social fed the fantasies of poets, playwrights, composers, and dreamers who pictured primitive man—especially the American Indian in his primeval forest—living in Edenic splendor and mutual beneficence. Beaumarchais embraced Rousseau's vision as his own—and extended it to include not only American Indians, but also the colonists living in what he imagined was complete freedom and harmony with man and nature in the North American wilderness.

To break the routine of reading, Beaumarchais played his wife's old harp, often growing so frustrated with its complexities that he ripped it apart and rebuilt its pedal mechanisms to make it easier to play.[14] Then, on a visit to the palace at Versailles, he stumbled into a chance conversation about his reinvented harp—and music generally—with Charles Lenormant d'Étioles, the abstinent spouse of Madame de Pompadour. Knowing his wife had stretched out in the king's bedroom suite behind the long, glittering wall of the great Hall of Mirrors, Lenormant was usually too embarrassed to appear at the palace. He compensated for his humiliating celibacy, however, by staging banquets, galas, and masquerade balls at his own Château d'Étioles, where he converted one of the largest rooms into a concert hall and theater, with a fully equipped stage for popular lewd comedies. Beaumarchais had honed his skills in the genre as a youth, and Lenormant invited the watchmaker to the château to perform and present original plays of his own. At Lenormant's behest, Beaumarchais wrote a series of short plays that won the nobleman's admiration and friendship —both for the scripts and for Beaumarchais's incredible ability to sit at his harp and improvise short, witty songs. Often rude or lewd or both, they evoked gales of laughter—especially when they portrayed outrageous behavior by the aristocracy. In one of his airs, he invited the audience to let themselves go, in the modern sense, saying and doing anything they pleased. The time was right for such behavior, he said, and he was not there judge them.

> Oser tout dire, oser tout faire,
> C'est le bon siècle d'à présent;
> Mais blâmer n'est pas mon affaire;
> Rions; moi, je suis né plaisant.

> Dare to say anything, dare to do anything;
> Now, right now, is the best time for you;
> I won't judge you—that's not my affair;
> Let us laugh; it's what I was born to do.[15]

Beaumarchais's reinvented harp drew so much attention from other musicians and instrument makers that it became the rage of court society—and a new source of income for the former watchmaker. The sounds of Beaumarchais songs and compositions resounded across Paris and Versailles and reached the ears of the king's reclusive daughters. Inevitably, they summoned the inventor of the new harp to their private apartments to teach them its intricacies, and, as his new watch mechanism had done, his new harp catapulted him farther along the path to fame and fortune.

Beaumarchais suppressed his shock when he entered the private apartments at Versailles, where the reverential portraits of the king's daughters he'd seen along the palace's public halls metamorphosed into the grotesque genetic realities of Bourbon family beaks and bottoms. Even their father the king gave them vulgar nicknames: he called Madame Louise, the youngest at twenty-two, *Chiffe* (spineless); Madame Sophie, twenty-five, *Graille* (a fat glutton); Madame Victoire, the fattest of the lot at twenty-six, *Coche* (a beamy boat); and Madame Adelaide, by far the prettiest at twenty-seven, *Loque* (a wreck). Although each was addressed as "Madame," Mesdames were all unmarried *demoiselles.* Louise was impossibly shy, kept her head bowed, eyes darting from side to side; Sophie was "slow-witted and dull"; Victoire was fat. Only Adelaide claimed a modicum of charm and good looks—but her explosive temper unnerved every potential suitor.

It was into this den of hapless harridans that twenty-seven-year-old sieur de Beaumarchais brought his disinterest, charm, smile, wit, and musicianship in 1759—along with a touch of melancholy to befit his status as a forlorn young widower—and, indeed, an orphan. Still mourning the loss of his mother, he was not entirely disinguous in finding solace and comfort in the presence of the four matronlike princesses. His demeanor combined with his soft, seductive songs to send the four maidens into swoons of rapture. They invited him to be their music master; he accepted, but humbly refused all compensation and, over the next four years, taught them to play the harp and guitar, composed scores of melodies easy enough for them to perform, and, when they were troubled, simply played, sang, or read to them—or listened to their woes. They adored him; he became a great friend of their brother, the heir-apparent to the throne; and, each evening, when the king invaded their apartment for his ritual visit, he too grew enchanted by the young man's amazing skills, erudition, and evident affection for his otherwise repulsive daughters.

As Beaumarchais was playing the harp one evening, the king terrified his daughters by bursting into the apartment unexpectedly, without being announced. As others snapped to their feet, the eyes of the music master were closed, his mind focused on his music, and he failed to stand—an error punishable by imprisonment or worse. The king had ordered one royal attendant drawn and quartered by horses before the palace gates for far less a misstep. Realizing his potentially fatal error, Beaumarchais sprang to attention amid the clatter of his falling chair and harp. In an unprecedented response that left attendants gasping, the usually fierce-faced king smiled, put his hand on the young man's shoulder—actually touching a commoner with his divine digits—and begged him to continue playing.

A wave of envy and rage surged through palace halls and antechambers, with infuriated courtiers turning their backs on Beaumarchais as he passed. Some sneered aloud of needing their watches and clocks repaired. One courtier actually stopped Beaumarchais to ask that he rewind a watch.

Embarrassed by the snickers and smiles that surrounded him, Beaumarchais first tried excusing himself, saying "I no longer practice the art, Monsieur."

"Please, Monsieur," the taunter retorted, "do not refuse me this one favor."

As onlookers all but doubled over in laughter, Beaumarchais smiled, took the watch, turned it over in his hands, and let it fall to the marble floor and shatter.

"I'm so sorry," he cried. "I'm afraid I've become clumsy. Please excuse me, Monsieur."[16]

The insults did not cease. One envious courtier planted a rumor that reached the ears of the princesses, contending that Beaumarchais and his father were bitter enemies. Warned by one of the princess's attendants, Beaumarchais rushed to Paris and fetched his father, promising a private tour of the palace. When the princesses saw their young instructor walking the corridors with an old man in tow and determined his identity, they confronted their music master.

"We were told you had quarreled," said Princess Adelaide.

"I, Madame?" he responded. "I pass my life with him. . . . If you will deign to see him he will testify to the attachment which I have never ceased to have for him."[17]

The malignant rumors kept surfacing, however, until Beaumarchais had no choice but to challenge a young nobleman to a duel—an illegal exercise he had only read about in adventure tales.

"They mounted their horses and rode to the walls of Meudon, beneath which they fought," wrote the contemporary historian Paul Philippe Gudin de La Brenellerie, whom Beaumarchais had met at the Étioles château. Also born to a Protestant watchmaker, Gudin was short, fat, slow—and tied tightly to the apron strings of his mother, who envisioned her son as the next Voltaire. Gudin eventually produced an unreadable thirty-volume history of France, along with innumerable dramas and poems, which drew nothing but ridicule when he tried reading them at literary salons. Only Beaumarchais had had the kindness to compliment the little man at a reading one evening. In doing so, he won a close, loyal, and trusted friend for life. Gudin attached himself to Beaumarchais for the next thirty years, becoming his first biographer, his "Boswell," and, most importantly on this particular day, his second at the duel at Meudon. Still the deft juggler with acrobatic quickness, Beaumarchais hopped aside to dodge the first thrust, the second, the third—then, on instinct, without realizing it, "he had the good fortune," according to Gudin, "to plunge his sword into the bosom of his adversary":

but when he withdrew it, he saw the blood stream out and his enemy fall to the ground and, evidently seized by remorse, he thought only of the best way to help him. He put his handkerchief on the wound to stop the flow of blood and keep his adversary from fainting.

"Fly," said the latter, "fly, Monsieur Beaumarchais. You are lost if you are seen—if it becomes known that you have killed me."

"You must have help," Beaumarchais insisted, "I'll get you some help."

He mounted his horse, galloped into the village of Meudon, found a surgeon and galloped back with him to the spot where the wounded man lay. During the eight days through which he lingered, the young knight refused to reveal the name of the man who had wounded him so severely.

"I have what I deserve," he insisted. "To please persons for whom I had no esteem, I insulted an honest man who had never offended me in any way." He carried with him to the tomb the name of the person who had deprived him of life.[18]

Before the young nobleman died, the guilt-stricken Beaumarchais confessed to the princesses, who immediately appealed to their father to protect the music master from criminal prosecution, "and his paternal goodness," according to Gudin, "made him reply, 'Arrange it in such a way, my children, that I may not hear of it.' The princesses took all the necessary precautions to bury the story of the duel with its victim."[19]

The knight's untimely death did little to ease the mistreatment of the music master by envious courtiers. While attending a ball in Versailles ten days after the duel, he stopped to watch a group of noblemen gambling at cards in an anteroom. One of them casually asked Beaumarchais to lend him thirty-five louis (about $1,000 in modern currency). To appear gracious, Beaumarchais agreed, anticipating repayment by evening's end. After three weeks, he wrote to the man, and received a written promise of repayment the next day. None came. A second letter three weeks later went unanswered for three more weeks, and Beaumarchais again wrote: "Inasmuch as you broke your written promise to repay me, Monsieur, I am not surprised by your failure to reply to my last letter. . . . You owe me neither civility nor respect, but you do owe me thirty-five louis."[20]

A few days later, Beaumarchais received an indignant reply with what amounted to a virtual challenge to another duel: "I know that I am unfortunate enough to owe you thirty-five louis, Monsieur, but I deny that this in any way dishonors me so long as I intend eventually to repay you. You shall have your thirty-five louis on Saturday; I give you my word. But I don't know whether I shall be able to close this matter with moderation."[21]

Astonished by the man's gall, Beaumarchais snapped back, "I shall await the result of your third promise at my house all Saturday morning; you say you cannot vouch for your moderation, but I can assure you I do not want to aggravate an already unfortunate situation for which I am not responsible. If, after this assurance, you intend to exceed the limits of civilized behavior—a situation I do not at all desire—you will find me, Monsieur, ready to respond appropriately to any insult." The money arrived two days later by messenger—without further correspondence.[22]

"The envy toward him resulted in strengthening his character," Gudin recalled. "He learned to control himself, master his impetuosity and passions and retain a coolness and presence of mind. He turned everything that seemed about to destroy him to his advantage and used every threat against him to rise to superior circumstances."[23]

3

Last Night Poor, Wealthy Today!

NOT EVERYONE AT Versailles turned their envy of Beaumarchais into insults or injury.

The great financier Joseph Pâris-Duverney had made a fortune with his two brothers as arms merchants to the French army during King George's War between France and England from 1740 to 1748. He doubled the size of his fortune supplying arms to the French army in the great Seven Years' War from 1756 to 1763, the world conflict which, as noted, began in the American wilderness when Lieutenant Colonel George Washington ambushed a squadron of French troops and killed its commander.

As a price for a near-monopoly supplying arms to the French military, Pâris-Duverney agreed to finance building the École Militaire, an elaborate and ornate training school for officers on the Champs de Mars, a huge stretch of flatland on the river Seine in what was then the countryside between Paris and Versailles but now lies behind the Eiffel Tower. Construction began in 1751, but with the outbreak of the Seven Years' War, the king lost interest. His generals needed officers on battlefields around the world immediately; there was no time to lose sending them to school; they could hone their skills under fire. Without royal sponsorship, Pâris-Duverney faced a halt to construction and loss of his investment—until he learned of the ambitious young Beaumarchais and his curious ties to the royal family.

"He wished to make my acquaintance," Beaumarchais noted. "He offered me his friendship, assistance and influence to see if I had enough influence to succeed in doing what . . . he had tried in vain."[1]

Joseph Pâris-Duverney, the legendary
French financier who opened the way for
Beaumarchais's successful entry into the
world of international trade.

CABINET DES ESTAMPES, BIBLIOTHÈQUE
NATIONALE, PARIS

Unlike other retainers, Beaumarchais's disinterested relationship with
the princesses allowed him to be frank, and when he explained that he
could make his own fortune if they accompanied him on a visit to the
École Militaire, they happily agreed. On the first pleasant day that followed, they asked Beaumarchais to accompany them to the school and
enjoyed the excursion so much they convinced their father to visit it with
them and renew his official sponsorship. Pâris-Duverney, in turn, all but
adopted Beaumarchais as a son and pledged to help him reap riches. "He
initiated me into the secrets of finance, of which he was a consummate
master. Under his guidance . . . I invested in a number of ventures in which

The completion of the École Militaire, the French training school for army officers, resulted from Beaumarchais's influence with King Louis XV's daughters.

RÉUNION DES MUSÉES NATIONAUX

he helped me with money, influence and advice. . . . I started making my fortune."[2] Beaumarchais would later put what he learned from Pâris-Duverney to good use in the American Revolution.

As Beaumarchais's fortune flowered, he used his money to buy a more substantial footing in the nobility, spending 85,000 francs (about $300,000 in today's currency) for a more prestigious sinecure as a secretary to the king, which paid him a token salary for doing nothing, but gave him unlimited access to the palace and all royal functions. It was what manor-born aristocrats snidely called *une savonette à vilain*—a soap to lubricate entry of the low-born into the highest levels of society. Pâris-Duverney loaned Beaumarchais 500,000 francs ($1,750,000) to buy an even more prestigious post as *Lieutenant-général des chasses aux baillage et capitainerie de la Varenne du Louvre*, which put him in a judge's prestigious robes. His judicial powers were somewhat less grand than his robes, though, limited as they were to fining poachers who trespassed in the king's hunting preserves in the forests surrounding Paris. He nonetheless carried the intimidating title of Lieutenant-General of the Court, and he took his work, if not his title, seriously, carefully studying Montesquieu's massive—and classic—work on French laws, political science, and social philosophy, *De l'esprit des lois* (The Spirit of Laws). The French political philosopher classed government into three categories: despotism, based on fear; monarchy, based on honor; and the republic, based on virtue, with individual liberty most likely to survive in small republics in which governors remain close to the governed and aware of their needs.[3] Having seen the French monarch abandon all sense of honor and turn despot, Beaumarchais grew enchanted with Montesquieu's descriptions of republican government, and he displayed Montesquieu's influence from the bench.

In his new post, Beaumarchais was subordinate to but one man—the Captain General, who, at the time, was the duc de La Vrillière, a pompous minister at Versailles who loathed riding to Paris to deal with peasant poachers and routinely left court business to his lieutenant general. Aware of the duc's disdain for the court, the minister of justice did not bother consulting the duc when he acceded to the request of Pâris-Duverney to appoint Beaumarchais. The duc, however, grew furious at what he perceived as both a discourtesy and the degradation of being on the same bench with the son of a commoner—a clockmaker at that. From the first, the duc de La Vrillière despised Beaumarchais, who nonetheless dutifully appeared on the bench in his judicial robes every Thursday. Although charged with fining poachers according to the value of the rabbits, birds, deer, or other animals they killed in the king's woods, Beaumarchais routinely dismissed cases against poor or hungry peasants—politely wishing them *bon appetit* and incurring even more of the duc's wrath. Montesquieu was taking hold of his mind as well as his heart.

Beaumarchais's newfound wealth permitted him to buy a magnificent 60,000-livre (about $250,000) mansion that still stands on the tree-lined rue de Condé, down the gentle slope from Queen Marie de Medici's seventeenth-century Palais du Luxembourg, and only a few steps from the

Place de l'Odéon. From his window he gazed at the palace and its magnificent woods, gardens, fountains, and statues—an ensemble that was not as grand as Versailles, but then he was not a king. Not yet! At his insistence, his widowed father abandoned the clock-repair business and retired to a life of leisure and luxury in his son's new home, with the Caron daughters who had yet to find husbands.

"I bless heaven in my old age," his father wrote, "for giving me a son with such an excellent heart. . . . My soul leaps with joy at owing my happiness, after God, to him alone."[4] Shortly after he had moved to his son's elegant mansion, however, Père Caron found another source of happiness in a neighboring mansion, where the lovely widow Madame Henry lured him into her arms.

In 1764, Caron's two older sisters left for Madrid after the older of the two married an architect, and he agreed to the younger girl's coming along as her sister's companion. Within weeks of their arrival, a young writer, Don José Clavijo y Fajardo, wooed and won the younger sister's heart and signed a marriage contract to wed her immediately after his appointment as Keeper of the Crown Archives. Once in his new post, however, he abandoned the young lady, who wrote to her father in shame and despair. Irate over his sister's mistreatment, Beaumarchais prepared to go to Spain to avenge her disgrace. After disclosing his plans to Pâris-Duverney, the wily old financier gave his protégé a second, more profitable incentive for going. France had ceded Louisiana to Spain as part of the peace settlement after the Seven Years' War, and, with the cession, French merchants lost trading rights in New Orleans. Pâris-Duverney and a group of French bankers wanted to establish a Spanish company to allow French *négriers*—slave traders—and other French merchants to continue their commerce under the Spanish flag and profit from the growing need for African labor and European supplies to develop resources in the Spanish Americas. To bribe the right officials and obtain the concession, he gave Beaumarchais letters of credit totaling 200,000 livres (about $800,000 in modern currency).

On May 1, 1764, Beaumarchais left for Madrid, and eighteen days later he pounded at the door of his sister's suitor demanding satisfaction, either in the field at sword point or at the altar. The young man chose the safety of the altar, apologized to Beaumarchais's sister, and reaffirmed his marriage proposal—even signing a document admitting his caddishness and declaring his affianced "pure and without blemish." Once rid of his irrational French tormentor, however, the young Spaniard slipped away again. Beaumarchais scoured the city, found him, and again extracted a pledge that he would marry the poor girl—but he again disappeared. After the resourceful Beaumarchais found him the third time, the Spaniard claimed he had previously offered to marry a chambermaid and, by law, could not marry Beaumarchais's sister until the chambermaid renounced her claim or died.

By now, however, the Frenchman's farcical daily chase and the Spaniard's clever escapes had become targets of sustained laughter in salons across Madrid, with newspapers turning the drama into serial cartoons. When Beaumarchais called Clavijo's bluff and demanded that the Spaniard marry the chambermaid, Clavijo ran to the police and accused his would-be brother-in-law of plotting against Spain. Facing arrest and deportation, Beaumarchais rode off to the palace with his letters of introduction from the French king's daughters to their cousin Spanish king Carlos III. After listening to the sumptuously attired Beaumarchais's entertaining description of his sister's dishonor, the king ordered the false fiancé fired and banned from government employment for life. Fearing arrest, the would-be archivist fled to a monastery outside the Madrid city walls.

"The coxcomb," Beaumarchais wrote in triumph to this father, "is completely crushed. His post is given away. He is now left with the choice of turning capuchin monk or leaving the country."[5]

With his sister's honor restored, Beaumarchais used his newfound friendship with the king to insinuate himself into Spanish court society. His chivalry in protecting his sister's honor combined with his good looks, wit, and musical talents to make him one of the most admired figures in Madrid. "If an inhabitant of Madrid sent you any news of me," he wrote his father, you would learn that your son was amusing himself here like a king; he spends all his evenings at the house of the Russian ambassador's wife and at milady Rochford's, the British ambassador's wife; he dines four times a week with the commander of engineers, and drives about Madrid in a coach and six; he goes to the royal palace to see ministers . . . and takes one of his meals every day at the French ambassador's. . . . Lord Rochford dotes upon me, goes to the Prado with me, sups with me, sings duets with me, and laughs aloud with me in the most astonishing fashion for an English diplomat.[6]

Women doted on him as well. "I have this afternoon been to the French ambassador's in the carriage of Mme. la Marquise de La Croix, who has the goodness to drive me everywhere," he boasted to his father. "She is a charming lady with great standing here because of her intelligence and grace as well as rank. I would die in this dull city if it were not for her delicious company." The marquise was a niece of the Bishop of Orléans and wife of a lieutenant general in the Spanish king's artillery. Her beauty and musical gifts had made her a centerpiece of Madrid's diplomatic set; her attraction to her handsome and talented compatriot Beaumarchais was instant.

"In the room where I am writing," he announced to his father a few weeks after meeting the marquise, "is a great and beautiful lady . . . who overwhelms me with kindness. I admit that without the charm of such delightful company, my business in Spain would not be enjoyable. But you must not conclude that I am neglecting my business."[7]

Indeed, he was not. After submitting a plan to supply slaves to the Spanish colonies, he proposed establishing a French trading company in Madrid to handle *all* imports and exports of the Louisiana Territory. He then proposed that the Pâris-Duverney interests develop agricultural and manufacturing facilities in undeveloped areas of Spain . . . and on and on. "The most comprehensive and lofty projects," he told his father,

are no strangers to my mind: My mind conceives and comprehends with ease that which would immediately check ordinary, indolent minds. . . . I have now managed to make myself absolute master of the enterprise for supplying *the entire provisions for the whole of the troops of Spain, Majorca, and the garrisons on the coast of Africa;* and those of all persons living at the king's expense. It amounts to more than twenty millions a year. My company is organized, my officials are appointed. I have four cargoes of corn on the way from both New England and from the south. . . . I have signed the celebrated agreement which entitles me to treat with the . . . Minister of War and Finance. Every one in Madrid is talking about it. . . .

Good night dear father; believe me, you must not be astonished at either my success, nor the opposite if it should befall me. . . . I shall soon be thirty-three. At twenty-four, I still worked in a shop. I am now at the prime of my life; my mind and body will never have greater vigor. . . . I have made up my mind that, over the next twenty years, my long labors will produce great success and permit retirement in tranquillity. In the meanwhile, I laugh; my inexhaustible good humor does not leave me for a moment. I do not tell you all now, but you may rely on my never forgetting your welfare. It is my part to work, yours to rest. The time will come when you will enjoy your old age as you deserve, free of care, among your loving children.[8]

In an afterthought, Beaumarchais told his father of the "delightful suppers" he had attended with the highest levels of Madrid society and the verses he had been writing for Spanish *seguedillas*. "I chose the most popular air, a soft, touching, charming melody, and wrote words to it. . . . My last *seguedilla* is in the hands of every one who speaks French in Madrid."[9] (The *seguedilla* is a Spanish dance to whose music poets often added four or seven short verses. The most famous Beaumarchais *seguedilla* appears near the end of chapter 12, just before the section titled "Coda.")

His songwriting success provoked an interest in theater, which he attended regularly. He began writing to great literary figures, including Voltaire, to whom he sent original work for criticism. In his reply, Voltaire diplomatically sidestepped any criticisms of Beaumarchais's writing, but he "compliments me, playfully, on my thirty-two teeth, my lively philosophy, and my age."[10]

After a year in Madrid, Beaumarchais returned to France in March 1765, traveling across the Pyrenées Mountains through the worst storms of the year. By early April, he arrived back in Paris to find both his house and the palace at Versailles in a state of utter turmoil. At home, his father had married the widow Madame Henry and moved out of the rue de Condé to new quarters, which the old man blithely charged to his son's account. Beaumarchais had no sooner adjusted to the departure of his father than his youngest sister, "Tonton," the liveliest, most lovable of his lovely bevy of sisters, left the rue de Condé to marry her own longtime beau, leaving Beaumarchais with but one sister to join him in song at the harpsichord.

When Beaumarchais went to Versailles, he learned that Madame de Pompadour had died and that his good friend, the prince and heir apparent, was ill and apparently approaching the same fate. Adding to the somber mood, his long absence from their salon had cost him the patronage, if not the friendship, of the princesses, who had found new distractions that left them little time for the songs and patter of the clockmaker's son. Beaumarchais was wealthy enough by then, however, to pursue a life of leisure, and he decided to quit palace life, sell his palace sinecures, and pursue a writing career. He retained his judgeship in Paris and resumed his Thursday appearances on the bench, but spent the rest of his time writing a variety of plays, ranging from what were called *parades*—one-act comedies with carefully constructed plots—and *scènes*, which were short pieces, usually involving a domestic dispute filled with off-color jokes using puns that were at one and the same time appropriate for the situation, but had obscene double meanings. Injecting his own original wit to refresh age-old plots and characters, he soon found his little comedies in demand in scores of manors and châteaus, where noblemen and their ladies, families, and friends enjoyed rehearsing and staging *parades* and *scènes* for their own amusement.

Confident he had learned his skill well enough to write a full-length presentation, he convinced the king's daughters to sponsor his first play,

Eugénie. It opened on January 29, 1767, to a chorus of hisses, whistles, and jeers. A long, tedious, melodrama, its *five acts* and *sixty-two scenes* depicted Lord Clarendon's tiresome attempts to lure the innocent virgin Eugénie into bed by staging a fake marriage ceremony. Along the way, His Lordship and Eugénie's brother take turns saving each other's lives and become close friends—until the brother discovers all and challenges Clarendon to a duel to salvage his sister's honor. Ah, but no need! His Lordship trips over his own devices and falls in love with the tender lass he tried to deceive. Rather than risk the life of her brother, who is now his friend, he repents and marries Eugénie—and they all skip happily offstage together. On opening night, a chorus of audience catcalls accompanied their departure.

Intent on purging himself of the critical humiliation, Beaumarchais followed the advice of a critic, cut the play by one-third, and rewrote the rest. The result drew audience cheers and new, revised reviews by critics for what was then considered a long run of twenty-three performances. England's legendary David Garrick—author of twenty plays, as well as his nation's greatest actor—commissioned a translation of *Eugénie*, renamed it *The School for Rakes*, and acted in it himself. Unfortunately, a number of French noblemen who saw Eugénie in both its original and revised formats thought they recognized themselves in the character of Lord Clarendon; they left the theater determined to wreak revenge on Beaumarchais.

Even the most successful playwright did not earn enough from the theater to cover costs of daily life in Paris, let alone live in the style of Beaumarchais. After his triumph in the theater, Beaumarchais sought new opportunities in finance and, as ever, in romance. After seeing the original presentation of *Eugénie*, a wealthy Paris silk merchant and his wife who were friends of Beaumarchais blamed the play's initial failure on Beaumarchais's having lived alone too long without a wife. An inveterate busybody who dabbled in matchmaking, the merchant's wife told Beaumarchais she planned to ride with a friend in an open carriage the following day under the shade of the chestnut trees along the Allée des Veuves—the Widows' Alley—near the Champs Elysées. Her friend, she said, was a beautiful and charming young widow whom she would introduce to Beaumarchais if he happened to ride by at the same time.

Poised majestically atop his magnificent horse and dressed in his most elegant horseman's gear, Beaumarchais high-trotted to his friend's carriage the next day and all but bounded off his mount to take the hand of Mme. Geneviève-Madeleine Lévêque. Née Watebled, Madame Lévêque was the beautiful blond widow of a judge—in her early thirties, wealthy, merry, and bright. The last two traits were as important as the others, if not more so in a house filled with as much merriment and wit as the Beaumarchais mansion. Song and laughter reigned every moment of the day, as Beaumarchais, his father, his sisters, or friends gathered regularly to regale each other singing in harmony or in boisterous rounds at the dining room table. Standing apart discreetly were the smiling domestics he continually rescued from hardships and untold cruelties in and about the theater neighborhoods and nursed back to health.

When the family wasn't singing, Beaumarchais and the others fell into the grip of what had become the latest Parisian after-dinner pastime— the *charade*, a word game in which players figured out the "punny" definition of a word from two interrelated clues, as in "Mon premier, c'est . . . ; Mon deuxième . . . ; Mon tout . . ." (My first can weigh a lot . . . ; my second is a lot of weight . . . ; my sum is a great American general. Answer: *Washington = Washing + ton*.) Laughter and song inevitably led to love and, in April 1768, Beaumarchais married Geneviève. Eight months later, she bore him his first child, a son, Pierre-Augustin-Eugène.

As Beaumarchais reveled in the joys of fatherhood, the French government launched a program to rebuild its navy and replace ships that the British had destroyed in the Seven Years' War. In desperate need of lumber for shipbuilders, it offered eight-year concessions to entrepreneurs to harvest trees in the king's forests. Never one to miss an opportunity to profit from government enterprises, Pâris-Duverney sent for his protégé Beaumarchais, and they established a jointly owned company to exploit 2,400 acres of prime forest at Chinon, near the confluence of the Loire, Indre, and Vienne Rivers just south of Tours. They agreed it would be best for Beaumarchais to take personal command of the enterprise to ensure maximum profits. Several days after arriving at his new job, he wrote to his wife:

> You asked me to write you, my dear love, about my work. I have to resolve misunderstandings between directors, managers, clerks; handle a budget of more than 100,000 crowns [more than $1.2 million], visit harbors, oversee 200 lumberjacks in the forest, arrange transport of wood from 280 acres, supervise building of new roads from the forest to the river and repair of old ones, order three or four thousand tons of hay and oats for thirty dray horses, oversee construction of gates and sluices on the River Indre to give us waterways on which to ship wood during the entire year, supervise loading of 50 barges that are waiting to carry their cargoes to Tours, Saumur, Angers and Nantes, sign leases for seven or eight farms to supply food and other provisions for our workers, oversee the bookkeeping for receipts and disbursements. That, my dear wife, is a brief description of my labors. . . .
>
> You see, my dear love, we do not sleep here as much as in Pantin [his wife's country home just north of Paris], but the work I do is far from disagreeable. This retreat is not for the pretentious. . . . If I were mean enough to wish you the misfortune of living in a desolate country in want of all pleasures, I would beg you to come to me. . . . Adieu, my love; good-night; I am going to bed. And my son, my son. How is he? I have to laugh to myself when I think that I am working here for him.[11]

Besides writing to his wife, Beaumarchais, now thirty-eight, spent his free time writing a second full-length play—*Les deux amis* (The Two Friends)—which opened in Paris on January 13, 1770 . . . and closed ten nights later. Beneath the poster outside the theater someone scrawled beneath the title: "By an author who has none." It was the story of a tax collector who tries to save a friend from bankruptcy by borrowing from the public till. One critic called it "an absurd story of loans—without interest."[12]

The failure of his second play marked the beginning of an avalanche of woes for Beaumarchais. In midsummer, his patron Pâris-Duverney died;

four months later, his wife died in childbirth, losing Beaumarchais's sec-
ond child; then his little son fell ill and followed his mother to the grave.
Adding to family losses was the death of his father's second wife. Pierre
Caron moved back into his son's rue de Condé mansion, but with only
Beaumarchais and his sister Julie still in residence, a dismal silence crushed
all semblance of life in every room.

The death of Pâris-Duverney had dire consequences for Beaumarchais.
While the budding playwright was earning his way into the old man's
heart, a ne'er-do-well great-nephew of the great industrialist had seethed
with bitterness watching his great-uncle lavish affection and investment
opportunities on the low-born Beaumarchais.

"I hate that man like a lover loves his mistress," the comte de La Blache
growled about Beaumarchais.[13]

Although La Blache had not worked a day in his great-uncle's industrial
empire, he nonetheless inherited every penny, and when Beaumarchais presented two promissory notes from the old man for 90,000 pounds (about
$360,000 today), La Blache declared them forgeries and claimed that Beau-
marchais actually owed the estate 139,000 livres (more than $50,000). He
filed suit against Beaumarchais in October 1771, winning a judgment of
56,000 livres, and began a relentless vendetta to destroy him. La Blache fed
rumors to the press that Beaumarchais had poisoned both his wives and
lost his post as Versailles music master for making unwanted overtures to
one of the king's daughters. Already despised by many noblemen at Versailles as an unscrupulous *arriviste*, Beaumarchais saw his name smeared
in scandal sheets.

Despondent over the accumulation of crushing setbacks—and with
nothing else to occupy his time—Beaumarchais turned to his favorite
pastime: writing plays—and even expanding them to include music. He
usurped a ubiquitous plot dating back to theater in ancient Rome: that
of a lecherous old man determined to thwart the marriage of two angelic
young lovers and ravish the young lady himself—only to have his quick-
witted servant thwart his ambitions by helping the young lovers disguise
themselves and elope. Beaumarchais added more than a touch of original-
ity to the tired tale by turning it into political satire, replacing the ser-

vant with a barber named Figaro whose biting wit and ingenious schemes "shave" onstage aristocrats, while mocking their offstage counterparts—including the royal family. Beaumarchais peopled the rest of his play with hilarious caricatures of men and women he knew intimately—commoners as well as aristocrats. Although political satire was a dangerous art form under the absolute French monarchy, news of political unrest in America had combined with the writings of enlightened French philosophes—Rousseau and others—to provoke widespread dissent and criticism of the social order in France. Beaumarchais laced Figaro's words and actions with biting wit and intelligent defiance of the ruling class that made the barber one of the most beloved characters in theater history. His arrival onstage could not have come at a more appropriate time.

Early in 1770, an ugly confrontation between British soldiers and the Sons of Liberty in New York City had left both sides with cuts and bruises, but no fatalities. Boston was the scene of far uglier incidents: when a small mob broke down the door of a Tory shopkeeper, a friend came to his help and fired his musket at the mob, wounding a nineteen-year-old and killing an eleven-year-old. "Young as he was," the *Boston Gazette* proclaimed, "he died in his country's cause."[14]

Rabble-rouser Samuel Adams turned the boy's funeral into the largest ever held in America—an enormous mass mourning of a martyr that stretched more than half a mile, with more than 400 carefully groomed, angelic children leading the coffin and 2,000 mourners walking behind, followed by thirty chariots and chaises.

"Mine eyes have never beheld such a funeral," Massachusetts attorney John Adams all but sobbed. "This shows there are more lives to spend if wanted in the service of their country. It shows too that the faction is not yet expiring—that the ardor of people is not to be quelled by the slaughter of one child and wounding of another."[15] The news shocked French philosophistes such as Beaumarchais, who had long believed the British had created an Edenic society in America.

Worse was to come in Boston, of course, when a squad of seven Redcoats fired into a mob of thuggish demonstrators at the customhouse, leaving five dead and eight wounded. Elevated to near sainthood by silversmith/

Paul Revere's engraving of the Boston Massacre inflamed anti-aristocratic passions in Europe as well as America by portraying British Redcoats slaughtering innocent civilians in Boston on March 5, 1770. In fact, hired thugs incited the British to fire by pelting them with stones. (This is a copy of a drawing by John Singleton Copley's half-brother, Henry Pelham.)

LIBRARY OF CONGRESS

engraver Paul Revere, their deaths elicited outrage against the ruling classes among English and French intellectuals, especially after copies of Revere's incendiary engraving reached Europe, showing British soldiers, muskets drawn, slaughtering helpless, unarmed townsmen.

Horrified by the slaughter in Boston, Beaumarchais increased his assault on the ruling class. Calling his play *Le Barbier de Séville*—"The Barber of Seville"—he set the action in Spain to make it more difficult for Versailles noblemen to recognize themselves in the characters onstage —and possibly retaliate against him in court or on the dueling pitch. To the mix of melodrama and hilarity, he added music—*seguedillas* that he had embraced while visiting Spain and for which he wrote words. The result was a brilliant precursor of the nineteenth-century operetta and twentieth-century musical comedy that evoked uneasy laughter among some aristocrats—and undisguised outrage among others for its insulting treatment of the nobility:

> COUNT: I think this rascal must be Figaro.
>
> FIGARO: The very same my lord.
>
> COUNT: I hardly recognized you, you good-for-nothing. Don't come near me!
>
> FIGARO: That's strange. I recognized you immediately—by the kind words with which you have always honored me.

But Beaumarchais did not protect Figaro from equally sharp barbs:

> COUNT: What have you done since I last dismissed you?
>
> FIGARO: On my return to Madrid . . . I tried the theater. . . . They hissed me, but if I could only try again . . .
>
> COUNT [interrupting]: You would take your revenge by boring them to death.

Recognizing his need for Figaro's help in wooing the beautiful Rosine, the count calls him "my friend" and tells him, "You shall be my savior and my guardian angel."

> FIGARO: How quickly my usefulness has closed the distance between us.
>
> COUNT: Your merry anger delights me. . . . What gave you such an optimistic philosophy?
>
> FIGARO: Continual misfortune. I always laugh at everything for fear I might cry.[16]

Figaro, of course, was a caricature of Beaumarchais himself—indeed, his alter ego. The origin of his name remains uncertain. It may have been a contraction of *Fils Caron* (son of Caron) at a time when the *s* in *fils* was silent, but an equally plausible origin is the Spanish colloquialism *picaro*, or *ficaro*, meaning "rascal." As the comedy unfolds, the barber Figaro helps

A contemporary drawing of the beloved barber, Figaro,
the revolutionary hero of Beaumarchais's popular
play, *Le Barbier de Séville*.

Music composed by Beaumarchais for "Je suis Lindor"—one of several
beautiful songs he created for *Le Barbier de Séville*. The combination of
music and song in a play was a first in the history of French theater.

his former master, the handsome young Count d'Almaviva, gain entrance to the house of the elderly lecher Doctor Bartolo (modeled after Beaumarchais's father) so the count can woo Bartolo's beautiful young ward Rosine. Mocking *Romeo and Juliet*, Beaumarchais lets the count woo Rosine from the street beneath her balcony—as he clumsily strums a guitar and sings "Je suis Lindor"—one of several beautiful songs Beaumarchais created for the play—a first in the history of French theater:

> Je suis Lindor, ma naissance est commune;
> Mes voeux sont ceux d'un simple bachelier;
> Que n'ai-je hélas! d'un brilliant chevalier,
> À vous offrir le rang et la fortune.

> Tous les matins ici, d'une voix tendre,
> Je chanterais mon amour sans espoir;
> Je bornerai mes plaisirs à vous voir,
> Et puissiez vous en trouver à m'entendre.

> My name is Lindor—of common birth;
> With but a young man's hopes to offer.
> Alas, I've no great knight's exalted name
> Nor rank or fame or wealth to proffer.

> In tender tones to thee each morn,
> I'll sing of my love, my hopeless love.
> I'll turn from every joy to see your face,
> To know you've heard me from above.

Although Bartolo schemes to keep Rosine for himself, she falls in love with the handsome young count. In the end, Figaro's complex but witty strategies overcome the parries of Bartolo and ensure a happy ending with the marriage of the count and Rosine—all while skewering the aristocracy with hilarious dialogue, replete with insulting or lewd double entendres, or both. As a reward, the count rescues Figaro from the tedium of barbering and gives him a sinecure as his valet and steward of the castle, with relatively luxurious quarters in the count's castle outside Seville. Beaumarchais offered his comic opera to the Théâtre Français (later, the Comédie Française), which agreed to stage the play the following year.

A torrent of misfortunes would prevent its opening, however.

In February 1772, while Beaumarchais was still writing *The Barber of Seville*, the court appointed a state's attorney, or *rapporteur*, to meet with litigants in the La Blache lawsuit and summarize their positions for the judges—a common practice in France to save time hearing testimony in court. Under normal circumstances the litigant who paid the state's attorney the largest bribe inevitably won the most flattering presentation of his case to the court. As Beaumarchais prepared his case for the *rapporteur*, police suddenly trooped down his street, pounded on his door and, when he showed himself, arrested him by order of the Captain General of the Court for the Conservation of the King's Pleasures—Beaumarchais's superior on the court where he served as lieutenant general. As he howled in protest at the impossibility of such an order, police clamped him in irons and carted him off to prison and an unlit dungeon packed with half-starved thieves, cutthroats, and political prisoners.

Inexplicably locked away in filth and darkness, with no prospects of release, Beaumarchais faced financial and personal ruin. Not only would he be unable to present his case to the *rapporteur* or the judges, but the Théâtre Français also canceled the opening of *The Barber of Seville*. As he searched his mind for an explanation for his fate, he grew convinced that La Blache was responsible for his imprisonment and he wrote in desperation to his friend Gudin. He thought back to his father's observation when the king's clockmaker Lepaute had stolen his invention for making wrist watches: "C'est normal," his father had declared. It's normal for the upper classes to step on those beneath them. "C'est comme ça"—that's life and the way things are.

"In all totalitarian countries," an older and wiser Beaumarchais now wrote to his friend Gudin, "dukes and peers with whom I can never associate ... punish those they cannot inculpate with justice. Those in power always prefer to punish rather than judge; in their eyes, being right is always a crime?"[17] Like others with sympathies for the oppressed, Beaumarchais was beginning to think and talk like an American revolutionary.

Ironically, it was not La Blache who was responsible for Beaumarchais's ill fortune. More curious than any plot he would ever conceive, the events that provoked his imprisonment began with an invitation he received from a theater devotee, the duc de Chaulnes, to the salon of his mistress, the actress Mademoiselle Ménard. Ménard had abandoned the theater because of the duc's jealous rages and physical assaults on her and her co-stars—sometimes leaping onstage in a mad, jealous rage to attack them whenever their roles called for mutual embraces. As the beautiful Ménard and handsome Beaumarchais exchanged pleasantries, smiles, and laughter, Chaulnes's paranoia reached explosive levels, and, a few days later, he brutally assaulted Ménard before rushing out to find Beaumarchais at the courthouse. Along the way, the powerfully built duc pounced on Beaumarchais's fat little friend Gudin like a "bird of prey," and threw him bodily into his coach. As a crowd formed, Gudin shrieked and leaped out the other side. The duc reached for his head, grabbed a fistful of hair, but was left with only a wig that set off roars of laughter from onlookers.

Driven to even more rage, the duc flew up the courthouse steps, raced into the courtroom, and, according to Beaumarchais, threatened "to kill me, tear out my heart and drink my blood." Faced with arrest, the duc relented but challenged Beaumarchais to a duel. Later, after Beaumarchais had returned home, the duc broke into the house, seized Beaumarchais's ceremonial sword, and rushed at him. As they fought, servants rushed to their master's aid. "Disarm this madman," cried Beaumarchais, blood streaming from his face, where Chaulnes had scratched him. As they pulled the duc off his victim, the most powerful of them—a gargantuan cook with a log in hand—prepared a final blow, but Beaumarchais shouted, "Don't hurt him; he'll say I tried to assassinate him in my house."[18] The servants loosened their grip—only to have the crazed noblemen leap at Beaumarchais once again. This time, the servants seized Chaulnes and locked him in a study, where, after devouring a meal prepared for Beaumarchais, he flew into a rage, breaking glass and howling vows to kill Beaumarchais.

Police arrived and led the duc back to his own home. Gudin describes the aftermath:

> That evening, Beaumarchais was as cheerful and assured as if he had passed a tranquil day. He visited old friends . . . recounted the day's adventures . . . assured the ladies that he would not allow a madman's conduct to spoil the evening's pleasures. . . . He was as calm, gay, and brilliant as usual during supper, and spent part of the evening playing the harp and singing Spanish *seguedillas.* He was always like that—throwing himself entirely into things at hand without thought of what had happened or might follow. . . . He never spoke ill of his enemies, even of those he knew to be the most intent on ruining him.[19]

Beaumarchais had a simple explanation for his friend: "Why should I lose the time I have with you, my friend, reliving things which will only make us miserable. I try to forget the folly of those about me, and think only of the good and useful; we have so many things to say to each other that these other topics should never find a place in our conversation."[20]

But the duc de La Vrillière, who so resented Beaumarchais's appointment to the bench, would not allow Beaumarchais to forget the folly of those about him. Although a tribunal that handled disputes between noblemen sentenced Chaulnes to prison and cleared Beaumarchais of all blame, de La Vrillière seethed with outrage that a duke had been sent to prison while a commoner—the low-born son of a clockmaker—was free. On February 24, 1773, he ordered Beaumarchais arrested and imprisoned, explaining to the chief of police, "The man is too insolent."[21] Beaumarchais refused at first to believe such pettiness could propagate such outrageous injustice, but as days turned into weeks, his resentment turned into rage as he looked around his dungeon and saw the cruelties inflicted on commoners by the privileged. Within a few months, he would transfer that rage onto the French stage and, ultimately, to the battlefields of America.

4

So You Mistreat Some Poor Devil...
Till He Trembles in Disgrace!

BEAUMARCHAIS LANGUISHED in prison for a month, scratching out letters to de La Vrillière protesting his arbitrary and unjust incarceration. The Captain General ignored the letters, insisting that Beaumarchais was "too insolent" for a commoner and deserved a lesson in humility. Beaumarchais appealed to his friend Antoine Gabriel de Sartine d'Alby, the Spanish-born chief of police—who was also born a commoner, with the added burden of the name *Sardine*. After escaping the tortures of adolescence, he changed his piscine surname to *Sartine*, moved to the French cathedral city of Albi, and began a new life as a French government official. After transfer to Paris, he organized the cleaning and illumination of the dirty and dangerous Paris streets and won promotion to police chief. Sartine d'Alby asked the Captain General to rescind the arrest order—only to meet with a stern rejection, without even an attempt at a justification.

"I have been denied justice because my adversary is a nobleman," Beaumarchais lamented.

> I have been imprisoned because I was insulted by a nobleman. Soon they will say that it was very insolent of me to have been assaulted by a nobleman. What do they mean by saying, "He has boasted too much in this affair?" Could I do less than demand justice and prove, by the conduct of my adversary, that I was in no way wrong? What a pretext to ruin an offended man to say, "He has talked too much about his case."[1]

Antoine Gabriel de Sartine d'Alby, the Spanish-
born chief of police in Paris and a close friend of
Beaumarchais, tried without success to arrange
the playwright's release from prison.

After signing his letter, Beaumarchais grew despondent. For the first
time in his life—and he vowed it would be the last—he found his ascent
in life blocked by forces too powerful to manipulate or defy. For the first
time, he was unable to call on his once-inexhaustible good humor to laugh
at his troubles. Then, a note arrived—in a child's hand:

Monsieur,

I am sending you my purse because one is always unhappy in prison. I am
very sorry that you are in prison. Every morning and every evening I say an
Ave Maria for you. I have the honor to be, *Monsieur*, your very humble and
very obedient servant.

Constant.[2]

With tears streaming down his cheeks, Beaumarchais found paper and pen to reply:

Mon cher petit ami Constant [My dear little friend Constant],
I received your letter with deepest gratitude. I have divided its contents with my fellow prisoners, according to their needs. I kept the best part of your gift for your friend Beaumarchais—by that I mean the prayers, the *Ave Marias*, which I need most—and I distributed the money in your purse to the poor sufferers around me. So, while intending to help but one man, you have earned the gratitude of many. That is the usual fruit of good deeds such as yours. Good day, my little friend Constant.

Beaumarchais.[3]

Beaumarchais sent his thanks to the boy's parents—his old friend Charles Lenormant d'Étioles, who had remarried after the death of his first wife Mme. de Pompadour and sired the little boy Constant. "My thanks and compliments," Beaumarchais wrote:

Your care instilled and developed his beneficence in an age when morality consists of protecting one's own interests. L'Abbé Leroux [the boy's teacher] has not been satisfied to teach his pupils to define the word virtue; he has taught them to love it. . . . Happy parents! to have a son six years of age capable of such a deed. I also had a son; but he is no more.[4]

On March 20, Sartine sent Beaumarchais a note warning that no one could survive tilting against authority or the aristocracy in an absolute monarchy. Beaumarchais would almost certainly languish in prison indefinitely if he did not replot the course of his life. Consciously or unconsciously, Beaumarchais realized the truth of his friend's warning. As one of his own onstage characters in *Le Barbier* warns Figaro, "A wise man does not start a quarrel with the great and powerful."[5] So Beaumarchais began revising the plot for his—and Figaro's—life with a letter to the duc de La Vrillière:

Monseigneur:

The dreadful affair of the duc de Chaulnes has produced a series of misfortunes for me, of which the greatest is having incurred your displeasure. . . . If in my grief, any of the steps I have taken have displeased you, I disavow them at your feet, Monseigneur, and beg you to grant me your generous pardon. . . . My entire family tearfully joins their prayers to mine. Every one, Monseigneur, praises your indulgence and goodness of heart. By a single word, you can fill the hearts of a multitude of honest people with joy and add their gratitude to the deep respect with which we—and especially I—are all your very humble and obedient servants.

Beaumarchais.[6]

It was Figaro redefined. Instead of demanding a pardon, Beaumarchais appealed to the duc's pompous self-depiction as a defender of justice. He asked the duc to consider releasing him for but a few hours each day to give his side of the La Blache lawsuit to the *rapporteur* for presentation to the judges. Satisfied by Beaumarchais's apparent contrition, the duc ordered the playwright released from prison during the day to attend to the La Blache case, but he was to return to his cell at night.

The duc's decision came too late, however. La Blache had already fed the *rapporteur* the "facts"—and funds—to win his case. The *rapporteur*—a short, fat, bearded brute of an Alsatian named Louis Valentin Goëzman—refused to see Beaumarchais. After combing a list of contacts, Beaumarchais found one with access to the *rapporteur*'s wife, who offered to open Goëzman's door for 100 louis (about $3,600). The bribe did indeed open Goëzman's door—but not his mind. After a few gruff questions, the Alsatian ended the interview abruptly and walked out, leaving Beaumarchais to choke on his words. With only days to go before trial, Beaumarchais asked for a second interview, but, without more cash, he could only offer Madam Goëzman a diamond-studded watch he had made. She accepted it, but demanded an extra fifteen louis (about $500) "for Goëzman's secretary." When Beaumarchais arrived for his second interview, however, Goëzman refused to see him. La Blache had offered more. On Goëzman's recommendation, the court declared the Pâris-Duverney promissory notes to Beaumarchais void and affirmed Beaumarchais to be 56,000 livres (more than $200,000 modern) in debt to La Blache.

The decision ended Beaumarchais's daily sorties and left him incarcerated full time, unable to raise cash to pay the court's award to La Blache. The latter obtained court orders to seize all the playwright's assets, including his home and everything in it. Beaumarchais's family fled—one of his sisters to a nearby Paris convent and two other sisters to a convent in Picardy, seventy miles north of Paris. A fourth, widowed sister died while her brother was in prison, leaving him the guardian of her little girl and of her husband's two sons by his first marriage. A fifth Beaumarchais sister and her husband took the orphaned children into their crowded home temporarily. With his son's funds seized, old Père Caron and Beaumarchais's stepmother moved to a rented room.

As creditors sank their teeth into Beaumarchais's other assets, courtiers who despised Beaumarchais for his rapid penetration of their aristocratic sancta joined the feeding frenzy, swooping in like vultures to salvage whatever flesh remained on the skeletal remains of Beaumarchais's vast enterprises.

"My courage is exhausted," he wrote to police chief Sartine.

> Public opinion has turned against me: My credit has fallen to less than nothing, my business is ruined, my family, of which I am the patriarch and sole support is in despair. I have done good all my life, *Monsieur*, but those disposed to evil have done nothing but tear me apart . . . and calumniate me from a distance. . . . I have enough courage to withstand my own misfortunes, but not enough to stem the tears of my father, a respectable man of seventy-five who is dying of grief over the abject state to which I have fallen. I do not have enough courage to ease the anguish of my sisters and nieces, who feel the horror of my detention and know how it has devastated my affairs.[7]

Beaumarchais remained in prison another month. On May 8, 1773, with the duc de La Vrillière satisfied that financial ruin had suitably humbled the insolent playwright, he ordered Beaumarchais released, an object of disdain by the vast majority of titled society, with only a handful of acquaintances able to conjure up a modicum of pity. Rather than risk scandal, the *rapporteur* Goëzman and his wife returned the watch and the 100 louis Beaumarchais had paid to obtain a fair hearing. His wife, however, pocketed the fifteen louis she had collected, and, after he left prison, the bankrupt Beaumarchais wrote to Madame Goëzman asking that she return them (more than $500 at a time when laborers earned about $1 a day). Assuming that Beaumarchais would not risk a public admission that he had bribed a judge's wife, she simply ignored his request. It was a bad decision that pushed Beaumarchais beyond the limits of his patience and provoked him to unsheathe his only weapon—his pen—a weapon he had used successfully as a youth to expose the king's clockmaker Lepaute as a thief. Motivated by even greater despair and desperation, Beaumarchais invested his last sou to publish a series of five pamphlets, or *mémoires*, one after the other, detailing events leading to his imprisonment and exposing the corruption that pervaded the French judiciary.

"The questions before us," he began simply in his first tract, "are whether it is necessary to bribe a judge with gold to get a fair trial and whether bribing judges is a punishable crime or simply an unfortunate fact of life in France."[8] Laced with Figaroan humor, dialogue, and biting sarcasm, his answers proved an enormous literary, social, and political success, selling by the thousands, in every café, salon, and château—reaching the hands (and eyes) of virtually every literate man and woman in France, including the king. His thirty-eight-page first pamphlet read like a play, at times evoking tears, at times disgust, at times gales of laughter. It also evoked additional charges against Beaumarchais for attempting to corrupt a judge, for which he could be sentenced to life behind a galley oar. Like Figaro, Beaumarchais remained undeterred:

> When my sister tried to protect our family savings by offering Goëzman's secretary fifty, instead of 100 louis, he refused indignantly: "When you offer a bribe, Madame, you must do so honestly."[9]

Unlike his maudlin letters of self-pity from prison, Beaumarchais allowed facts and events in the case to evoke sympathy for his plight and expose corruption—often lampooning himself:

Unlike many other aristocrats, my nobility is not uncertain; you don't have to accept my word for it. My nobility is my legitimate property, for which I have a fine parchment with a large, yellow wax seal. No one can challenge its authenticity, because I still have the receipt for its purchase twenty years ago.[10]

The first pamphlet laid out his case; the subsequent ones described appearances at court, where each party could examine and cross-examine his adversary. When the court clerk asked whether Madame Goëzman and Beaumarchais knew each other, she snapped that she neither knew nor wished to know him. Beaumarchais, in turn, agreed in part: "I do not have the honor of knowing *Madame*, but after looking her over, I can't help conjuring a wish that differs from hers."[11]

When the laughter subsided, the examination began.

Beaumarchais asked whether he had not given her 100 louis. "That is false," she cried out. "No one ever mentioned anything about 100 louis!"

"Did you not hide the 100 louis in a vase?"

"That's not true!"

"Did you not promise to arrange an audience for me with your husband in exchange for the 100 louis?"

"Filthy lie!"

He asked her about the 100 louis sixteen times, and sixteen times she denied any knowledge of them. Finally, he asked about the fifteen louis.

"I insist, Monsieur, that no one ever said a word to me or offered me fifteen louis. What point would there be to offer me fifteen louis after I refused 100 the day before?"

"The day before what, Madame?"

"My dear Sir: the day before . . . of course . . . the day before the day . . ." She stopped suddenly and bit her lips. Beaumarchais finished her sentence for her: "The day before the day that no one spoke to you of fifteen louis?"

"Stop this, Monsieur! Leave me alone," she stood and shouted, "or I'll slap your face. What do I care about fifteen louis. You're trying to confuse me and make me contradict myself with all your nasty, twisted questions. Well now I swear I will not answer anything anymore!"[12]

The publication of Beaumarchais's real-life trial transfixed Paris and Versailles for seven months, from August 1773 to February 1774. His pamphlets—and the dull, boorish responses by Goëzman and his wife—restored Beaumarchais's reputation and popularity. More than 4,000 copies circulated across Europe, making his name among the best known in Europe and inspiring Hessian poet Johann Wolfgang Goethe to write a popular drama based on Beaumarchais's improbable adventures. They enthralled Voltaire, who himself had been imprisoned, exiled, and eventually forced to flee France to Ferney, Switzerland, to avoid prosecution for his writings. "No comedy was ever more amusing, no tragedy more touching," he commented on the Beaumarchais pamphlets. "What a man! He unites everything—humor, seriousness, argument, gaiety, force, pathos, every kind of eloquence . . . and he confounds all his adversaries, and he gives lessons to his judges."[13] And in England, Horace Walpole reacted with "horror" over the French "mode of administering justice. . . . Is there a country in the world in which this Madame Goëzman would not have been severely punished?"[14]

In January 1774, the Théâtre Français took advantage of the publicity surrounding the Beaumarchais trial to revive his first play, *Eugénie*. As crowds fought their way into the theater each night, critics who had demeaned Beaumarchais for not belonging to the Poet's Society restored his literary reputation with glowing reviews. The Théâtre Français announced it would produce *The Barber of Seville* the following month. Celebrities across Europe joined Voltaire, Goethe, and Walpole in supporting Beaumarchais—among them, the French philosopher Jean Le Rond d'Alembert, coeditor with Diderot of the monumental *Encyclopédie*.

The trial reached a climax when one of the judges withdrew from the case and all but admitted that Goëzman had shared bribes with him. He sent Beaumarchais a six-page plea for help in salvaging his reputation: "I have read your last memorial [pamphlet], *Monsieur*," the judge wrote. "I yield to your prayers by resigning as your judge." Admitting that he feared "the public will condemn me," the judge pleaded to Beaumarchais "to mention my resignation in your next pamphlet as an honorable act."[15]

With the court itself tarred by the same brush as one of the parties before it, the remaining judges retired to consider the case, despising Beaumarchais for having exposed the corruption that pervaded their institution. With angry crowds repeatedly chanting "Beau-mar-chais!" outside the courthouse, the judges deliberated for twelve hours before deciding to strip Goëzman of his judicial robes, expel him from the judiciary, and disbar him. They imposed token fines on Madame Goëzman and three intermediaries in the bribery schemes and ordered Madame Goëzman to return the fifteen louis. Although the court restored Beaumarchais's property and assets, it fined him for publishing his four pamphlets and bringing dishonor on the courts. Calling them an illegal attempt to influence a court decision, the judges ordered them burned by the public executioner. Finally, they stripped all participants of their civil rights and citizenship for an indefinite period—the Goëzmans for soliciting and accepting bribes, and Beaumarchais for giving them.

As word of Beaumarchais's sentence reached the crowds outside, a roar of outrage enveloped the courthouse, forcing the judges to slip out the back door to escape retribution. The crowds cheered as the playwright emerged; they followed his carriage to his sister's home and were still cheering there the next morning when he emerged. Two days after the trial, the prince de Conti, a Bourbon relative of the king, joined with one of the king's grandsons, the comte d'Artois—the future King Charles X—in inviting Beaumarchais to the prince-royal's festival the next day. "We are of a sufficiently illustrious house," Conti proclaimed, "to show the nation what is her duty toward one who has deserved so well of his country."[16]

Despite restoration of his popularity—and property—Beaumarchais remained in legal limbo, in so-called civil degradation—in effect, a "nonperson," without the rights of a citizen, and therefore unable to prevent La Blache from returning to court to collect the judgment awarded earlier. Only a "letter of relief" from the king could delay collection of the judgment until Beaumarchais could appeal to a higher court for a reversal. Although the king had always liked Beaumarchais and was himself amused

Boston patriots, disguised as Indians, dump British tea overboard on December 16, 1773. News of the Boston Tea Party stimulated French support for the American Revolution. The scene in this engraving—created in 1846, more than seven decades after the actual event—was largely the product of Nathaniel Currier's imagination.

LIBRARY OF CONGRESS

by the Beaumarchais pamphlets, he was annoyed by the music master's having brought discredit to the court system. And after reading *The Barber of Seville*, the king grew irate at Figaro's insolent barbs at the aristocracy. He ordered censors to ban the play and told Police Chief Sartine to silence the playwright's voice. He wanted none of the so-called tea parties and other popular stirrings of England and America to spread to France. Although American Patriots had held their Boston Tea Party in mid-December 1773, the news did not arrive in France until the end of January, just as the Beaumarchais trial reached its tumultuous end. Although Beaumarchais appreciated the humor of Patriots disguising themselves as Indians to dispose of British tea, Sartine told the playwright that his only hope for a "letter of relief" was not humor, but a grand gesture of obeisance. "I counsel you not to show yourself in public anymore. Above all, do not write anything, because the king wishes that you publish nothing more about this affair."[17]

Beaumarchais responded appropriately, recognizing that "royal power was a rock," as Gudin put it, "against which prudence might well fear to throw herself. He therefore adopted a wise policy of submitting . . . to the king, obeying him and keeping silent."[18] Walking away from the adoring throngs of Paris, he went into self-imposed exile in a forgotten hamlet across the northern French border in Flanders and sent a letter of contrition to a close friend who was a banker and counselor to the king.

"What has pierced my heart more than anything else," Beaumarchais wrote to his friend, knowing that the letter would reach the king,

> has been the unfavorable impression recent events may have given the king about me. Some have told him that I was seditious and intent on notoriety, but no one told him that I was merely defending myself. . . . You know, my friend, that I always led a quiet life and never would have written about public matters if powerful enemies had not united to ruin me. Should I have allowed myself to be crushed without trying to defend myself? Is it a reason to dishonor me and my family if I did so vigorously? Is it a reason to sever the ties from society of an honest subject who might well have been employed usefully in the service of king and country? I have the strength to support undeserved misfortune, but my father is dying of sorrow after seventy-five years of honor and hard work; my sisters are weak and helpless.[19]

His letter was enough to sway the king—especially Beaumarchais's stated willingness to serve his monarch. The king had not read idly of Figaro's machinations on behalf of his liege, the comte d'Almaviva, in *The Barber.* Nor was he unaware of Beaumarchais's (and Figaro's) talent for undermining the credibility of those in authority. Beaumarchais's friend at court replied that the king felt he could use that talent and promised a letter of relief to allow Beaumarchais to recover his estate if he undertook a difficult secret mission with zeal—and succeeded.

"The sweetest thing in the world, my dear friend," Beaumarchais replied, "is the generosity of your sincere friendship. Everyone tells me that I have a reprieve; add to this the news that it is the king's free will that I obtain it. May God hear your prayers, my generous friend."[20]

In March 1774, after a month in exile, Beaumarchais returned to Paris, and, according to his friend Gudin, attracted swarms of admirers, including a Swiss lady of considerable wealth, "endowed with beauty, a tender heart and a firmness of character capable of supporting him in the cruel combats that would be his destiny." Gudin insists she "burned with a desire" to see him:

> Under the pretext of busying herself with music, she sent . . . to beg him to lend her his harp. Beaumarchais understood. He replied, "I lend nothing, but if the lady wishes to come here, I will hear her play and she may hear me." She came. It was difficult to see Beaumarchais without loving him. What an impression he made, regarded as the defender of oppressed liberty, avenger of the public . . . his charm, looks, voice, bearing. . . . The attraction of the first moment increased from hour to hour as each discovered excellent qualities in the other. . . . Their hearts were united from that moment by a bond which no circumstance could break and which love, esteem and time . . . rendered indissoluble.[21]

Still without his civil rights, he could not marry her; nevertheless, the starstruck Marie-Thérèse Amélie de Willermaulaz became his full-time companion and lover, adding a gay, cheerful presence—and stately good looks—to his life and eventually taking full responsibility for preserving the atmosphere of song, laughter, good cheer, good food, and good wine that had characterized every Beaumarchais home since his childhood.

Shortly after Beaumarchais met Marie-Thérèse, Sartine came from the palace with details of the mission Beaumarchais was to undertake for the king: Théveneau de Morande, a French writer of little consequence living in London, had extorted large sums from French notables by detailing their sexual adventures—but not their names—in a periodical he edited called *Le Gazetier cuirassé ou Anecdotes scandaleuses de la Cour de France*—"The Journalist in Armor or Scandalous Anecdotes from the French Court." Morande's audacity peaked with the printing of a tale entitled *Mémoires secrets d'une femme publique*—"The Secret Memoirs of a Prostitute"—which purported to relate the early life of Madame du

Marie-Thérèse Amélie de Willermaulaz,
who became Beaumarchais's full-time companion,
lover, and mother of his child, before restoration
of his civil rights allowed them to marry.
AUTHOR'S COLLECTION

Barry before she became the king's mistress. After Madame de Pompadour died in 1764, Louis XV spent four years experimenting with a procession of women, until his keen eye spotted the beautiful twenty-two-year-old Jeanne Bécu, who, according to Morande's version of her biography, was dining with his valet. Insisting she was the illegitimate daughter of a seamstress, Morande said Bécu had gone to work in a Paris brothel at fifteen, where the owner appropriated the young beauty as his own at first, then used her and other young girls to win favors at court by taking them to the king's summer palace in Compiègne, north of Paris, for the pleasure of the king's servants. When the fifty-eight-year-old king saw her, according to Morande's lascivious tale, she so aroused his lust that he snatched

Madame du Barry was the successor to Madame de
Pompadour as King Louis XV's official Royal Mistress.
She was the target of a libelous pamphlet that
Beaumarchais, acting as a secret agent for the
king, succeeded in suppressing.

RÉUNION DES MUSÉES NATIONAUX

her up and took her to his royal chamber, despite his valet's warnings that
she had slept on the streets and might transmit venereal disease. To mini-
mize scandal, Morande explained, the king ennobled her by ordering her
to marry Count Guillaume du Barry, who barely finished uttering his oath
of marriage when the king seized Madame's arm and, exercising his *droit
du seigneur*—the right of a lord to sleep with his vassal's bride on the wedding night—he led her back to the royal bed to consummate her wedding.

The king's prime minister, the duc de Choiseul, was but one of many
critics at court who found the king's behavior disgraceful. Eager to promote his own sister for consideration as the king's royal mistress, he described du Barry as "contemptible scum and a danger to the king at his age
and declining health." The king ignored Choiseul and his other critics,

however, and, toward the end of April 1769, he presided over a "formal presentation at Court of a whore from the streets of Paris and her elevation to the rank of Royal Mistress."[22]

When Morande threatened to reveal the name of *la femme publique*, King Louis asked his brother monarch the British king to have his agents kill Morande and seize materials with any references to Madame du Barry. Time after time, however, Morande escaped—and, with each escape, he increased the price for documents relating to Madame du Barry. Having read *The Barber of Seville*, the king decided that only a brilliant scamp like Figaro would be able to outsmart Morande, and he called on Figaro's creator to go to London.

Although Beaumarchais arrived at Morande's door in disguise under the name of Ronac (an anagram of Caron), Morande turned out to be warm and amusing, with winning ways that quickly turned Beaumarchais into a friend and confederate. As a master designer of intricate plots, Beaumarchais appreciated Morande's bravura in exposing aristocratic life in France, and, in the aftermath of his outrageous imprisonment by the duc de La Vrillière, he shared Morande's deep loathing for the aristocracy. Indeed, his abhorrence for French nobility had already spawned a sense of comradeship with Americans and their rebellion against British rule. The people of Boston had thrown British tea into the sea rather than pay exorbitant taxes to drink it, and city after city in America was following suit in the spring of 1774. A mob disguised as Indians boarded a tea ship in New York City in March and dumped its entire cargo into the water. In April, a tea ship tied up in Annapolis, Maryland, only to a have a mob set fire to it and destroy its cargo. A ship attempting to land tea in Greenwich, New Jersey, met the same fate. Infuriated by colonist insolence, the British monarch and his parliamentary aristocrats punished them by closing Boston to all trade—in effect threatening the city with starvation. Beaumarchais would equate the response of Britain's parliament with the sort of injustice that he had suffered at the hands of the French judiciary. In his mind and heart, he was at one with American patriots—none of whom he had ever met. They were creations of his imagination—godlike defenders of individual liberty.

Before their conversations had ended, Beaumarchais decided to team up with Morande by taking a copy of the du Barry pamphlet back to Versailles with Morande's conditions for destroying all copies. Less than a week after going to London, Beaumarchais was back in Versailles displaying the pamphlet to the king's secret-service director, whose agents had tried for months to lay hands on it—and Morande—without success:

"You must be the devil," said the king's man incredulously as he looked at the pamphlet.

"It is only Monsieur de Beaumarchais, at your service, my lord."[23]

On April 8, Beaumarchais returned to London with 20,000 livres (about $80,000 today) for Morande and a king's contract to pay Morande 4,000 livres annually if he destroyed the pamphlets and swore an oath of allegiance that would subject him to summary execution for disloyalty. With Beaumarchais watching, Morande burned the pamphlets on the evening of April 24, 1774. With his newfound wealth, he went into legitimate journalism, becoming editor of *Le Courier de l'Europe*, to which Beaumarchais would frequently contribute under a pseudonym.

When Beaumarchais returned to France, he all but sprinted to Versailles to claim his royal reprieve and resume his storied life where he had left off before being swept up by a torrent of prejudice, calumny, and villainy. To his dismay, Louis XV was ill with smallpox and died a few days later—without leaving a word in writing to confirm his authorization of the Beaumarchais mission and recompense. The new king and his ministerial appointees knew nothing about it. The few officials who did know were unwilling to risk their futures by intervening on Beaumarchais's behalf after the new king and his Austrian queen, Marie Antoinette, expressed their disgust for Madame du Barry and exiled her from the palace. Beaumarchais was left with nothing to show for his London adventure—not even his travel expenses, let alone his civil rights or a "letter of relief" to stave off impending bankruptcy and imprisonment. Astonished by what he called "the strange fate that pursues me," Beaumarchais lamented, "If the king had lived for eight more days, I would have recovered my civil rights. I had his royal word for it."[24]

Beaumarchais tried to salvage some advantage from his service to the late king: "I hope you don't want me to remain without civil rights because of a decision by a discredited court," he reasoned with his friend, Police Chief Sartine. "All Europe has absolved me of its odious and absurd judgment, but I need a new decree to destroy the one it issued. I shall not cease to work toward this end. I hope your good offices will help attain this important object."[25] Sartine could only suggest that Beaumarchais await an opportunity to serve the new king as he had the old.

Beaumarchais decided to provide the opportunity for himself.

The threat of a scandalous revelation had provoked Beaumarchais's mission for the old king, he reasoned. A similar threat to the new king might yield the same results. This time, however, Beaumarchais intended to collect his just rewards in advance.

5

I'm the Busiest, Cleverest Fellow I Know

WITHIN DAYS of Sartine's suggestion that Beaumarchais await an opportunity to serve the new king, a scandalous document appeared mysteriously—indeed, miraculously—under Sartine's door at Versailles. It was entitled *Avis à la branche espagnole sur ses droits à la couronne de France, à défaut d'héritiers* (The Rights of the Spanish Branch [of the Bourbon Kings] to Claim the French Throne in the Absence of Any Heirs to the French King). The potentially explosive document stated with certainty that twenty-year-old king Louis XVI was unable to procreate and sire an heir, thus giving the Spanish Bourbons the right to claim the French throne.

The pamphlet devastated the royal couple. After four years of marriage Louis and his queen had indeed failed to produce any children. Theirs was the usual arranged royal marriage—in this case allying France and Austria by the union of the French heir apparent with Archduchess Marie Antoinette, a daughter of Austrian empress Marie Theresa.

Marie Antoinette's new husband, however, was taciturn, portly, and disinterested in society and sex. He was happiest alone in a quiet room, in a comfortable chair, studying history books and maps—and making delicate little metal trinkets with his fat little fingers. In contrast, his queen was a wildly outgoing beauty, raised in a ceaseless whirl of balls and entertainment in Vienna and the nearby summer palace of Schönbrun. Only nineteen when crowned queen of France, she had chafed beside her all-but-impotent fat prince during the four last dismal years of Louis XV's reign. With the old man's death, she abandoned her husband to his maps and

The Austrian-born queen of France, Marie
Antoinette, and her husband, King Louis XVI, also
were about to become targets of libelous pamphlets
when Beaumarchais stepped into the picture. Again
acting as secret agent to a king, Beaumarchais pursued
the mysterious author of the libelous materials into
the Vienna Woods.

RÉUNION DES MUSÉES NATIONAUX

trinkets and staged a nonstop frenzy of balls, banquets, and theater galas
that illuminated the skies over Versailles and Paris. Up all night, asleep all
day, she had as little inclination as her husband to mate and breed royal
heirs. The document proclaiming royal sterility, however, cast a different—and dangerous—light on their behavior and threatened to provoke
pretenders to the throne from the rival French House of Orléans or the
Spanish Bourbons to plot the overthrow of the timorous king. The king
and his counselors knew they had to destroy the pamphlet and its author.

Additional information materialized from no-one-knew-where naming the author as one "Guillaume Angelucci," an Italian adventurer living in England as "William Atkinson." An apparent master of disguises, the evil Angelucci successfully eluded all efforts by French—and English—agents to find even of a trace of his existence, past or present. All they learned was that he had the resources to flood Europe with copies of the document by publishing simultaneous editions in different languages in England and Holland.

The circumstances surrounding the document resembled so closely those of the du Barry pamphlet that Sartine approached the king and proposed Beaumarchais as the ideal agent to root out Angelucci and suppress publication of the document that threatened the royal family with scandal. Beaumarchais all but leaped at the opportunity to serve his king, but demanded, as a reward, an immediate "letter of relief" and restoration of his civil rights after he found Angelucci and destroyed the libelous document. Beaumarchais also demanded a written order from the king to guarantee his compensation if and when he succeeded in his mission:

> The Sieur de Beaumarchais, charged by my secret orders, will start for his destination as soon as possible; the discretion and energy he invests in their execution will be the most agreeable proofs which he can give me of his zeal for my service.
>
> Louis.
> Marly, July 10, 1774.[1]

Beaumarchais put the document in a gold locket he hung from his neck, pledged his "head, heart and arms" to the king's service, and within days wrote to Sartine from London that he had found Angelucci alias Atkinson, paid him £1,400 (about $5,000 in today's currency), and burned 1,000 copies of the pamphlet in Angelucci's possession. Using his anagrammatic name of Ronac, he and Angelucci, he said, would leave immediately for Holland to destroy copies there.

Beaumarchais's next letter described the successful completion of his mission in Holland—only to end with a horrifying, hastily scribbled addendum, breathlessly detailing the treacherous Angelucci's escape with an unburned copy. Writing that his quarry was fleeing to Nuremberg, Beaumarchais pledged to catch him and burn the last copy of the infamous document.

"I am like a lion," he wrote to Sartine. "I am out of money, but I have my own diamonds and jewelry that I will sell and, with rage in my heart . . . I shall travel day and night to find that abominable man. . . . I shall strip him of his papers and kill him."[2]

Beaumarchais followed Angelucci across Germany, detailing every step of the melodramatic chase in letters to Sartine. He wrote that he had trapped the villain at the forest of Neustadt, near Nuremberg, that Angelucci was on his horse and tried galloping away into the woods, but Beaumarchais had been too quick. He leaped from his coach, raced into the woods on foot, and, with Herculean strength, caught Angelucci's boot and wrestled him off his horse to the ground. With Angelucci pleading for his life, Beaumarchais searched the man's pockets, opened his valise, and lay hands on the last copy of the document that might have disgraced the French royal couple. He destroyed it immediately before turning his attention to his cringing prisoner. After receiving assurances that Angelucci would return to Italy and never again threaten the French royals, he allowed him to flee, even giving him a few banknotes to pay for his passage.

As Beaumarchais left the forest, though, two robbers set upon him and wounded him with a knife.

"Mein Gott," the coachman cried out when he saw the bleeding Beaumarchais approach.

"I immediately urinated on my handkerchief," Beaumarchais wrote, "and applied the urine-soaked cloth to my wound."

When he got to town, he applied a clean bandage—this time choosing *eau-de-vie*, or fruit brandy, instead of urine, as a more appetizing antiseptic. After learning that Angelucci had masterminded the attack, Beaumarchais asked for an audience with Empress Marie Theresa to obtain help in tracking the mysterious Italian who was blackmailing the king and queen of France:

EMPRESS: How did you acquire such zeal for the interests of my son-in-law
and, above all, my daughter?

BEAUMARCHAIS: I was one of the most unfortunate men in France toward the close of the last reign, Madame. The queen . . . did not disdain to
show some sympathy for me. . . . In serving her now, without even a hope
that she will ever know, I am only acquitting an immense debt. . . .

EMPRESS: But, what was the need for you to change your name, Monsieur?

BEAUMARCHAIS: I am only too well known throughout Europe, Madame. If I appeared under the name of Beaumarchais, I would no longer
be free to work secretly as so delicate a mission requires; that is why I
begged the king to let me travel under the name of Ronac, as indicated
in my passport.[3]

That evening a squad of soldiers stormed into his room and charged him
with being an impostor, liar, and adventurer. His coach driver had filed a report saying that Beaumarchais had staged the entire Neustadt Forest scene
and, indeed, had stabbed himself with a razor. After seizing his papers and
other possessions, police placed him under house arrest, posting guards by
his door twenty-four hours a day. He sent an urgent appeal to Sartine, and
after a month's imprisonment, a letter arrived from Versailles, assuring the
Austrian government that Beaumarchais/Ronac was a personal envoy of
the king. The empress ordered Beaumarchais released, and along with her
apologies, she sent him 1,000 ducats (about $6,000 in modern currency).
In a grand, theatrical gesture, however, Beaumarchais returned the money,
saying, "I accept no favors but from my master." Warned that he was "taking a great liberty to refuse the empress's favors," Beaumarchais replied
indignantly, "Monsieur, the only liberty which cannot be taken from a
very respectful but cruelly outraged man is the liberty to refuse favors. For
the rest, my master will decide."[4] The empress replaced the money with a
diamond ring that Beaumarchais would wear the rest of his life.

Although no one in the Austrian court believed a word of Beaumarchais's fantastic adventure—no Angelucci or Atkinson ever surfaced
anywhere—Marie Antoinette and King Louis XVI received him as a
hero. In the song he composed describing his quest, he compared himself

to Robin Hood and captured the hearts of the royals, their ministers, and the French people:

> Toujours, toujours, il est toujours le même.
> Jamais Robin ne connut le chagrin,
> Le temps sombre ou serein,
> Les jours gras, le carême,
> Le matin ou le soir,
> Dites blanc, dites noir,
> Toujours, toujours, il est toujours le même.[5]

> Ever faithful, ever true; he is ever faithful and true.
> Robin Hood was never sad,
> In either good times or in bad,
> In days of plenty or of need,
> Mornings or nights, on bright days or drab.
> He is ever faithful and true . . . etc.

France hailed and feted Beaumarchais as a near legend. The king promoted Sartine to minister of the navy and ordered the royal treasury to reimburse Beaumarchais 72,000 livres (just under $300,000) for both his missions —the earlier one for Louis XV as well as the mission for Louis XVI. Beaumarchais took advantage of his celebrity to petition the court to annul the judgment in the La Blache case, and the court complied. With his assets no longer attached, he used the 72,000 livres from his mythical hunt for Angelucci to recover his spacious house on the rue de Condé and moved back with his mistress, Marie-Thérèse Amélie de Willermaulaz, his father, his two sisters, a third, widowed sister, and her daughter and two sons. He went on to raise his two fatherless nephews as his own sons.

Beaumarchais's father, seventy-six-year-old André Caron, also moved back into the house on the rue de Condé. Although he suffered the agonies of arthritis, he nonetheless continued his constant hunt for women. Closest at hand was the housekeeper, who was just as constant in her hunt for money. Knowing that the old man's son had ample reserves, she teased the old man mercilessly with aphrodisiacal whispers, light touches, and promises of *peut-être demain, mon chéri* (maybe tomorrow, dearie)—if only she could find the money today for her sick mother, father, brother, and so on. Beaumarchais suspected what she was up to, but had no evidence to confront her and was powerless to dissuade his sexually starved father from the chase.

Once he settled into his home again, Beaumarchais asked for and won permission to stage *The Barber of Seville*, but made the mistake of revising it from a four-act hilarity to a biting, five-act drama. Laced with bitterness and anger, Figaro echoed Beaumarchais's own pent-up rage at the injustices he had suffered:

> I have seen the most honest men nearly crushed by slander. . . . At first, a slight rumor, skimming the ground like the swallow before the storm, *pianissimo,* it murmurs, and twists and leaves behind its poisonous trail. An acquaintance hears it and *piano, piano,* slips it gracefully into your ear. The evil is done, it sprouts, crawls, travels on, and *rinforzando* from mouth to mouth, it flies like the devil; then, suddenly, I don't know how, you see slander arising, hissing, swelling, and growing before your eyes. It flies forward, extends its flight, whirls, envelops, tars, bursts, and thunders, becomes a general cry, a public *crescendo,* a universal chorus of hate and admonition. Who can withstand it?[6]

The play opened on February 22, 1775, to a packed house, but proved too bitter for an audience seeking laughter and entertainment. When Figaro complained of having been "welcomed in one town, imprisoned in another, everywhere rising above circumstances . . . mocking the foolish, braving the wicked," hissing interrupted him; the audience had not come for angry diatribe. Some began to leave—one by one at first, then in small groups . . . By the end the house was almost empty. The Théâtre Français canceled the following day's performance.

"People had expected a masterpiece," according to Jean-François de La Harpe, a contemporary literary critic. "The length of the speeches was wea-

Le Théâtre Français in Paris, where a packed house cheered performances of Beaumarchais's new play, *Le Barbier de Séville*, in February 1775. The great nineteenth-century French writer Gustave Flaubert called Figaro's fiery monologues, which assailed aristocratic privilege, one of the causes of the French Revolution.

RÉUNION DES MUSÉES NATIONAUX

risome, the bad jokes repulsive. Beaumarchais counted too much on his popularity and encumbered his play with useless scenes and jokes that were often coarse, destroyed all its charms and gave it the character of burlesque. The failure was complete."[7]

Always the optimist, refusing to let failure deter him, Beaumarchais set to work that evening. Three nights later, *The Barber* reopened as a shorter, four-act play that sent its audience into rapt laughter from the first scene to the last. It played to full houses until the end of the season and ensured Beaumarchais's place among the greatest French playwrights in history and unquestionably the finest of his era. Actors—professionals and amateurs alike—staged it across France. In Versailles, Queen Marie Antoinette insisted on staging it at the Petit Trianon—and starring as Rosine, with her brother-in-law the comte d'Artois, the future King Charles X, playing Figaro.

Beaumarchais's alter ego Figaro joined the ranks of the most popular characters ever to appear on the French stage—like Beaumarchais himself, a multifaceted, multitalented genius whom circumstance forced to become a metaphorical barber. Beset by more powerful, evil-minded, high-born characters, he laughs, sings, dances, and cleverly schemes his way over, around, and under impossible hurdles to success—a simple commoner shaving his enemies and manipulating the world to his own advantage.

A tiny gust that extinguishes a candle, Figaro reminds his audience, *can ignite an inferno.*

As unique in the French theater as Falstaff on the British stage, Figaro was an entirely new character in French drama: *human* in every respect— at times cheerful or sad, daring or cowardly, forthright or scheming, scrupulous or not, but incapable of pure evil, he was ready to do whatever was needed to ensure the survival of humanity and human success. For 150 years, the French stage had presented only classical characters of heroic dimensions created by Corneille and Racine. Although Molière's satires of manners introduced humor, his characters were buffoonish archetypes rather than individuals, and, more often than not, they were *aristocratic* archetypes. For the first time, theater audiences were able to see *themselves* (or at least elements of themselves and what they would like to be) onstage, expressing their thoughts, their emotions. Figaro was not only human—thoroughly human—he was the *petit bourgeois* in the Age of Enlightenment: a *citoyen* "born free" under Jean-Jacques Rousseau's *Contrat social*, surrendering some personal rights to the common good but demanding, in return, equal status, equal opportunity, and a modicum of mutual assistance from others. His speech, mannerisms, interests, and life required an entirely new type of theatrical presentation. He represented as much of a revolution on the French stage as he soon would in French streets.

> Le vin et la paresse
> Se partagent mon coeur.
> Si l'une et ma tendresse,
> L'autre fait mon bonheur.

Wine and idleness
Share my heart;
The first is my love,
The other my joy.

The Théâtre Français reaped a fortune from the play, but after a month's performances, Beaumarchais had not a sou to show for his success—not even an accounting of theater receipts. From the time a century earlier when Molière had formed his own theater company—during the reign of Louis XIV—the law required theaters to give playwrights about 10 percent of the profits from all performances of their plays—unless total receipts fell below 1,200 livres for the first two performances. With that rule in mind, theaters often failed to publicize productions until the third performance, thus ensuring empty houses the first two nights—and allowing theaters and actors to keep all subsequent revenues for themselves. By the time Figaro walked onstage, theater companies had not only stopped paying playwrights, they had stopped sending them financial statements. But they had never faced Figaro.

When *Barber* opened, Beaumarchais was intent on rebuilding his fortune, and after a month of seeing his play performed to packed houses, he shocked the theater managers and actors by demanding an official tally and share of receipts—in other words, by claiming his authorship rights. In a backstage scene that mirrored Figaro's onstage confrontations, one irate actor demanded, "At least tell us how many times you expect us to play it for your profit before the play belongs to us."

"Why should it ever belong to you?" Beaumarchais retorted.

"Because that's the arrangement most authors make."

"That does not mean I have to do the same."

"They are very satisfied, Monsieur, by the honor of seeing their plays performed time and time again. So tell us how many times you want us to play it for your profit—six, eight, ten times? Tell us!"

"I want you to play it 1,001 times!"

"You are not very modest, Monsieur!"

"I am as modest as you are just. You want to inherit from people before they are dead."[8]

The Théâtre Français claimed it had no written records of receipts and could not provide any. With the malicious smile that had become his trademark, Beaumarchais bid his tormentors adieu and invited twenty-three of the nation's leading authors and composers to join him to form the powerful Société des Auteurs et Compositeurs Dramatiques. Under his leadership, the group threatened a writers' strike and forced all theater companies in France to agree not to present any play without the author's consent and to pay playwrights 12 percent of *gross profits*. As Figaro the barber put it,

> Overwhelmed with debts and light on cash;
> Welcomed in one town, imprisoned in the next;
> Praised by some, blamed by others;
> Making the best of good weather, enduring the bad;
> Mocking the foolish, braving the wicked;
> Laughing in my misery and shaving all.[9]

Early in 1775, French foreign minister comte de Vergennes watched the uncanny Figaro and his creator manipulate the world onstage and off—and enlisted the playwright's help with a problem of state that would tie Beaumarchais's fortunes to the American Revolutionary War. The problem had baffled the king's intelligence bureau for a decade and threatened to involve the nation in an unnecessary war with England that it could not afford. At the heart of the problem was a rogue French spy in London, Chevalier Charles Geneviève d'Eon de Beaumont, who had served heroically as an army captain during the Seven Years' War and been an effective spy before and after the conflict. Although a fierce, dangerously skilled swordsman, his prewar espionage had raised some questions—and eyebrows—about his gender.

In the buildup to the Seven Years' War, French King Louis XV had tried unsuccessfully to lure Russia from the British to the French side. Then a mysterious French beauty appeared at the czarina's palace and so stunned the court with her grace, bearing, and intellect that the czarina embraced her as a personal aide for French cultural and political affairs. As the two grew closer, Mademoiselle Lia de Beaumont revealed herself to be the Chevalier d'Eon. Instead of arousing the czarina's fury, she/he provoked gales of laughter, admiration, and deep affection that resulted in Russia's alliance with France in the Seven Years' War with Britain. Hailed at Versailles for his diplomatic victory, the Chevalier d'Eon marched off to battle (in a man's uniform) to win his nation's highest military honor—the Cross of Saint Louis.

Although France eventually lost the war and her vast empire in Asia, Africa, and North America, French King Louis XV immediately began plotting to avenge his nation's defeat. Among other things, he ordered the comte de Broglie, the commanding general of the army, to draw up plans to invade England and sent the Chevalier d'Eon to England to ingratiate himself at court, elicit military secrets, and survey British ports and military defenses.

D'Eon proved himself as remarkable in London as he had been in St. Petersburg, appearing alternatively as the stunning Mademoiselle de Beaumont or the handsome Chevalier Charles d'Eon in formal military dress in ballrooms and diplomatic functions—without arousing suspicions that he might be she or she he. The chevalier won the friendship, trust, and favors of King George III and his queen. At least one d'Eon biographer—and there were many—claims he fathered English queen Sophia Charlotte's son—the future King George IV. And while Monsieur d'Eon was seducing the queen, the svelte Mademoiselle de Beaumont was seducing courtiers with fine brandy and the promise of sexual favors for hints of military secrets to send to General de Broglie.

After a violent falling out in which d'Eon challenged the French ambassador's authority in London, Versailles ordered d'Eon home and cut off his salary. D'Eon refused to return and threatened to reveal military secrets to the British government and turn over letters from King Louis XV

La Chevalière d'Eon was a transsexual who, as a
male, had been a French officer and spy. Posing as
a woman, he/she extracted money from the French
government by threatening to reveal French military
secrets to the British. French foreign minister
Vergennes sent Beaumarchais to England as a
secret agent to foil d'Eon's plan.

AUTHOR'S COLLECTION

revealing plans to invade Britain. Louis XV's ministers relented and
bought d'Eon's silence by letting him remain in London, a retiree on full
salary. With Louis XV's death, however, salary payments to d'Eon ended.
The chevalier sent angry demands to Versailles for back pay and an additional 300,000 livres (about $1.25 million modern) that he claimed the
late king owed him for private services. The new foreign minister, comte
de Vergennes, sent agents to arrest him and bring him back to France, but

d'Eon was too clever, rapidly switching disguises and leaving agents embarrassed and befuddled about his/her identity. One agent was so taken in by Mademoiselle de Beaumont that, instead of arresting her, he all but swooned over her beauty and proposed marriage.

"It cannot be denied that she was a phenomenal person," wrote M. de Flassan, a contemporary historian and archivist.

> Nature was deceived in giving her a sex so much in contradiction with her
> . . . character. Her mania for playing the part of a man and for deceiving
> all observers rendered her sometimes ill-tempered. . . . For the rest she deserved esteem and respect for the constancy with which she concealed her
> sex from scrutiny. The brilliant part this woman played in missions of a
> delicate nature . . . proves that she was more fitted for politics by her wit and
> knowledge than many men who have followed the same career.[10]

After each farcical encounter with French agents, d'Eon increased his threats and blackmail demands. Foreign Minister Vergennes decided that only Figaro would be able to untangle the d'Eon affair, and he asked Beaumarchais to go to London to see if he could retrieve the secret correspondence of Louis XV from the dangerous *chevalier/chevalière*.

"You are enlightened and prudent," Vergennes told Beaumarchais. "You know what men are, and I am not uneasy about your arriving at a good result with Monsieur d'Eon, if it is possible to do so. If the enterprise fails in your hands, it must be taken for granted that it can never succeed."[11] Vergennes said he was particularly interested in retrieving a damaging letter of Louis XV asking d'Eon to assess which English harbors would be most open for landing invading French troops.

A master of espionage himself, Vergennes had honed his skills for thirteen years as French ambassador in Turkey. Appointed ambassador to Sweden in 1771, he masterminded the coup d'état that overthrew King Gustave III, before being called by the new king, Louis XVI, to head the Foreign Affairs Ministry at Versailles in 1774. A fierce nationalist like his predecessor Choiseul, Vergennes was intent on rebuilding the French empire —if possible, without plunging the nation into a costly war with her ancient enemy Britain. Like Choiseul before him, Vergennes saw the incipient rebellion by American colonists as a possible means of weakening Britain and opening the way for French repossession of Canada.

As Vergennes spoke to Beaumarchais about the d'Eon mission, the shots at Lexington resounded around the world, provoking consternation and anger in London and cheers in France. Versailles ministers smiled or laughed at the vision of ill-clad farmers with outdated muskets humiliating the vaunted British Redcoats and laying siege to British-occupied Boston. In Philadelphia, representatives of the twelve other British colonies agreed to form a Continental Army to join the Massachusetts rebels under the overall command of Virginia's General George Washington. As Vergennes related the latest news from America, he told Beaumarchais to report any interesting developments in the British political scene that might be of interest to Versailles. Beaumarchais agreed to serve Vergennes on condition that Louis XVI would fulfill his late grandfather Louis XV's pledge to restore the playwright's civil rights. Vergennes agreed.

Too well known by then to travel undercover as Monsieur de Ronac, Beaumarchais went to London festooned in the ostentatious garb and other accoutrements that befitted his reputation as a theater celebrity and carefree bon vivant. Accompanied by his friend Gudin, he pretended he was going to London to savor what promised to be a triumphant English presentation of his *Barber of Seville*, which had been playing to standing-room-only audiences in Paris. By the time he reached London, Beaumarchais was beginning to enjoy his double life as a government spy. A master at plotting intrigue on the stage, he was equally skilled at plotting it in real life and as addicted to living a life of adventure, espionage, and speculation as he was to writing about it. He had become every bit as cunning, resourceful, and witty offstage as his fictional alter ego Figaro was in *The Barber* onstage. Indeed, Beaumarchais had become Figaro.

Once in London, Beaumarchais immediately called on his old friend Lord Rochford, who had been British ambassador to Spain and befriended Beaumarchais when the playwright was in Madrid. Now Britain's Foreign

Secretary and close confidant of King George III, Rochford had enjoyed singing duets in harmony with Beaumarchais when the two were in Madrid and rejoiced at the chance to resume their songfests in London. The playwright was equally enthusiastic and used each interval between songs to refill His Lordship's wine glass and extract state secrets from his devotee. After one evening of wine and song, the ever-effusive Rochford indicated that d'Eon frequented the home of the rebellious John Wilkes, a bitter parliamentary opponent of the king and an outspoken supporter of the rebellious American colonists. Like Beaumarchais, Wilkes had been the perpetual victim of what Rousseau called the inequalities among men in a class society. Twenty-seven years older than Beaumarchais, Wilkes had won election to Parliament in 1757, at the age of thirty-two, only to land in prison for seditious libel after founding an anti-Tory weekly and criticizing a speech by King George II. Released because of parliamentary privilege, he was expelled from Parliament on trumped-up charges that he was the anonymous author of a second libelous article. Declared an outlaw, he fled to France, but returned to face trial and again went to prison. His Middlesex constituency reelected him three times, only to have Parliament invalidate each of his elections and provoke rioting among his constituents. The rioting spread to London's lower- and middle-class neighborhoods, which saw Wilkes as a champion of commoners and the disenfranchised majority.

When American colonists began boycotting British imports to protest Parliament's heavy duties on tea and other staples, English merchants joined the Wilkes camp and, under the banner of "Wilkes and Liberty," elected him, successively, alderman of London in 1770, sheriff in 1771, and lord mayor in 1774—a post he still held when he first met Beaumarchais. After the Minutemen fired the shots at Lexington, Wilkes became an open advocate of American independence and a secret agent for Boston's Sons of Liberty. As each of the colonies established a "committee of correspondence," it turned to him to help find military aid overseas.

"For a long time," Wilkes mocked the British monarch, "the king has done me the honor of hating me. On my side, I have always rendered him the justice of despising him."[12]

After Beaumarchais's old friend Théveneau de Morande had introduced the French playwright to Wilkes, the latter immediately invited the celebrated creator of Figaro to his dinner table, where Beaumarchais pretended to feign disinterest in d'Eon and sat in rapt attention as dissident Americans talked of the latest developments in the struggle for freedom in their homeland. The Second Continental Congress had convened in Philadelphia and declared the colonies in a "state of defense" and invited "fellow sufferers" in Canada to join the struggle. It declared the Patriot forces laying siege to Boston a "Continental Army" and voted to raise six companies of riflemen from Pennsylvania, Maryland, and Virginia to join them. It appointed as commander in chief Virginia's George Washington —the man who had ignited the Anglo-French conflagration in North America eighteen years earlier and set off the worldwide Seven Years' War.

Before Washington reached Massachusetts, however, the British commanding general in Boston declared martial law and proclaimed the Americans besieging the city to be rebels and traitors—subject to summary hanging if taken prisoner. On June 17, the British spotted Patriots building a fort atop Breed's Hill on the Charlestown peninsula across the harbor from Boston. British ships landed 2,400 troops and laid a barrage on the hilltop as the Redcoats edged up the slope. A murderous rain of Patriot fire forced the British to retreat. A second attempt to scale the hill met with similar results. On the third attempt, the British discarded their extra gear and charged up the hill with bayonets fixed. The firing from the top gradually diminished—and then ceased. The Americans had run out of powder. The British overran the hilltop and assaulted and captured neighboring Bunker Hill. When they were done, 100 dead and 267 wounded Americans lay strewn across the two hilltops, but the assault had cost the British 1,045 casualties and elevated their American victims to martyrdom. Bunker Hill became a cause célèbre for anti-British colonists.

Two weeks later, on July 3, 1775, Washington arrived in nearby Cambridge to take command of the Continental Army, only to find his 14,500 troops in danger of annihilation. They were out of arms and ammunition. With enough powder to issue only nine cartridges per man, Washington sent a desperate plea to Congress: "I need not enlarge on our melancholy situation," he wrote to President John Hancock. "It is sufficient to say that the existence of the Army and salvation of the country depends upon something being done for our relief both speedy and effectual and that our situation be kept a profound secret."[13]

Congress responded with two resolutions that left Parliament and the king utterly confused—along with quite a few Americans, including George Washington. On July 5, Congress passed an "Olive Branch Petition" that expressed deep attachment to King George III and great hopes for restoring harmonious relations with Britain. But the following day, it issued a "Declaration of the Causes and Necessities of Taking Up Arms" and declared Americans ready to die rather than live enslaved under the very monarch it had claimed to venerate the previous day. The contradictory congressional declarations confused the French Minister of Foreign Affairs, the comte de Vergennes, and left English foreign minister Lord Rochford—as well as his friend Beaumarchais—completely "puzzled . . . by what is going on in America."[14]

D'Eon was too skilled an agent not to sense the real purpose of Beaumarchais's visit to the Wilkes house, and, according to Gudin, he "paid the most delicate attention to Beaumarchais. . . . He had a woman's voice . . . and confessed with tears that he was a woman. It appeared that was to be d'Eon's strategy with Beaumarchais." Comparing himself to Joan of Arc, he displayed scars from battle wounds on his legs and appealed to Beaumarchais as a "guardian angel" for help in his dispute with Versailles.[15]

Always an admirer of good acting, Beaumarchais agreed to meet the chevalier privately the next day and then turned his attention to the interesting American appeals for arms. Before ending his service as America's colonial agent in London and returning home, Benjamin Franklin had turned London into a center for American agents to "treat with English, Dutch and French armorers and merchants to furnish and ship war matériel to the colonies."[16] A few merchants were already selling small quantities of arms to the American rebels, but the American War of Independence was obviously doomed without huge infusions that only an experienced arms trader such as Beaumarchais could provide. In discussions with Americans at Wilkes's home, he sensed an opportunity to use the skills he had acquired with Pâris-Duverney to improve his fortune and help the Americans. With more than 1,000 miles of unprotected coastline, the rebels had no difficulty finding isolated beaches where small ships could land supplies undetected by British authorities. Long Island's north shore, he learned, had already been the site of several landings, including one with 10,000 pounds of powder for Connecticut rebels. One ship from Bayonne, France, had carried about thirty tons of powder to a landing site in Rhode Island, near Providence. Some French arms dealers were shipping arms to the French West Indies under the guise of resupplying French troops. Then, when British cruisers were out of sight, they set sail for St. Eustatius or some other Dutch isle, where American vessels ostensibly picking up shipments of sugarcane would pick up arms as well and bury them in their holds beneath the stacks of cane stalks.

After several dinners together at Wilkes's home, d'Eon came to Beaumarchais's lodgings, where the two spies talked forthrightly. D'Eon "drank, smoked and swore like a German horseman,"[17] not only reiterating his financial demands but insisting on his right to return to France without risk of retaliation by the French government. He particularly feared imprisonment in the Bastille.

"But Monsieur," Beaumarchais assured him, " the French government does not put women in the Bastille." The playwright went on to explain that if d'Eon returned to France as a woman, her gender would render her immune from prosecution and punishment, although she would also lose certain civil rights accorded only to men. After much parrying, the two agreed on monetary terms, and, with d'Eon looking on, the playwright penned what seemed to be a letter to the king on d'Eon's behalf:

> One's heart can only pity this creature who is persecuted so much yet is of a gender to which everything is usually forgiven. I presume to assure you that treating this astonishing creature with skill and kindness will restore her fealty as a loyal subject who will return all the papers relating to the late king on reasonable terms.[18]

The letter was as much a ruse as d'Eon's continual costume changes. Beaumarchais sent the letter to Vergennes knowing it would never reach the king's eyes because of the impertinent use of "you" instead of *Votre Majesté*. Vergennes immediately understood what Beaumarchais had done and sent him a confidential note approving the terms, but reminding the playwright "not to neglect to impress upon your Amazon . . . not to reenter the kingdom [of France] in other than women's clothes." Under no circumstance was she to wear her cross of Saint Louis in women's clothes.[19]

Beaumarchais made a quick round-trip to Versailles to retrieve d'Eon's official amnesty papers and money, but when the two met to make the exchange, d'Eon withheld key documents. The ever-suspicious Beaumarchais—still the deft juggler of his youth—proved equally cunning by slipping blank paper amid the currency notes to shortchange d'Eon without diminishing the size of the money pack.

Beaumarchais sent d'Eon a sarcastic note the next morning, beginning, "Ma pauvre Chevalière or whatever it pleases you to be with me . . . ." He then demanded that d'Eon surrender all the documents if he/she wanted all his/her money. The chevalier agreed.

"She conducted me to her house," Beaumarchais wrote to Vergennes, "and drew from beneath the flooring five cardboard boxes, well sealed and labeled 'secret papers, to be remitted to the King alone.'"[20]

With a coach waiting to carry him and the documents to the English Channel and a boat to France, Beaumarchais handed d'Eon a large deck of currency—actually dealing out the bills to prove they contained no blank paper—then rode off to the coast. After recounting it later, however, d'Eon found the packet 40,000 livres short. Beaumarchais's quick hands had removed them even as he dealt them—"to obtain some further advantages . . . over this impetuous and cunning creature."[21]

The infuriated d'Eon retaliated by telling all of London that she and Beaumarchais were lovers. He published a letter he said he had sent to the playwright:

By a blind confidence in you and your promise, I disclosed the mystery of my sex to you: Out of gratitude, I gave you my portrait, and you promised me yours. There have been many other engagements between us . . . including our approaching marriage. But according to what I hear from Paris, this was mere persiflage on your part. . . . That would be contemptible and a breach of faith. . . . Why did I not remember that men are only on earth to deceive the credulity of girls and women.[22]

When Beaumarchais returned to London, he found himself the target of a barrage of jokes, which failed to undermine his own sense of humor. "Every one tells me that this crazy woman is mad about me," he wrote to Vergennes. "She thinks I have treated her with contempt. . . . Who the devil would ever have imagined that, to serve the king in this affair, I would have to become the gallant knight of a captain of dragoons? This adventure has become absurd."[23]

The "adventure" came to an abrupt end, with d'Eon sending letters to Vergennes abusing Beaumarchais, but evoking only gales of laughter at the palace. Both Vergennes and Beaumarchais ignored the letters, and Beaumarchais withheld all further payments to—and all contact with—the chevalier.[24]

Beaumarchais's "triumph" over d'Eon did not come without its costs, however. During his absence in London, his father, André Caron, had taken advantage of his son's absence to marry the housekeeper—a price she had demanded for her sexual favors. Unfortunately, the marathon bedroom adventures that followed the wedding proved too much for the old man, and he died—but not before signing a paper acknowledging an enormous financial debt to his widow-to-be. Although Caron had no legal basis for willing his son's money, the housekeeper threatened to sue Beaumarchais and again drag his name in the mud of a public scandal. He gave her 6,000 livres (about $25,000 today) to disappear in silence.

6

Plotting and Pocketing

IN THE COURSE OF his encounters with d'Eon at the Wilkes salon, Beaumarchais formed his first friendship with an American—a superbly educated Virginian, who seemed more English than American. A member of the storied Lee family, Arthur Lee had been born at the family's eastern Virginia estate, Stratford, in 1740, but spent most of the next forty years abroad, studying at Eton for six years before earning a medical degree at the University of Edinburgh, traveling on the continent, and then earning a law degree at London's Inns of Court. Mentored at one time or another by Samuel Johnson, James Boswell, Adam Smith, and other British luminaries, he returned to Virginia for a brief but unsuccessful attempt to practice medicine. While there, he plunged into the growing political and economic disputes with the mother country, writing a series of letters to American and British newspapers, gaining some celebrity as a pamphleteer, and winning the friendship of such American dissidents as Boston's Samuel Adams and Philadelphia's John Dickinson. He returned to England in 1770, and when Massachusetts named Benjamin Franklin as colonial agent in London, Samuel Adams helped win Arthur Lee's appointment as Franklin's assistant and designated successor.

Lee had just won admission to the London bar when the world heard the shots at Lexington in the spring of 1775. Invited with other Americans to celebrate at John Wilkes's lodgings, he met and quickly attached himself to Beaumarchais. Poised, charming, and witty, Lee was more than eloquent in expounding the American cause: the deep hatred for Britain that Americans now shared with the French; the desperate need for arms,

Arthur Lee replaced Benjamin Franklin as American
agent in London and was first to enlist Beaumarchais
in the American fight for independence.

ammunition, technical assistance, and funding in the fight for liberty and
independence; and the advantages to France of American independence.

"We offer France, as reward for its secret aid," Lee promised Beaumarchais, "a secret treaty of commerce. This treaty will give France, for a
certain number of years after peace is established, all the advantages of that
commerce with which for a century America has enriched England. This
trade will pass to France, and in addition, we agree to guarantee French
possessions [in the West Indies] to the full extent of our power."[1] Beaumarchais immediately envisioned opportunities to profit from the sale of
both arms to America during the war, and a wide range of French merchandise in the peace that would follow if he helped the Americans win
their independence from Britain.

American independence was inevitable, Lee argued. At best, the British
would be able to muster forces of 25,000 to 40,000 men. The Americans
were raising an army of 50,000, with 50,000 other able-bodied men ready
to volunteer to fight at their side. If the French refused to provide aid, the

Americans would obtain it from other nations, who would then reap the wealth from unfettered trade with America after the war. Lee also warned that if, through lack of French aid, the Americans lost the war, Britain would emerge as the world's most powerful nation militarily and economically. As such, it would almost certainly extend its North American empire across the West Indies, seizing the French Caribbean islands that provided France with sugar—at that time, its most important import.

Lured by the prospects of huge personal profits at first, Beaumarchais planned to convince Vergennes that the near-bankrupt French treasury stood to profit handsomely if the Americans won independence from Britain and awarded France special trading privileges. But as the summer's conversations with Arthur Lee progressed, another motive crept into Beaumarchais's thinking as he envisioned selling arms to the Americans: he grew genuinely sympathetic to the plight of simple American farmers —commoners like himself—defending their homes, fields, and fruits of their labor from plunder by powerful, insensitive English aristocrats in Parliament—much as he had defended his home from seizure by powerful, insensitive French aristocrats in Paris.

"Go to France, Monsieur," Lee urged Beaumarchais. "Go to France and display this picture of affairs. I am going to shut myself up in the country until you return. . . . Tell your ministers that I am prepared to follow you, if necessary, in order to confirm in Paris this statement of the case."[2]

"The Americans will triumph," Beaumarchais now wrote passionately to the comte de Vergennes, "but they must be assisted in their struggle, for if they lose, they will turn against us for not having helped them. We are not yet ready for war ourselves, but we must prepare and, while doing so, we must send secret aid to the Americans in the most prudent way."[3]

Beaumarchais's letter to Vergennes opened a stream of secret correspondence between the two, culminating in a massive Beaumarchais proposal addressed to the king himself. Called *La paix ou la guerre*—"Peace or

War"—and addressed *Au Roi seul*—"To the King alone"—it is one of the most important and least known documents of the American Revolutionary War. It put France on the path toward the alliance with the American revolutionaries that ensured their victory over England and the birth of a free and independent new nation: the United States of America.

"The famous quarrel between America and England," Beaumarchais predicted to the king,

> will soon divide the world and change the system of Europe. . . . While a violent crisis is approaching with great rapidity, I am obliged to warn your majesty that the preservation of our possessions in America, and the peace which your majesty appears to desire so much, depend solely upon this one proposition: *we must help the Americans.* I will now demonstrate it. . . .
>
> Let us look at all the hypothetical outcomes of the current crisis. . . . Is there a single one of them which does not instantly lead to the very war you wish to avoid? If the English triumph over the Americans, their victory would embolden them to expand their American empire by seizing the French West Indies. And if they lose the war, they would seize the French West Indies as compensation for loss of the mainland.

"What, then, is to be done . . . to have peace and preserve our islands?" Beaumarchais asked rhetorically. He then answered his own question, asserting that the only way to keep France out of war and preserve her Caribbean possessions was to prevent England and America from triumphing over each other—and that meant providing the Americans with enough military and financial assistance to put them "on an equal—but not a superior—level of strength with England."

> Believe me, Sire . . . economy of two or three millions now will certainly make you lose, before two years, more than three hundred. As for the danger of drawing upon us the storm of war with England which you wish to avoid, I reply that we will not incur that danger if we adopt the plan I propose of secretly assisting the Americans without compromising ourselves. . . . And if your majesty does not have a more clever man at hand to employ in this matter, I will undertake and answer for the execution of

the arrangement without anyone being compromised, persuaded that my zeal will supply my want of talent better than the talent of another could replace my zeal.[4]

Unlike Louis XV, King Louis XVI opposed war as a general principle —especially against a fellow monarch. He believed deeply that monarchs were spiritual brothers: God had placed them all on their respective thrones; they ruled by divine right. In his letters, England's George III had addressed him as "Monsieur mon frère" and signed himself "Votre bon frère George." The thought of conflict against a "brother monarch," therefore, disturbed Louis XVI, and, indeed, the thought of any conflict disturbed him. He revered tranquillity—in his chambers, his palace, his gardens, his nation, and his world. Louis XVI was determined not to repeat the errors of his predecessor on the throne—his grandfather, Louis XV, who had bankrupted France with endless military adventures. Louis XVI had ascended the throne unsteadily. Led by strict handlers during his childhood, he metamorphosed into a portly, compulsively taciturn young man with a disability that impeded sexual arousal. His father—the only legitimate son of the long-lived King Louis XV—had died when Louis XVI was but ten years old and never ruled. Louis XV died ten years later, leaving a bevy of illegitimate sons, but only his twenty-year-old grandson as a legitimate heir to succeed him on the throne of France.

In contrast to his grandfather, Louis XVI showed little appetite for society or sex after he mounted the throne—even spurning his stunningly beautiful wife Marie Antoinette. He loathed the late-night excitement of his wife's perpetual masked balls and other garish entertainments; he wanted nothing more than the quiet of his private study. Round and ungainly, he was happiest reclining in a deep, comfortably cushioned chair, studying history books and poring over maps. For one so languid, he was surprisingly dexterous—thus his keen interest in making trinkets. Whenever Vergennes or other ministers approached the king to remind him of his divine role on the French throne to conceive princes and restore French rule over the world, Louis simply waved them off without looking up or saying a word.

French king Louis XVI plots the reconquest of North America after approving
Beaumarchais's scheme to provide secret military aid to American rebels
in their struggle for independence from Britain.

RÉUNION DES MUSÉES NATIONAUX

When, therefore, Beaumarchais relayed Arthur Lee's message, along
with his own masterful "Peace or War" policy statement, Vergennes did
not respond immediately—or pass *La paix ou la guerre* on to the king. He
remained confused by the contradictory "Olive Branch" and "Arms" proc-
lamations of the American Congress in early July. He questioned American willingness "to die rather than be enslaved," as Congress had stated in
its proclamation on the "Necessities of Taking Up Arms."[5]

Vergennes also suspected Lee of maintaining secret ties to the British
government. Lee was "in constant touch with spies from the British Foreign Office," according to Vergennes's own agents.[6] Before approaching the
king with a request for aid to the Americans, Vergennes wanted to hear
directly from American leaders in America whether they would welcome
an alliance with France. He was well aware that many Americans retained

vivid memories of the massacres of the French and Indian War. At the time, Washington had called the French "our perfidious false and cruel enemies,"[7] and, like most Americans, he would certainly not welcome a French return to Canada or any other part of North America.

Vergennes also recognized that the rebels represented a minority of Americans—probably not more than one-third. In an all-out war against Britain, there was considerable doubt whether the huge Tory population would fight for independence. Indeed, many might join the British and fight against their own countrymen to preserve British rule—and control of their properties. A third consideration was the possibility of an early, peaceful resolution of the Anglo-American dispute. A large number of influential English merchants, bankers, and even parliamentarians opposed the harsh measures Parliament had inflicted on the Americans.

"Reflect how you are to govern a people who think they ought to be free, and think they are not," pleaded the eloquent British parliamentarian Edmund Burke to his colleagues. "Your scheme yields no revenue; it yields nothing but discontent, disorder, disobedience; and such is the state of America, that after wading up to your eyes in blood, you could only end just where you began."[8]

The American colonies collectively represented Britain's largest trading partner, and most men of commerce in Britain opposed measures that disturbed that relationship. Given enough time, Vergennes reasoned, the British themselves might dismiss the British government and effect a peaceful resolution of their problems in America. Premature French intervention might provoke an unnecessary war that could cost France the last vestiges of empire in the rich Caribbean sugar islands.

And still another reason Vergennes hesitated to respond to the Lee-Beaumarchais request for aid was the weak condition of the French army. The French military was unprepared for war with Britain. He would not have been as reluctant if King Louis's cousin, Spanish king Carlos III, had expressed some willingness to support the French effort to help the Americans. Although Spain had more to lose than France from British expansionism in the Americas, Carlos's ministers feared that an American victory in a war of independence against England might inspire settlers in Spanish colonies to rebel and wrest control of the rich, ore-laden lands in Mexico and South America.

To try to resolve his questions, Vergennes decided to send an English-speaking agent to America to determine how American leaders *in America* might respond to French aid. He chose the army's most distinguished intelligence officer, Achard de Bonvouloir.

Just as Bonvouloir's ship was losing sight of the French coast, George Washington, the commander in chief of America's Continental Army, was opening a mysterious letter from someone who identified himself only as "A Friend to America":

> I beg leave to propose to your Excellency's consideration, that a good Schooner . . . should proceed as soon as may be, to Havre de Grace [Le Havre] . . . with a suitable person on board (your Agent) who should immediately on his arrival there go to Paris or Versailles . . . with letters from your Excellency to the prime minister of France, requesting an immediate supply of ten thousand barrels [2.2 million pounds] of powder, with one hundred tons of lead: for the payment of which the Continental Congress will make provision. Your reasons to induce the French minister to grant this supply will so strongly coincide with the national politics of France, it seems highly probable he will be glad of the opportunity of supplying or even of giving it, though in some covered way. If your agent succeeds, he can easily procure under the auspices of the French minister five or six vessels . . . of 100 tons each, to bring the powder and lead. . . . Another schooner, alike circumstanced, might be sent to Cadiz, and the business perhaps negotiated with the Spanish governor for a like quantity of powder and lead. If not, your agent might proceed to Madrid . . . and settle the business with the prime minister.

"A Friend" suggested that Washington could reduce shipping costs by sending the French vessels back to France loaded with American tobacco and other valuable produce. He also offered Washington a choice of "fire-arms, flints or tinplates for making cartridge boxes," but warned against British spies. "Should it be known to the English . . . the vessels will be stopped; or taken by English cruisers."[9]

Although the identity of America's early "friend" remains a mystery, only Beaumarchais had the theatrical instincts to conceive of and time the elements of so intricate a plot so perfectly. Although an American (possibly Arthur Lee) penned the words, it almost certainly was a translation of a French original. It could, of course, have been the work of other French agents, such as Bonvouloir—or even of Foreign Minister Vergennes—but its contents presaged the very plan that Beaumarchais was preparing for implementing his "Peace or War" policy that was already in the hands of Foreign Minister Vergennes.

Disguised as an ordinary French business man, Bonvouloir reached Phila-delphia just before Christmas 1775 with an introduction to a prominent French intellectual who took him to meet members of the Congressional Committee of Secret Correspondence, which acted as a liaison between each of the state committees of secret correspondence organizing the war ef-forts in their jurisdictions. The members of the Congressional Committee —Benjamin Franklin, John Dickinson, Benjamin Harrison, John Jay, and Thomas Johnson[10]—had all tried without success to determine whether England's ancient European enemies—especially France, Spain, or Holland —might provide military aid to the rebellious colonies. In addition to basic military supplies—arms, ammunition, tents, and the like—the Americans needed artillery officers capable of calculating cannon-fire trajectories and engineers to plan construction and destruction of fortifications.

Bonvouloir followed his instructions from Vergennes to the letter, re-iterating his feigned status as a private businessman but adding his assur-ances that French sentiment favored the Americans. Although he could promise no French government military aid, he declared that France was "well-disposed" toward the Americans and saw no obstacles to American merchants buying arms and other supplies from French merchants in exchange for produce—tobacco, rice, and the like. As a personal service to the committee, he agreed to try to find retired French army engineers who might be willing to come to America.

After his meeting, Bonvouloir wrote a long, pleasant letter about his travels to his friend the French ambassador in London. Between the lines was a detailed report in invisible ink—milk—for relay to Vergennes. Bonvouloir said America had more than enough troops to wage successful war against England but lacked arms and ammunition. "Every one here is a soldier," he declared. "The troops are well clothed, well paid and well led. They have about 50,000 paid troops and an even larger number of volunteers who refuse any pay. You may judge for yourself how men of this caliber will fight. The members of the committee all said that they have sworn to fight to the end for their freedom and that the enemy will have to chop them to bits before they will surrender."[11]

Bonvouloir went on to give Vergennes a thorough technical evaluation of the American situation. He lauded the skills of American marksmen, American mastery of unconventional warfare in the wilderness, and George Washington's inspiring leadership. But they had many disadvantages—the lack of a navy, for one. Moreover, the rank-and-file troops were farmers, fishermen, carpenters, and craftsmen who lacked training, discipline, ammunition, clothing, food, and other basic supplies such as tents and blankets—and Congress had no money to fill those needs. Moreover, Americans were far from united in support of the war: at least one-third remained loyal to Britain.

British forces, on the other hand, were well equipped, well trained, and well disciplined, and they had enough financial resources to hire foreign mercenaries and continue the war indefinitely. The powerful British navy controlled the coastline and offshore waters and would have no trouble transporting troops to America and supporting them with offshore firepower. The British would, however, face certain disadvantages: their troops were unfamiliar with American terrain, and their leaders were arrogant. British officers tended to underestimate the strength, skills, and will of

American fighters, and they were often unwilling to abandon traditional linear warfare to adapt to frontier conditions. British soldiers were over-dressed and carried too much equipment for fighting in American forests, where every tree, bush, and boulder could hide an American marksman, on his knees or belly, rifle at the ready. In addition, the distance of supply lines to navy ships on the coast would put the British army at a disadvantage if fighting spread inland.

As Bonvouloir was meeting with members of the American Congress, Beau-marchais reappeared at Versailles—somewhat incensed that Vergennes had failed to reply to his last messages from London. Vergennes had not only refused to see Arthur Lee at Versailles, he had also failed to transmit the "Peace or War" policy statement that Beaumarchais had prepared for the king. More intent than before on providing French aid to the Americans, Beaumarchais penned another letter addressed "To the King alone—very important." In it, he scolded the king for his reluctance to turn on England, "that natural enemy, that jealous rival of your success, that people always systematically unjust to you":

> When have the usurpations and outrages of this people ever had any limit but that of its strength? Has [England] not always waged war against you without declaring it? Did it not begin the last one, in a time of peace? Did it not humble you by forcing you to destroy your finest seaport [Dunkerque]? Has it not recently subjected your merchant vessels to inspection on the northern seas?—a humiliation which would have made Louis XIV rather eat his hands than not atone for it?[12]

Under any monarch other than the withdrawn and self-absorbed Louis XVI, Beaumarchais's blunt language would have sent him to the torture chamber before being drawn and quartered. But Beaumarchais had known Louis as a boy in the salons of his aunts, the four daughters of Louis XV. He was a gentle man who had long enjoyed the playwright's songs and plays and genuinely admired Beaumarchais's wit. Although Vergennes agreed with Beaumarchais's thinking, he found the language so offensive that he withheld it from the king.

A few days thereafter, Bonvouloir's first report arrived, along with news that seemed to confirm Beaumarchais's assessment: A force of about 1,000 Americans under Brigadier General Richard Montgomery had captured Montreal, while Benedict Arnold had reached the St. Lawrence River with a force of more than 600 volunteers and was about to lay siege to Quebec. In the South, 900 Virginia and North Carolina militiamen defeated a loyalist army recruited by the Earl of Dunmore, the British governor of Virginia. Before fleeing to the safety of British ships offshore, Dunmore avenged his defeat by burning the port city of Norfolk and leaving it useless to either the British or Americans. Nonetheless, the Americans had put the British to flight and freed Virginia from British control. The largest, richest, and most heavily populated of the thirteen British colonies, Virginia had joined Massachusetts in declaring its independence from Britain.

Buoyed by Bonvouloir's report, Vergennes prepared a long and detailed policy statement for King Louis XVI that summarized all the findings of his agents—Bonvouloir, Beaumarchais, and others. Entitled *Reflexions*, Vergennes's historic paper reflected the conclusions of Beaumarchais's "Peace or War"—that the goal of colonial rebels was "no longer a redress of grievances, but a determined effort to cut their ties to England." He warned that if no one aided the rebels, Britain would probably defeat them and "retain the mercantile benefits of her American trade."

> England will thus be able to prevent the American colonies from dealing with other nations, while accumulating all the benefits of exclusive trade with those colonies. It is to prevent England from gaining this double advantage that makes it imperative for France to intervene in the current dispute.... England is France's natural enemy.... her cherished, long-standing goal is, if not the destruction of France, at least our emasculation, humiliation and ruin. For centuries, that has been England's primary motive for the many wars she has waged against us.[13]

Vergennes's momentous statement proposed indirect intervention in the American Revolution as a relatively low-cost opportunity to exact revenge against England for the humiliation of the Seven Years' War and to restore French hegemony on the North American continent without firing a shot. "The power of England will diminish," he assured the king, "and ours will increase accordingly; English commerce will suffer an irreparable loss while ours will increase accordingly; it is very probable that . . . we may be able to recover part of the possessions that the English seized from us in America, such as . . . Canada."[14]

Although George Washington had no way of knowing it, a nobleman and king in France's Palais de Versailles—and a scheming French playwright lurking in a palace antechamber—were about to decide the fate of the American Revolution and whether Washington himself would survive as the heroic father of his country or die a traitor on a London gibbet. To strengthen his argument to the king, Vergennes placed the critical Beaumarchais "Peace or War" document in the king's hands. Vergennes told the king that Beaumarchais would implement the aid program by drawing from stockpiles of surplus French arms from the Seven Years' War and sell them to independent trading firms that would carry them to America and trade them for tobacco, cotton, lumber, and whale oil that would normally flow to Britain. "This exchange of traffic," Vergennes explained, "could be made without the government appearing involved in any way."[15]

After reluctantly approving the broad principles of the scheme, the king asked his foreign minister for a more detailed plan. Vergennes then turned to Beaumarchais, who drafted a plot worthy of any he ever devised for Figaro onstage. He proposed that the royal treasury provide him with 1 million livres (about $4 million today) to set up a private foreign company, thus concealing the French government's involvement from the British. He would then use half the money to buy surplus military supplies from the king's army—in effect channeling the king's money back into his treasury via the war ministry while ridding the military of surplus matériel. At the time, French military depots bulged with obsolete arms and ammunition from the Seven Years' War. Although technological advances had rendered much of the artillery worthless in European warfare, it was more than adequate for American rebels in the wilderness. The French military had, for example, about 400 cannon dating back to the seventeenth century and still bearing the back-to-back double L's of Louis XIV.

After using half the king's money to buy surplus war equipment, Beaumarchais would lend the other half to the American government to purchase supplies from him, thus refilling his coffers with more of the king's money to buy more war supplies from the king's army. The Americans would repay the loan and buy all future supplies by filling the empty arms ships with tobacco, rice, indigo, lumber, and other commodities for transport back to Beaumarchais, who would sell them on the French market and recoup the money he had loaned to the Americans. In effect, the king's initial million-livre investment would find its way back into the royal treasury after only two shipments of arms to America, after which the king—and Beaumarchais—would reap nothing but profits from the arms trade with America.

Except for King Louis XVI, the comte de Vergennes and sieur de Beaumarchais, no one in France or America would know the ultimate destination of the arms. And when the arms eventually reached American shores, no one in France or America would know exactly how they got there. French shippers, longshoremen, and sailors would know only that they were transferring surplus war matériel from the French homeland to reinforce defenses of the French sugar islands. In some cases, the ships might sail directly from France to America, but in other cases, they would, indeed, sail to the French sugar islands, where smaller ships would then pick up the cargoes to transfer them, ostensibly, to other ports in the French islands—but, in fact, to American ports to the north.

Although the British would eventually discover the source of some of the supplies and protest to the French government, the French Foreign Office would simply express its regrets but insist that, as a neutral nation, it had no powers to prevent merchants from trading and no way of knowing the destination of old and useless weapons after an infinite number of trades on world markets. In the end, the surplus supplies would simply vanish from France and reappear in America, with no money changing hands and without any contacts between American and French authorities. And while French arms produced a stalemate in the fighting in America, French manufacturers would use the time to resupply the French military with modern equipment and bring French forces to a par with those of the British.

After Vergennes finished reading the Beaumarchais plot to the king, Louis and his foreign minister stared at each other for several minutes then burst into peals of laughter at Beaumarchais's preposterously cunning scheme. It was pure Figaro and they loved it—so much so that the king not only agreed to the plan, he authorized Vergennes to enlist his Bourbon cousin the Spanish king in the project. Beaumarchais had convinced Europe's oldest, most despotic monarchy to support a rebellion against a kindred monarch by commoners who proposed governing their country themselves.

"Receive all my compliments, sir," Vergennes wrote to Beaumarchais. "After having assured you of the King's approbation, mine may not appear very interesting to you; however, I cannot help applauding the wisdom and firmness of your conduct, and of renewing to you the expression of my esteem."[16] Vergennes had several reservations, however: he would not deal directly with American rebels for fear of provoking war with Britain. He and Beaumarchais then worked out a plan whereby the French government would lend rather than give Beaumarchais's firm the 1 million livres and attempt to coax the Spanish government to do the same. Beaumarchais would then raise an additional 1 million livres of his own from private sources. He would then draw military supplies from French government stocks, which he could either buy outright with cash or replace with approved modern weaponry. In any case, the French government was to have no vested interest in the Beaumarchais company, which would sell its arms to the Americans for tobacco, rice, or other products, which Beaumarchais could resell in French markets. Beaumarchais's company was to be self-supporting, with Beaumarchais expected to bear any losses but reap all profits.

Citing the *Pacte de Famille*, which tied the Bourbon kings of France and Spain by treaty and blood, the king sent word to his cousin the Spanish king to consider matching the French investment. Vergennes wrote to his Spanish counterpart warning that if the English defeated the American rebels, they would almost certainly seize rich Spanish colonies in Florida and the Caribbean, as well as the gold and silver mines of Mexico. By "keeping the flames of the American rebellion burning," he asserted, Spain and France would keep the British too distracted to attack elsewhere.[17] Vergennes predicted that the internecine war would leave both sides exhausted and reduce England to a second-rate power, allowing the Spanish to expand northward along the Mississippi River and the French to repossess Canada. The two Bourbon kings would control almost all of North America and shrink the British colonies to an impotent strip of land between the Appalachian Mountains and the Atlantic Ocean.

7

I Wish to Serve Your Country
as if It Were My Own

IN MID-JANUARY 1776, when the Beaumarchais scheme was still under consideration at Versailles, America's portly commander of artillery, General Henry Knox, waddled into Cambridge at the head of an exhausted column. He and his men had just completed an improbable 300-mile journey to Fort Ticonderoga, New York, and back. On their return to Cambridge, they had dragged forty-three cannon and sixteen mortars through the snow, over ice-covered streams and ponds. On the night of March 4 and into the early morning hours of March 5, a force of 2,000 Americans under General John Thomas captured Dorchester Heights overlooking Boston, allowing Knox to put his artillery in positions to rake the entire city and harbor with cannon fire. Two days later, British commander Lord Richard Howe ordered British forces to evacuate Boston, and by March 17, all his troops, along with about 1,000 Loyalists, had boarded British troop ships in the harbor. On March 26, the British fleet sailed off to Halifax, Nova Scotia, leaving Boston and the rest of Massachusetts an independent state in the hands of Americans and their forces.

When news of the British evacuation of Boston reached Europe, Spanish king Carlos III agreed to match his French cousin's 1-million-livre investment in the Beaumarchais scheme, and on May 1, Louis XVI signed a check for 1 million livres, with the payee left blank. Before the king turned it over to Beaumarchais, however, Vergennes warned the playwright that the two monarchs "shall have no further hand in the affair because it would compromise the government too much in the eyes of the English."[1] Vergennes reiterated the need for Beaumarchais to raise additional funds from private investors—wealthy aristocrats and merchant bankers—to disguise the royal funds. "In the eyes of the English and American governments, the operation must assume the aspect of a speculation by an individual," Vergennes declared.

> To appear so, it must be so. We are secretly giving you a million francs. We shall get Spain to contribute an equal sum; with these two millions and the cooperation of other parties who may invest in your enterprise, you will establish a large commercial house and, at your risk, supply America with arms, munitions, equipment, and all other necessary matériel for carrying on a war. Our arsenals will give you arms and ammunition which you can replace or pay for. You will not demand money of the Americans because they have none; but you will demand payment from the produce of their soil, and we will help you distribute it in this kingdom. . . . After our initial support, the operation must afterward feed and support itself; but because we reserve the right to favor its continuance or put an end to its operation, you shall render us a regular accounting of your profits and your losses, and we will determine whether to grant you fresh assistance or discharge you of liability for previous grants.[2]

In mid-May 1776, Beaumarchais established a company under the Spanish name "Roderigue Hortalez et Cie." to conceal its ties to the French government. On June 10, 1776, a month before the Americans declared independence, Beaumarchais signed one of the most valuable receipts in world history—and certainly *the most important* receipt in American history:

> Received of M. Duvergier, in conformity with the orders of M. de Vergennes, dated the 5th instant . . . the sum of one million, of which I am to render an account to the said Sieur Comte de Vergennes.
>
> Caron de Beaumarchais
Good for a million of livres tournois.
Paris, June 10, 1776.[3]

As a further precaution, Vergennes had asked the French king to make his check out to Vergennes's fifteen-year-old son Duvergier, who then en-

dorsed it over to Hortalez et Cie. Later in the month, Beaumarchais noti-
fied Arthur Lee in a carefully worded letter that omitted any reference to
the French government. He wrote it in cipher and addressed it to "Mary
Johnston"—Arthur Lee's code name for all arms transactions.

"The difficulties I encountered in my negotiations with the minister,"
read the deciphered message from Beaumarchais, "have made me decide to
form a company that will send the supplies of powder and stores to your
friend at Cap François, Santo Domingo, against return cargoes of tobacco."[4]
He signed it "Roderigue Hortalez & Co."

Two months later in early August, the Spanish ambassador issued a
check for 1 million livres to the French treasury and gave Beaumarchais
a receipt that permitted him to draw from the Spanish funds. By then,
Beaumarchais had also lured several appropriate private investors into the
venture from the port cities of Nantes, Le Havre, and Bordeaux—ship
charterer Jean-Joseph de Monthieu, the shipowners of *Les Frères Man-
taudoin*, merchant-trader Pelletier Du Doyer, and financier-banker Joseph
Peyrera of Bordeaux.

With Beaumarchais's huge international political, military, and economic
scheme set to begin—and with more than 3 million livres in government
and private funds in his accounts—the French playwright approached Vergennes about a delicate problem. It might prove embarrassing to the French
king, Beaumarchais suggested calmly, if participants in the scheme learned
that the central figure managing their millions was a convicted felon. Vergennes blanched. Within days, the attorney general appeared in court and
asked the panel of judges to reverse the financial judgments against Beaumarchais in the La Blache lawsuits, to restore Beaumarchais's civil rights,
and to reinstate him to his seat on the judge's bench. Without bothering
to deliberate, the judges voted unanimously in favor of Beaumarchais, provoking a chorus of cheers among spectators, who hoisted Beaumarchais on
their shoulders and carried him out of the courtroom to the nearest tavern.

"Monsieur le comte," Beaumarchais exulted to Vergennes. "I have just been judged *déblamé* [unconvicted], amid a universal concourse of applause. . . . I have four hundred people around me applauding and embracing me and making an infernal noise, which, to me, sounds like perfect harmony." Beaumarchais went on to thank the foreign minister and "begged" that his expressions of gratitude be placed at "the feet of the king."[5]

On June 7, 1776, Virginia's Richard Henry Lee—Arthur Lee's older brother—proposed a resolution in the Continental Congress in Philadelphia that the United Colonies "are, and of right ought to be, free and independent States." After three days of debate, Congress postponed voting on the resolution until July 1, while a committee of five—John Adams, Benjamin Franklin, Thomas Jefferson, Robert Livingston, and Roger Sherman —prepared a formal declaration of independence. On July 2, a British fleet with 150 troop transports sailed into New York Bay, landing the first 10,000 of what would be an army of 23,000 British and 9,000 Hessian troops. On July 4, Congress voted 12–0 for independence, with New York abstaining until its Provincial Congress approved. Informed on July 15 that the New Yorkers had approved the document, Congress voted to have the "Unanimous Declaration" engrossed on parchment. On August 2, fifty-three members of Congress added their signatures to those of John Hancock, the president of Congress, and Charles Thomson, the secretary. Within three weeks, 20,000 British and Hessian troops stormed ashore in Brooklyn, New York, and after five days, they had overrun American defenders, leaving 1,500 of the 5,000-man American force dead or wounded and its two commanding generals, William Alexander of New Jersey and John Sullivan of New Hampshire, prisoners. The British sent Sullivan to Congress in Philadelphia with a proposal for an informal peace conference on Staten Island.

The slaughter on Long Island began a sharp reversal of American fortunes, with the powerful British army chasing Washington's army northward to White Plains, then westward across the Hudson River and northern New Jersey through sheets of icy autumn rains toward the Delaware

River. They barely made it to safety on the opposite bank in Pennsylvania. By early December, desertions had reduced his army to only about 3,000 men. Sickness left 500 of the 700 Virginians unfit for duty. Only Washington's foresight in commandeering small craft along the river prevented the British from crossing and annihilating the Americans. British commander General Sir William Howe posted troops at Trenton and Princeton to wait for the river to freeze to cross on foot and wipe out Washington's crippled army and end the Revolution in the North. The British advance left New York and most of New Jersey in British hands—and the Redcoats almost in sight of the American rebel capital. On December 12, Congress fled Philadelphia for Baltimore and, all but conceding defeat in the struggle for independence, began debating terms of capitulation.

General Washington's aide, Colonel Joseph Reed lamented "that something must be attempted to revive our expiring credit. Our affairs are hastening fast to ruin if we do not retrieve them by some happy event."[6] The French *chargé d'affaires* in London confirmed the plight of Washington's force in his melancholy report to Foreign Minister Vergennes in Versailles: "The Americans can no longer hold their ground. They have no choice but surrender."[7]

In Paris, Beaumarchais had already begun the enormous task of saving Washington and his Americans by visiting seaports on the Atlantic to find the best facilities for handling large arms shipments to America and to determine sea routes where his ships would be least likely to encounter the British navy and British privateers. After returning to Paris and roaming her streets for a few days, he rented the largest, most lavish Paris town house he could find—large enough to house his family in one part of the structure and the offices of his new enterprise in a separate part. Rather than act secretively and draw the certain attention of curious British spies, he decided to operate so openly in Paris that spies would inevitably conclude that he was simply engaged in conventional foreign trade. For his offices, he settled on the elaborate former Dutch embassy on the rue Vieille du Temple in what is now the Marais district of Paris. The Hôtel des Ambassadeurs de Hollande, as it was still called, was ornate enough to serve as perfect theater for what would be the most elaborate and costly production of Beaumarchais's career. From the street, visitors passed through a huge wooden door into a courtyard before crossing to the door of the mansion itself. A reception room opened onto a grand gallery lined by floor-to-ceiling murals. At the other end were sculpted doors that revealed the main salon, with gloriously ornamented window openings and shutters.

Only a few people knew the true identity of Roderigue Hortalez, among them Gudin, who served as Beaumarchais's secretary, Gudin's brother, the cashier, and Beaumarchais's pregnant Swiss mistress, Mademoiselle Marie-Thérèse Willermaulez. Beaumarchais made an appropriately grand entry every day, nodding his head, smiling, all but bowing to visitors waiting to see him before disappearing into his own office. All ears turned, however, to the huge, hand-carved wooden door marked "Sr. Roderigue Hortalez."

A man clouded in mystery, his name elicited hushed whispers of awe from visitors to "Hortalez et Cie." None had ever had "the honor" of actually seeing him, but everyone recognized his deep, elegant voice in discussions behind closed office doors with Monsieur de Beaumarchais, who marched back and forth, in and out of his own and the banker's offices throughout the day.

Like Figaro, Hortalez was a larger-than-life character from the dramatis personae that peopled Beaumarchais's vast imagination—one that he exulted in playing with an authentic Spanish accent behind the closed door of his office to an audience of visitors who heard but never saw him. Beaumarchais was in his element at Hortalez et Cie., unseen on a world stage, cloaked lavishly in renown, money, and intrigue, alone and unseen, emoting to an invisible audience—often arguing or laughing, soliloquizing stentorian Spanish sounds and replying to himself obsequiously in French: "Oui, Monsieur! Tout de suite, Monsieur."

Beaumarchais and Roderigue Hortalez often disappeared for days at a time, with Hortalez or the sieur de Ronac or a mysterious Monsieur Durand, among others, appearing at army bases in all corners of France, to check inventories of arms, powder barrels, uniforms, and tents, before hopping into a carriage and riding full speed to Le Havre, Brest, Bordeaux, or Rochefort to check on port facilities, capacity, and available labor. A master of disguise and theatrical makeup, Beaumarchais never appeared as the famed playwright Beaumarchais, whose known ties to the French court would arouse suspicions of British agents.

Beaumarchais wrote in cipher to his friend Mary Johnston (Arthur Lee) in London that he hoped soon "to send to Cape François, on the island of San Domingo, a ship loaded with merchandise to the value of twenty-five thousand pounds sterling."

> On your part, do not fail to send a ship loaded with good Virginia tobacco, and let your friend send in the ship an intelligent, discreet, and faithful person, with powers to receive the . . . merchandise . . . and to make remittances in tobacco, which I can no more do without than your friend can do without what I send him. . . . Let him give his notes to my house for what he shall not be able to pay in tobacco.[8]

Beaumarchais's fictional plots onstage seldom proceeded without complications, however, and his real-life offstage plots were no different. Just as he was establishing his own huge arms-trading enterprise, another French entrepreneur barged into the clandestine Franco-American arms trade, backed by no less a man than Benjamin Franklin. A scientist like Franklin, *Monsieur le docteur* Barbeu Dubourg and Franklin were old friends, and, like the Philadelphia scholar, he covered costs of his unremunerative scientific pursuits by engaging in various business enterprises. Thus, when the Secret Committee of Congress, of which Franklin was a member, appointed Connecticut delegate Silas Deane to go to Paris to find military supplies and recruit engineers, Franklin suggested that Deane contact Dubourg. He gave the Connecticut merchant a letter of introduction, addressed to "Mon cher ami Barbeu Dubourg," calling him a "friend to the Americans" who was "prudent, faithful, secret, intelligent in affairs and capable of giving you very sage advice."[9]

Deane's instructions were not dissimilar to those that Congress had given Arthur Lee, but the Committee of Secret Correspondence believed that British agents had infiltrated the congressional membership and that the British-educated Lee might himself be working with the British government. Unaware that Lee had already succeeded in his mission and planned working with Beaumarchais, the committee issued these instructions to Deane:

> With the assistance of Monsieur Dubourg, who understands English, you will be able to make immediate application to Monsieur de Vergennes, *ministre des affaires étrangères* . . . acquainting him that you are in France upon business of the American Congress in the character of a merchant. . . . acquaint him that . . . the Congress . . . was not able to furnish . . . the quantity of arms and ammunition necessary for its defense . . . and you have been dispatched by their authority to apply to some European authority for a supply. France has been pitched on for the first application, from an opinion that if we should come to a total separation from Great Britain, France would be looked upon as the power whose friendship it would be fittest for us to obtain and cultivate. That the commercial advantages Britain had enjoyed with the Colonies had contributed greatly to her late wealth and importance. That it is likely a great part of our commerce will naturally fall to the share of France, especially if she favors us in this application, as that will be a means of gaining and securing the friendship of the Colonies. . . . That the supply we at present want is clothing and arms for twenty-five thousand men, with a suitable quantity of ammunition, and one hundred field pieces.[10]

Being businessmen themselves, the committee members realized that pure patriotism was not enough of an incentive for a merchant like Deane to undertake so hazardous a mission. Given the risks of a dangerous ocean crossing and the possibility of arrest and indefinite imprisonment—even possible execution—if captured by the British, they offered the Connecticut merchant a 5 percent commission on all purchases—in effect enough to yield him a large private fortune and fame as a hero of the American Revolution. The terms were much the same as those they had offered Arthur Lee for serving as agent in London and, before him, Benjamin Franklin.

Deane arrived in Paris in early June 1776, but neither he nor Dr. Du-

Silas Deane, a Connecticut merchant and
member of Congress, awarded contracts
to Beaumarchais to supply the American
Continental Army with arms, ammunition,
and other essential military supplies.

LIBRARY OF CONGRESS

bourg were aware of Beaumarchais or any French government plan to send
arms to America. When Deane approached the French scientist, Dubourg
saw an opportunity to profit handsomely by becoming Deane's sole inter-
mediary in the purchase of French arms. The Connecticut merchant was
too experienced to fall victim to such a scheme, however, and demanded a
meeting with Vergennes, who protested that France was neutral in the dispute between England and her colonies and had no intention of involving
herself by engaging in the arms trade. In an aside, however, he noted that
the government had no powers to restrict such trade in the private sector.

Elated that they were free to buy arms privately and ship them to America, Deane and Dubourg returned to Paris to draw up orders to private dealers for guns, ammunition, powder, and various other materials. The American military had other needs, however: engineers for road and bridge construction and demolition, and trained artillery officers to man and aim the big guns that Deane planned to buy in France. Dubourg gave Deane a list of well-known officers who, he believed, might be willing to go to America. Without ready cash for incentive bonuses and salary advances, however, Deane had to write to the Committee of Secret Correspondence before he could begin recruiting.

Having just translated Arthur Lee's pleas into a huge investment in Beaumarchais's military supply program for the Americans, Vergennes was, to say the least, puzzled at the appearance of another American with credentials from the same American Congress asking for exactly what Arthur Lee had requested and what Beaumarchais was about to deliver. After rejecting Deane's requests for French government assistance, Vergennes let the American know that someone unconnected with the government would contact him.

Four days later, Beaumarchais appeared at Deane's lodgings and disclosed that arms, ammunition, and military equipment worth more than 3 million livres were already on the way to French ports and would soon be en route to America. Beaumarchais's revelations astonished and elated the American—and all but crushed Dubourg's hopes of participating in the government arms trade. In a desperate attempt to insinuate himself into the trading arrangements, Dubourg met with Beaumarchais, who saw no reason to share prospective profits with anyone else and refused. Dubourg responded angrily with a letter to Vergennes questioning the playwright's morals and ethics:

> Everyone knows his wit, his talents. . . . I believe he is one of the most proper men in the world for political negotiations, but . . . the least proper for mercantile enterprises. He loves display; they say he keeps women; he passes . . . for a spendthrift and there is not a merchant in France who does not think of him in this way. . . . Therefore, I was very much astonished when

he informed me that you had charged him not only to aid you . . . but had concentrated on him alone the *ensemble* and the details of all the commercial operations.[11]

The letter startled Vergennes at first; then, knowing Beaumarchais's circumstances, he broke into laughter and sent it off to the playwright, who flew into a rage and immediately replied to Dubourg and sent a copy to Vergennes: "*Et bien*," he began, "how does it affect our business if I like pomp and splendor, and maintain young ladies in my house?"

The ladies who have been in my house for the last twenty years, sir, . . . are five in number—four sisters and one niece. To my great regret, two of these women have been dead for the last three years. I now keep only three, two sisters and my niece—which is still extravagant for a private individual like myself. But what would you think if you knew me better and learned that I carried the scandal so far as to keep men as well: two nephews—very young and rather good looking? You have reasons for writing evil of me to the comte de Vergennes without knowing me. . . . They were not exactly words from the Gospel, but I am not angry, because M. de Vergennes is not a small man.[12]

Fearful that he had damaged his standing at the Foreign Ministry, Dubourg sought to make amends by inviting Beaumarchais to sup with him, and by the end of the evening, Beaumarchais forgave the old man, knowing that Vergennes had already eliminated Dubourg as a player in the French arms trade with America and given Hortalez et Cie. a virtual monopoly.

With Deane officially empowered by the Committee of Secret Correspondence to generate the arms purchases in France—and Lee maintaining suspiciously close ties to British officials—Beaumarchais severed relations with Lee to deal exclusively with Deane. At best, Beaumarchais reasoned, Lee was agent for but a few American colonies, while Deane represented the Congress and, in effect, all thirteen colonies. Like Deane and other agents Congress had appointed, Lee had envisioned harvesting 5 percent commissions on the arms deals with France, thus ensuring himself a private fortune, and a possible rise to heroic status and high office in America. As the youngest of the Lee brothers, he stood to inherit next to nothing from the family's vast estates in Virginia—which was why his father sent him to London to study medicine and law and acquire other means of earning a living.

Deane's sudden appearance "enraged and disappointed" Lee, according to the contemporary historian Jared Sparks. "He [had] hoped to play the principal part in the enterprise. On hearing it was passing into the hands of Mr. Deane—a Connecticut merchant, no less—he hurried to Paris, accused Deane of interfering in his affairs, tried to cause a quarrel between Deane and Beaumarchais, and, not being able to succeed, returned to London vexed at his failure and furious with Deane."[13]

No less furious with Beaumarchais, he determined to wreak vengeance on both by writing to the Committee of Secret Correspondence accusing Deane and Beaumarchais of deceiving both the French and American governments by charging the Congress 3 million livres for what he said had been an outright gift of the French government. "M. de Vergennes, the minister and his secretary," Lee wrote to the Secret Committee of Congress, "have repeatedly assured us that no return was expected for the cargoes sent by Beaumarchais. This gentleman is not a merchant; he is known to be a political agent, employed by the court of France."[14] With two influential older brothers in Congress—the great orator Richard Henry Lee and the sedate but beloved Francis Lightfoot Lee—Arthur Lee's vicious accusations would haunt Deane and Beaumarchais for the rest of their lives.

Despite difficulties understanding each other, Deane and Beaumarchais muddled their way through a pleasant first meeting, each leaving with warm feelings about his new partner and Deane returning directly to his hotel to pen a letter of understanding between the two. "With regard to the credit we require for the provisions and ammunition which I hope to obtain from you," Deane wrote,

> twelve months have been the longest credit my countrymen have ever been accustomed to, and the Congress having engaged large quantities of to- bacco in Virginia and Maryland, together with other articles in other parts which they will ship as fast as vessels can be provided, I have no doubt but very considerable remittance will be made within six months . . . and for the whole within a year. I hope, however, that . . . you will be able to wait for whatever sum may remain due after the credit we shall agree on is expired, having the usual interest allowed you.[15]

After having Deane's letter translated, Beaumarchais replied two days later with friendly words, assuring Deane that he was ready to extend as much as 3 million livres in credit to the U.S. Congress and pledged that American ships arriving with tobacco in France would sail back filled with military equipment. "As I believe that I am to deal with a virtuous nation, it will be enough for me to keep an exact account of all I advance. . . . I wish to serve your country as if it were my own, and I hope to find in the friendship of a noble-minded nation the true reward of the labor which I willingly undertake for them."[16]

Beaumarchais's reply elated the Connecticut merchant, who had antici- pated great difficulties and usurious terms in the market for clandestine arms purchases. "I am of the opinion that your proposals . . . are just and equitable," he wrote to Beaumarchais.

> The generous confidence which you place in the virtue and justice of my constituents causes me the greatest pleasure . . . and permit me to assure you the United Colonies will take the most effectual measures to make you remittances, and to justify in every respect the sentiments you entertain of them.[17]

The warm feelings that developed between the two men—and the zeal with which Deane espoused American independence, individual liberty, and equal opportunity—inspired Beaumarchais to make the American cause his own. Indeed, the American Revolution symbolized the war he had waged against the aristocracy his entire life. In his heart, Beaumarchais and Figaro were both American. "The respectful esteem I have for the brave people who defend their liberty under your leadership," he wrote to the Committee of Secret Correspondence in Philadelphia,

> has induced me to form ... a large commercial firm for the sole purpose of serving you in Europe, there to supply you with necessaries of every sort ... clothes, linens, powder, ammunition, muskets, cannon or even gold for the payment of your troops, and in general every thing that can be useful for the honorable war in which you are engaged. Your deputies, gentlemen, will find in me a sincere friend, in my house a shelter, in my coffers money; and I shall assist them by every possible means in their transactions. . . . You may be certain, gentlemen, that my indefatigable zeal will ... facilitate all trade operations much more to your advantage than to mine. . . . One thing can never change or decline: my avowed and ardent desire to serve you to the utmost of my power.[18]

By November, Beaumarchais had convinced Deane of the sincerity of his belief in the American Revolution as a vehicle of change in the Western world's political and social order—a change that would permit social equality, religious freedom, and equal opportunity. Deane confirmed Beaumarchais's commitment in a letter to the committee:

> I should never have completed what I have, but for the generous, the indefatigable and spirited exertions of Monsieur Beaumarchais, to whom the United States are, on every account, greatly indebted, more so than to any other person on this side of the water. . . . Therefore I am confident you will make the earliest and most ample remittances. . . . I cannot in a letter do full justice to Monsieur Beaumarchais for his great address and assiduity in our cause; I can only say he appears to have undertaken it on great and liberal principles, and has, in the pursuit, made it his own.[19]

Despite the ease with which they worked together, both Deane and Beaumarchais recognized the fragility of the business they were in. The Treaty of Paris that ended the Seven Years' War specifically banned the very kind of arms traffic that the French foreign minister had sponsored. If the British ambassador to France, Lord Stormont, or his spies were to learn of the Beaumarchais-Deane arms deal and the role of French foreign minister Vergennes, Britain would almost certainly declare war against France—and France was not ready for war.

From the first, however, the deal with Deane began to fray at the edges. Although Deane asked the Committee of Secret Correspondence to send ships to France to pick up the French military supplies, Arthur Lee's letters infected the minds of committee members and, to Deane's immense frustration, the committee failed to respond. No American ships ever arrived in French ports.

"I shall not be able to provide them," Deane finally admitted to Beaumarchais in late August 1776. He asked Beaumarchais both to procure vessels and disburse the security for each charter—an enormous outlay that Beaumarchais had not anticipated. Beaumarchais faced the challenge of revisiting major French ports to charter or buy a fleet of cargo ships and find ship captains willing to risk their lives and the lives of their crews. Beaumarchais realized he could no longer manage his complex scheme without a confidential aide in the field—visiting military depots and ports, following up on shipments to America if necessary. He found the perfect candidate in Jean-Baptiste Théveneau de Francy, the brilliant younger brother of Théveneau de Morande, the "Journalist in Armor," whom Beaumarchais had helped negotiate a hefty cash settlement from King Louis XV for not publishing the libelous memoirs of Madame du Barry. Though brother of a brilliant swindler, Francy proved one of the most decent, honest, and loyal characters in the ever-twisting plot of Beaumarchais's life as an arms merchant.

By the end of November 1776, Beaumarchais had acquired three ships, but without the steady stream of American ships that Deane had promised, he needed more warehouse space to store materials while his ships shuttled materials back and forth to America. At Le Havre alone, 200 cannons and mortars had accumulated at dockside, with more than 20,000 cannonballs weighing four pounds each; 25,000 rifles with bayonets; 10,000 grenades; 290,000 pounds of gunpowder; and clothing, blankets, and tents for 25,000 men. Deane then added to Beaumarchais's burdens with a request for experienced artillery officers and engineers. Although Deane recruited many on his own—most notably, the marquis de Lafayette and Baron Johann de Kalb—Beaumarchais had to spend precious time in taverns and inns near major military bases, befriending officers to determine their political leanings. Acting on Deane's assurances that the U.S. government would reimburse him, Beaumarchais gave cash bonuses to those who espoused the American cause and promised travel expenses, high salaries, six months' pay in advance—and the highest leadership ranks in the army of the legendary George Washington. He recruited thirty officers—a dozen artillery officers, a dozen engineers, and the rest infantrymen—paying them all from Hortalez funds. Among the Beaumarchais recruits were the "count de Conway," Kazimierz Pulaski, and the young engineer/architect Pierre Charles L'Enfant, who would remain in the United States after independence and help design the young nation's capital city in Washington.

"Every time I think how we hold in our hands the destiny of the world," Beaumarchais wrote to Vergennes with an openness that few commoners would dare display to a person of high nobility, "and that we have the power to change the system of things—and when I see so many advantages, so much glory ready to escape, I regret infinitely not to have more influence . . . to prevent the evil on one hand, and aid the good on the other. I know too well your patriotism to fear offending you in speaking thus."[20]

At the end of 1776, the piles of military equipment on the docks at Le Havre and the arrival of three transport ships drew the attention of British spies, who reported their findings to British ambassador Lord Stormont. The last semblance of secrecy surrounding the accumulated armaments disappeared when Benjamin Franklin sailed into the port city of Nantes. Upon his arrival, Franklin immediately wrote to his *cher bon ami* Dr. Dubourg and reignited the latter's hopes—and all-too-public boasts—that he would play a major role in supplying French arms to America. Like Deane, Franklin arrived in France charged with obtaining arms, ammunition,

Benjamin Franklin, the venerable American
scientist, went to Paris to purchase arms and
ammunition from a French friend and associate,
only to be frustrated when he learned that the
French government had given a monopoly
on its arms trade to Beaumarchais.

military supplies, and loans from foreign governments—for which he too
stood to reap 5 percent commissions, a substantial private fortune, and the
thanks of a grateful nation. Unlike Deane, Franklin had had the foresight
to sail to France with a cargo of indigo he had bought in America. Its resale
at a profit on the Nantes dock filled the venerable doctor's pockets with an
abundance of cash—and left Dubourg crowing about his plans to buy arms
for America in partnership with Franklin.

"Is there no way to shut his mouth?" Beaumarchais complained to

Vergennes. "Dubourg must be made to keep silent and not compromise the ministry," he warned. "If while we close the doors on one side, someone opens the windows on the other, it is impossible for the secret not to escape."[21]

Although Beaumarchais had hoped to establish a friendship with Franklin, the American rebuffed his overtures after learning that Beaumarchais had already obtained a monopoly on purchases of French government arms and would therefore prevent Franklin from profiting from the arms trade.

As military supplies continued accumulating on the docks at Le Havre, British agents reported to the British government in London, which responded with ever-more-menacing warnings to the French government. Versailles replied unconvincingly with bland statements that the arms were destined for French forces in the French West Indies and that the government had no power to restrict private merchants. Beaumarchais, meanwhile, raced to Le Havre disguised as Durand to rid the docks of the troublesome supplies and get them on their way to America. Unfortunately, he reached Le Havre just as his popular play *Le Barbier de Séville* had opened in the local theater. Outraged by what he considered a careless and inferior performance, he threw off his disguise and insisted on leading rehearsals. No longer Hortalez, Ronac, Durand, or anyone else, he reverted to the irrepressible, flamboyant playwright, dashing about town, entertaining officers he had recruited, then storming into the local theater to promote performances of his plays. Spending half his time at the docks and half at the theater, he managed to oversee cargo loading at pier side and rehearsals onstage, coaching dockworkers and actors with equal verve—and unmasking himself before the world in the greatest performance of his life. The identities of Durand, Ronac, and Hortalez became clear to all. "His precaution of concealing himself under the name of Durand," said one officer, "became perfectly useless."[22]

After Lord Stormont learned of Beaumarchais's involvement in arms shipments, he issued "the most vehement remonstrances to the French government" and threatened war. Fearing the imminent outbreak of hostilities, Louis XVI ordered a halt to the Beaumarchais operations at Le Havre. The minister of war prohibited all army officers from leaving France, and Vergennes ordered the rest of the Beaumarchais fleet to remain in port. Beaumarchais, however, had spies of his own, one of whom galloped out of Versailles and reached Le Havre before the orders arrived from Vergennes. Beaumarchais ordered his ships to leave port immediately—only to have volunteer officers refuse to board unless Beaumarchais paid them a full year's salary instead of six months' as originally agreed. Beaumarchais had no choice but to comply or face bankruptcy if the embargo prevented his sale of military stores to America.

By the time the order from Versailles arrived to halt the sailings, the largest of Beaumarchais's three ships—the *Amphitrite*—was already under way with the largest share of Hortalez et Cie. stores on board. Its cargo included 52 brass cannon, 52 carriages for same, 20,000 four-pound cannonballs, 9,000 grenades, about 6,500 muskets, more than 900 tents, assorted tools—spades, pickaxes, and so forth—320 blankets, 8,545 black stockings, 4,097 shirts—and 1,272 dozen pocket handkerchiefs!

A jubilant Beaumarchais had climbed aboard to celebrate as the ship left the dock, and he disembarked with the pilot when the ship approached the end of the channel and the open sea. As he watched the *Amphitrite* sail off to America, Beaumarchais was celebrating more than the successful birth of his arms-trading business. A few weeks earlier, on January 5, 1777, his beloved Mlle. de Willermaulez had given birth to Beaumarchais's daughter, whom they named *Eugénie*, after his first successful play.

Among the officers on board the *Amphitrite* was Major Philippe Charles Tronson du Coudray, a self-styled engineer and artillery expert who had persuaded Deane to send him to America as chief of artillery with the rank of major general. Eager for his own share of profits from the arms trade, du Coudray tried commandeering the ship after it got under way, demanding quarters befitting his rank and challenging the captain for ultimate command of the ship. The captain ordered the ship to come about and put into Lorient, a port on the southern coast of Brittany. With two Beaumarchais ships trapped at Le Havre by Vergennes's embargo and the *Amphitrite* docked in Lorient, Hortalez et Cie.—and Beaumarchais—faced financial collapse. Its effort to supply French arms to the Americans seemed doomed, and with it the American War of Independence.

8

Figaro Here, Figaro There…

WHEN BEAUMARCHAIS learned of the *Amphitrite*'s return to port, he sent his trusted confidante Francy galloping to Lorient, where he confronted du Coudray, handing him a letter from Beaumarchais, who called du Coudray's conduct inexplicable. "As the real owner of the vessel 'Amphitrite,'" he wrote to du Coudray, "I order Captain Fautrelle to take the sole command of it. . . . Consequently, you will have the kindness, sir, to obey, or to find another ship and go where you please. . . . On receipt of this letter, you will kindly put Captain Fautrelle in possession of all the parcels, orders, and letters relating to delivery of the cargo of his ship."[1]

Beaumarchais sent Vergennes a plea to reverse his orders halting the departure of his ships. "I prostrate myself at your feet, Monsieur le Comte," Beaumarchais implored the foreign minister. "It serves no purpose allowing these ships to sit idly in port. As a personal favor to me, let the ships sail to Santo Domingo or let me order the artillery unloaded onto foreign vessels and let me satisfy the terms of my arrangements with my American friends."[2]

Beaumarchais was able to obtain a partial lifting of the embargo, with all arms on French ships to sail only to French territory and all arms bound for America thereafter to be carried on American ships. Beaumarchais gave Captain Fautrelle new official orders showing Port-au-Prince on the French island of Santo Domingo as his destination—but he gave the captain verbal instructions to change course for Portsmouth, New Hampshire, if possible, once he got under way, and to deliver his cargo directly to the besieged American revolutionaries.

The *Amphitrite* finally left port on February 6, 1777, with du Coudray remaining on shore to await another ship for America. On board was Beaumarchais's young nephew, whom the playwright had raised as his own son after the boy's mother had died. Inspired by his uncle's struggles against aristocrat oppression and praises for the American Revolution, Beaumarchais's nephew signed on with Silas Deane as a volunteer artillery officer—despite his uncle's admonitions that he was too young. When Francy discovered the boy on the *Amphitrite*, he wrote to Beaumarchais, who recognized the futility of trying to stop him. Describing the boy's impulses as childish, he nonetheless asked Francy to have one of the older officers watch over him and gave the boy his blessing. Within a year, he had earned promotion to the rank of major and wrote to his uncle on the eve of battle:

> Your nephew, my dear uncle, may be killed, but he will never do anything unworthy of one who has the honor of being related to you. This is as certain as that he will always feel the greatest affection for the best uncle living.[3]

As the *Amphitrite* sailed off to America in the winter of 1777, nothing but the disastrous news noted earlier was arriving from that far-off wilderness. Two months earlier, on December 11, 1776, the remnants of the American army—a mere 5,200—had barely escaped capture by crossing the Delaware River into Pennsylvania, where they lay on the frozen ground, without tents to shield them from the wind, sleet, and snow, and without a drop of rum to keep them warm. Death and desertions had reduced Washington's army to only 5,200 men—one-third of them too sick or hungry to serve. The desperate American commander in chief knew that if the ice on the river grew thick enough to allow the enemy to cross, he and his men faced annihilation. With New York and New Jersey in British hands, Congress had fled Philadelphia for Baltimore to draw up terms of capitulation in the evidently futile struggle for independence.

"It is with a heavy heart I sit down to write you," banker Robert Morris wrote to Deane from Philadelphia just before Christmas, lamenting that "the late unfortunate turn of American Affairs leaves no room for joy in the mind of any true friend of our country. I am now the only member of Congress left in this city and cannot pretend to give you a regular detail of our manifold misfortunes."[4]

Some congressmen believed Washington incompetent—and he was thinking much the same thing: "It is impossible . . . to give you any idea . . . of my difficulties—and the constant perplexities and mortifications I constantly meet with," he wrote to his brother. "Adieu my dear Sir—remember me affectionately to . . . the family. Your sincerely affectionate brother, George Washington."[5]

On the morning of December 22, his aide Colonel Joseph Reed came to him. "We are all of the opinion," he warned, "that something must be attempted to revive our expiring credit. Our affairs are hastening fast to ruin if we do not retrieve them by some happy event."[6] Three days later, Washington responded. In one of the most daring exploits in American military history, he led 2,400 troops through a blinding snowstorm on Christmas night across the ice-choked Delaware River and stormed the Hessian garrison guarding the town. Catching the Hessians asleep in their barracks at dawn on December 26, the Americans captured 918 of the 1,400-man garrison and killed 30, including the Hessian commander. The Americans suffered but five casualties.

After moving his Hessian prisoners into a holding area, Washington ordered his entire force into Trenton, where ample Hessian provisions reinvigorated their bodies and spirits. On January 2, 1777, a British force under General Lord Cornwallis approached from the east to counterattack. Washington established the semblance of a camp in defensive positions east of Trenton, but he led the bulk of his force around Cornwallis's flanks during the night and arrived near Princeton by dawn. With Cornwallis boasting that he would "bag the fox [Washington]," the British attacked what proved to be an illusory American camp east of Trenton, while the bulk of Washington's army now attacked the sides and rear of the British force. Fearful of being trapped, Cornwallis led a hasty retreat eastward and ceded all of western New Jersey to the Americans. By mid-January, Washington's courageous little army had cleared most of western New Jersey of enemy troops and sent American morale—both civilian and military—soaring. The news electrified the world. A band of untrained, half-starved, ill-equipped citizen-soldiers had defeated a larger force of the best-trained professional soldiers in the world.

Congress immediately returned to Philadelphia, and when news of Washington's victory at Trenton reached Versailles, France, "it produced the most vivid sensation," Deane wrote to Congress in a letter cosigned by Franklin and Arthur Lee. "The hearts of the French people are universally for us and the opinion for an immediate war with Great Britain is very strong, but the court has its reasons for postponing a little longer."[7]

At Versailles, Washington's triumph at Trenton provoked the comte de Vergennes to reverse his orders and allow Beaumarchais's two other ships to set sail for America. The *Seine* and the *Mercure* left for America with more arms and ammunition and thousands of tents, blankets, and articles of clothing, including 1,800 dozen pairs of worsted hose, 1,700 pairs of shoes, and 1,245 dozen pocket handkerchiefs.

As the *Seine, Mercure,* and *Amphitrite* bounded over the waves to America, Beaumarchais chartered two more ships and sent them off with more brass cannon, cannonballs, bombs, muskets, clothing, and bedding. By March, Beaumarchais added two more ships; by summer his fleet had grown to twelve; by autumn, twenty. "Never has a commercial affair been promoted with such vigor," Beaumarchais boasted to Vergennes. "May God bless it with success."[8]

After the *Amphitrite* had sailed, Deane wrote to Congress, "The eyes of all are on you, and the fear of your giving up is the greatest obstacle I have to contend with. . . . Monsieur Beaumarchais has been my minister in effect, as this court is extremely cautious and I now advise you to attend carefully to the articles sent you. . . . Large remittances are necessary for your credit, and the enormous price of tobacco, of rice, of flour and many other articles, gives you an opportunity of making your remittances to very good advantage. Twenty thousand hogsheads of tobacco [10 hogsheads = approximately 1 ½ bushels] are wanted immediately for this kingdom and more for other parts of Europe."[9]

Again, Congress failed to respond or reply.

In the spring of 1777, British Secretary of State for the Colonies Lord George Germain ordered his commanders in America to crush the insurrection or face dismissal and disgrace. General Sir William Howe, whose forces controlled New York City, and General John Burgoyne in Canada planned a three-pronged strategy aimed at capturing the rebel capital of Philadelphia, and isolating New England from the rest of the colonies by gaining control of the Hudson River Valley and the waterways to the Canadian frontier. While Howe sent one-third of his force from New York to capture Philadelphia, a second force would sail northward along the Hudson River toward Albany. Meanwhile, Burgoyne would march southward from Canada, along Lake Champlain and Lake George, to meet the troops from New York at Albany.

Rather than confront Washington's Continental Army in New Jersey, north of Philadelphia, Howe decided to approach from the south. He loaded 15,000 British troops onto a fleet of ships that sailed into Chesapeake Bay and up to its northern shore, where his army landed and began what he hoped would be an easy march toward the American capital. Burgoyne's campaign also started well, as he led 8,000 British troops and Indian warriors from the Canadian border southward, capturing Lake Champlain and overrunning Fort Ticonderoga, Mount Defiance, and, finally, Fort Anne. Hopelessly outmanned and outgunned, the Patriots —now reduced to raw recruits—deserted by the scores, knowing they were helpless to slow Burgoyne's inexorable advance to Albany. For them, at least, the American Revolution in the North seemed at an end . . .

. . . until a small band of farmers suddenly appeared on the outskirts of Bennington, Vermont, each carrying several muskets or more, firing into the air as they approached—shouting incomprehensibly about a ship . . . a French ship.

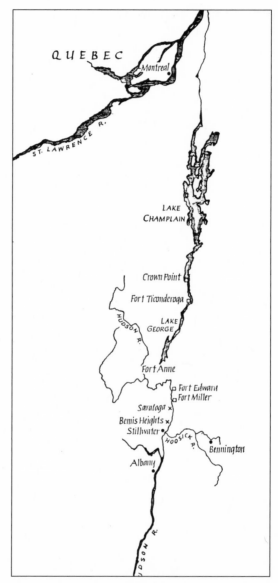

The Saratoga Campaign saw British General John Burgoyne
lead 7,700 British and German troops from Canada along Lake
Champlain and Lake George to Saratoga. Intent on reaching Albany
and isolating New England from the rest of the continent, he met
final defeat and was forced to surrender to the Americans
after a decisive battle at Bemis Heights.

On March 17, 1777, the 300-ton *Mercure*, the first of the three Beaumarchais ships that had set sail in January and early February, had appeared at the entrance to the harbor at Portsmouth, New Hampshire. As puzzled townsfolk gathered at pier side, the ship ran its colors up the mast. The ship was French, carrying 12,000 muskets, 50 brass cannon, powder and ammunition, 1,000 tents, and clothes for 10,000 men.

Spectators stared in disbelief at first, then, as sailors displayed the muskets to the crowd, townsmen began shouting, cheering, roaring, dancing, jumping aboard to hug sailors. Boys and men raced about town to find militiamen, militia commanders, and anyone in the military. Within a week the euphoria had metamorphosed into a carefully organized, determined effort to transport supplies to Saratoga by packhorse, wagon, and sheer human effort. Part of the shipment went to George Washington's army in New Jersey, but the rest traveled 150 miles to the American Northern Army, which was trying to halt Burgoyne's advance northeast of Albany, New York. Muskets were easiest to transport, with individual men and boys setting out on their own in small groups, each carrying several at a time on his back and outdistancing the heavily loaded wagons. As they crossed New Hampshire toward Vermont, they handed their extra muskets to unarmed volunteers and marched together to Saratoga, growing by the tens, the hundreds, and more. In Vermont, they crossed paths with men who had abandoned the front for lack of ammunition. Rearmed and reinvigorated by the arrival of arms and ammunition from France, they turned about and returned to war with the others.

As they neared Bennington, Vermont, their number had swelled to more than 2,000. They arrived in time to reinforce General John Stark's 500 militiamen, who were under attack by a contingent of 900 British troops and running out of powder. With their powder horns refilled with Beaumarchais supplies, the Americans slaughtered 200 Redcoats by the end of the day and captured the remaining 700—depleting Burgoyne's forces by 10 percent. The disaster at Bennington proved the first in a series of crushing defeats that the arrival of Beaumarchais ships would inflict on Burgoyne and his Redcoats in the coming days.

Nor was the war going well in the south. Although Howe had left New

York with 15,000 troops on July 23, it took him a month to reach the northern shore of Chesapeake Bay and land his men—and another month of
fierce fighting to capture Philadelphia. By then, Washington's winter triumph at Trenton had revived American spirits and doubled the number
of his fighting force to more than 10,000. By then, too, more French arms
from Beaumarchais were landing on American shores. Although the British had captured the *Seine*, the 480-ton *Amphitrite* lumbered safely over
the horizon into Portsmouth harbor on April 30 with twice as much cargo
as the *Mercure*—enough arms, ammunition, and supplies for 30,000 men,
according to Silas Deane's own inventory.[10] As more Beaumarchais ships
arrived in Portsmouth, supply lines formed to carry French muskets, balls,
powder, and other supplies to Washington's army. Although still outnum-
bered, the Americans used their fresh supplies of arms and ammunition
to begrudge Howe's invaders every inch of ground on the road to Philadelphia, ceding access to the city only after a fierce bayonet attack at the
Brandywine River southwest of the city sliced their numbers to levels that
made further resistance impossible.

By the time Howe's army marched into Philadelphia on September 26,
Burgoyne's army in the north was running out of food. Unaware that
Beaumarchais had successfully rearmed the Americans, Burgoyne ordered
his troops to decamp and advance to Albany. Waiting for him was a bat-
tle-tested force of Northern Army soldiers under General Horatio Gates,
a British-born officer who had planted his men on Bemis Heights, just
south of Saratoga. As men streamed in to support Gates with supplies from
Beaumarchais's *Amphitrite*, Burgoyne ordered 1,200 Hessians to attack the
American right flank, while 2,200 British troops charged the left flank and
the rest of the British army attacked the center. To Burgoyne's shock, the
Americans turned the encounter into a slaughterhouse, with General Dan-
iel Morgan's riflemen poised behind trees on the slopes of Bemis Heights
raining bullets on the advancing British troops as they marched in traditional linear style toward the forested hillside. Unaccustomed to fighting
in the North American wilderness, the Redcoats toppled onto each other
like toy soldiers, row after row, marching forward relentlessly, stepping over
their fallen comrades before dropping under the ceaseless rifle fire. The

British forces on either flank withdrew toward the center to save survivors and cover their retreat. At the end of the day, Burgoyne had lost about 600 men. The Patriots had lost only half that number, and whereas Burgoyne could not count on replacements, hundreds more farmers and their sons were streaming into the American camp to volunteer.

As supplies from the *Amphitrite* continued rolling into the American camp, Burgoyne put his troops on half-rations and resolved to break through the American left flank, which blocked the road to Albany. Again, the Americans routed the British, who suffered a loss of 700 troops captured, wounded, and killed. The Americans lost 150 men. By early October, the American army had swelled to 17,000, all of them now well armed by Beaumarchais. By then, he had doubled his fleet to forty ships. Some continued sailing into Portsmouth, but many followed safer routes to the French West Indies, where they distributed their cargoes to smaller American ships that sailed into hidden harbors along the Atlantic coast. By October 1777, Beaumarchais's ships had landed 200 field artillery pieces at Portsmouth, along with thousands of muskets, thousands of kegs of powder, and enough blankets, clothes, and shoes—and pocket handkerchiefs—in all, worth 5 million livres (about $20 million in today's dollars), or nine-tenths of the Northern Army's military supplies at the time.

As Patriot forces surrounded Burgoyne's army at Saratoga, Sir Henry Clinton sailed up the Hudson River from New York toward Albany to relieve Burgoyne. Clinton left New York on October 13, but his ships scraped bottom two days later, only midway up to Albany. Although his troops disembarked on the western shore of the river, they were already too late and too far away to save Burgoyne.

When the *Amphitrite* was preparing to cast off for its return to France, an American ship's captain arrived at Portsmouth with his officers and crew—and orders from Congress to seize command of the *Amphitrite* and sail off as a privateer to attack British shipping. Citing the command as a "reward for his zeal," the instructions directed him to split the proceeds of all prizes three ways, with "one third to the French owners, master and crew, one third to Congress," and one-third for the American captain "and his merry men." The American captain was John Paul Jones.

Appalled by the sheer gall of both Congress and Jones, the captain of the *Amphitrite* placed his hand on the handle of his sword and denied Jones permission to board his ship. To ease tensions, the captain of the *Mercure* stepped between the two men and offered to carry Jones as a passenger to seek a ship of his own in France, but Jones simply walked away. Congress subsequently offered him command of an American ship—the *Ranger.*

When the *Amphitrite* returned from America, Beaumarchais bounded onto the deck and pulled up in shock as he stared in disbelief into the empty hold: no tobacco, no rice, no flour—nothing. Although the smaller *Mercure* had returned carrying lumber for masts and spars from New Hampshire's white pine forests, the huge *Amphitrite* had returned to port empty—without American products to pay for the arms he had sent. In the weeks that followed, ship after ship returned in the same condition. All were to have picked up cargoes in such ports as Newport, Charleston, and Savannah before returning to France, but the Americans had evidently reneged on their deal. Beaumarchais had now sent more than 5 million livres (more than $20 million today) in arms to the Americans and received in return one load of lumber worth 19,000 livres (nearly $80,000).

Unbeknownst to Beaumarchais, Arthur Lee was responsible for the playwright's financial reversals. He had convinced Benjamin Franklin that the French arms Beaumarchais was shipping to America were an outright gift from the French king, and Franklin confirmed that "the first two millions granted to Beaumarchais by his majesty we understood to be a gift."[11] Lee confirmed Franklin's argument with a letter of his own to Congress asserting, "I think it is my duty to state to you some facts relative to the demands of . . . Hortalez. . . . The Minister has repeatedly assured us, and in the most explicit terms, that no return is expected for these subsidies."[12]

Convinced that all the arms, ammunition, and matériel on the Beaumarchais ships had been gifts of the French king, Congress not only refused to ship any commodities to Beaumarchais, it did not reply to his letters or even thank him.

"I am in despair," Beaumarchais wrote to Vergennes on July 1, citing debts of more than 500,000 livres. As creditors threatened to seize Beaumarchais's ships, Vergennes advanced him another 1 million livres to maintain the flow of arms to America, but Beaumarchais realized the advance was but a temporary solution to a much more serious problem: the failure of Congress to respond to his—and Silas Deane's—entreaties to pay Hortalez et Cie. for earlier shipments. Even his crews threatened to abandon him. Without return cargoes to provide them with commissions, ships' officers were selling cannons off their decks to realize some returns for their voyages. Beaumarchais decided to send Théveneau de Francy to America to learn the reasons and work out an arrangement for continuing to sell arms to America.

Sailing with Francy was a Prussian officer whom the French minister of war, comte de St. Germain, had enticed into volunteering to train the American army. "You are the very man America needs at this moment," St. Germain told Baron Friedrich Wilhelm Ludolf Gerhard Augustin von Steuben. "Here is your field of action, here is the Republic you must serve. If you succeed . . . you will acquire more glory than you can hope for in Europe for many years to come."[13] When Benjamin Franklin was unable to provide von Steuben with an advance on his salary or even his traveling expenses, Beaumarchais gave the Prussian 1,000 *louis d'or* and free passage to America.

Beaumarchais also gave von Steuben a letter of introduction to Congress: "The art of making war successfully being the fruit of courage combined with prudence, knowledge and experience," Beaumarchais wrote, "a companion in arms of the great Frederick, who stood by his side for twenty-two years, seems one of the men best fitted to second Monsieur Washington."[14] Weeks later, von Steuben stood on a field at Valley Forge barking orders at Washington's troops, teaching them to march in formation and teaching their officers the arts of warfare, strategy, and maintaining troop discipline.

"I congratulate myself for what I have learned of him and for having given so great an officer to my friends, the free men of America," Beaumarchais boasted to Francy after learning of von Steuben's appointment as Inspector General of the Continental Army. "Never have I made an investment which gave me greater pleasure. . . . Bravo! Tell him that his glory is the interest on my money."[15]

Francy arrived in America in December 1777 and spent the next three months cajoling Congress into honoring the contractual arrangements implicit in the exchange of letters between Beaumarchais and Silas Deane in 1776. He finally extracted a document on April 6, 1778, that included this admission: "Whereas, Roderigue Hortalès et Cie. have shipped or caused to be shipped . . . considerable quantities of cannon, arms, ammunition, clothing, and other stores . . ." It continued with a promise to honor outstanding bills of 24 million livres (more than $98 million) plus 6 percent annual interest, payable either in specie or "exports of American produce." The contract seemed to be a complete repudiation of Arthur Lee and a vindication of Beaumarchais "as the most zealous partisan of the American republic in France."[16]

The document did not, however, translate into any tobacco shipments, and after two months of fruitless attempts to obtain payment for his patron's arms shipments, Francy wrote in despair to Beaumarchais: "In spite of the most formal engagements, these people find the means of obstructing all business and a pretext for breaking the most solemn promises. This business would be one of the greatest commercial operations ever engaged in, if one could only rely on the good faith of these republicans. But they have no principle and I sincerely believe you should close all your accounts with them."[17]

On October 13, 1777, British General John Burgoyne asked for a ceasefire at Saratoga. Four days later, surrounded by a well-armed force three times larger than his own, he surrendered his army of more than 5,000 men to the Americans. After the surrender, Burgoyne at last reached Albany—as a prisoner rather than as a conqueror—while his men marched away to an internment camp near Boston. Clinton's troops, meanwhile, had reached the state capital of Kingston to the south and, hearing of Burgoyne's surrender, retaliated by burning the town to the ground before reboarding their ships and returning to New York.

When news of Burgoyne's surrender reached London the following month, gloom swept through the halls of Parliament. Prime Minister Lord North responded by sending a representative to Paris to try to negotiate terms of reconciliation with Deane and Franklin, but the Saratoga victory emboldened the Americans to refuse to discuss any topic but full independence.

Exulting in the news of the Saratoga victory, Beaumarchais warned Vergennes that "an emissary from Lord North arrived in Paris yesterday. . . . He has orders to gain the deputation at Passy [Franklin's residence] at any price. This is the moment or never . . . whichever of the two nations, France or England, recognizes first the independence of America, she alone will reap all the fruits, while that independence will certainly be ruinous to the one which allows her rival to get the advance."[18]

Using the American victory at Saratoga to convince Vergennes that the Americans would win the war if properly armed, Beaumarchais coaxed the foreign minister into urging the king to recognize American independence. And as the playwright predicted, the king's acquiescence made France the first nation to harvest the fruits of American independence.

On February 6, 1778, French representatives signed two treaties with the Americans. One was a treaty of amity and commerce that immediately granted France and the United States "most favored nation" trade status with each other. The other treaty formed a defensive military alliance that would become effective if and when France and Britain went to war with one another. The alliance included a French pledge to help the United States "maintain its liberty, sovereignty, and independence," and it gave the United States the right to conquer Canada and Bermuda. France won the right to seize the British West Indies. Both nations agreed to guarantee

each other's territorial integrity. On March 20, 1778, King Louis XVI officially received Franklin and Deane as representatives of the United States
of America.

Before leaving for Versailles, however, Deane learned that Congress had
recalled him. Although he could not know it then, his recall followed a
series of letters from Arthur Lee insinuating that Deane had embezzled
funds destined for American aid. Only the eloquence of New York's John
Jay, then secretary for foreign affairs, prevented Congress from adding a
censure to the recall.

Distraught by the unfeeling senselessness of the letter of recall, Deane
turned to his friend Beaumarchais, who had received word from Francy of
Deane's humiliation. "I am almost sure that it is the work of that famous
politician ... Arthur Lee," Francy wrote. "It is he who has alienated Doctor
Franklin from you."[19]

It was Deane who had taught Beaumarchais to love America and the
American cause, and Beaumarchais instinctively began plotting to save his
friend's reputation with a letter to Vergennes, who already suspected Lee
of being an agent for England. "To succeed in his design," Beaumarchais
wrote of Lee, "it was necessary to dispose of a colleague so formidable as
Mr. Deane ... by rendering him ... an object of suspicion to Congress."
Calling Deane a friend of France and French interests, Beaumarchais
urged Vergennes to bestow on Deane

> a particular mark of distinction, even the King's portrait or some such no-
> ticeable present to convince his countrymen that not only was he a credit-
> able and faithful agent, but that his personality, prudence and action have
> pleased the French Ministry. I strongly recommend his being escorted by
> a fleet or royal frigate. . . . Once justified before Congress, his opinion be-
> comes of immense weight and influence. . . . His enemies will remain dazed
> and humiliated at their own failure. . . . Upon the assurance that these
> considerations be regarded as just, I will neglect everything else until I have
> completely vindicated Mr. Deane.[20]

Beaumarchais's seductive words convinced Vergennes to send Deane a
portrait of King Louis XVI, with testimonial letters from the king's min-

isters. What Deane needed more than the king's portrait, however, was some hard cash. In accepting his assignment in France, he had counted on collecting a 5 percent commission on the sale of commodities that Congress was to have shipped to pay for military supplies. By the time of his recall, however, Congress had shipped so little that Deane had depleted his own resources and had borrowed money from Beaumarchais to pay for his food and lodging during his last months in France. Benjamin Franklin, of course, had foreseen such problems and brought a shipload of indigo he had purchased in America to sell when he landed in Brittany.

The world-renowned Admiral Comte d'Estaing led a French fleet that carried Deane home to America, and Vergennes's personal letter to the president of Congress confirmed Deane's "zeal, activity and intelligence in supporting United States interests."[21] Beaumarchais wrote that even as America's other ministers—Lee and Franklin—were "lacking in common civility towards me, I testify that my zeal, my advances of money, and my shipments of supplies and merchandise have been . . . due to the indefatigable exertions of Mr. Deane."[22]

Before leaving, Deane wrote a long farewell to his friend Beaumarchais, promising, first, to return in the fall to repay Beaumarchais's personal loans to him and then congratulating him for having "contributed more than any other person . . . to [the French government] resolution to protect America's liberties and independence. I shall . . . rely on being honored with a continuance of your . . . friendship. Wishing that you may ever be happy and fortunate . . . Silas Deane."[23]

As Deane sailed to America, word of the French fleet's approach provoked a British evacuation of Philadelphia and consolidation of their American forces in New York. When Deane's ship moored in Delaware Bay, he sent word of his arrival to Congress, which simply ignored him. And when he finally addressed that body, its members dismissed his every word, with the friends and relatives of Arthur Lee convinced that Lee had had no reason to lie about Deane and that his accusations were true.

While waiting for Francy to obtain redress from Congress, Beaumarchais heard from William Carmichael, Deane's secretary, who had preceded his patron home to America. "I have applied myself with my whole power to convince my compatriots of the injustice and ingratitude with which you have been treated," Carmichael wrote.

> I wish for the honor of my compatriots that it had never been necessary for us to plead for you.... Mr. de Francy is in Virginia and works sincerely and indefatigably for your interests.
>
> Your nephew spent several weeks with me, but is now commanded with his general to join the army.... He is a brave young man who makes himself loved very much.... He has all the vivacity of his age and desires to distinguish himself. General Conway assures me that he conducted himself like a young hero at the battle of the Brandywine. I take the liberty of entering into these details because I know they will delight his mother, since bravery has been a powerful recommendation to the fair sex, and she will be charmed to find so much in her own son.[24]

The ships in the Beaumarchais fleet that had not been seized by the British continued carrying arms to America, and to replace his missing ships, he chartered or bought ever-larger ships, with more guns to protect themselves against privateers and warships. "I struggle against obstacles of every kind," Beaumarchais complained to Francy,

> but as I struggle ... I hope to conquer with patience, and courage, and very much money.
>
> I still hope that ... you will send me ... a cargo that will deliver me from the horrible pressure in which I find myself. I do not know whether I flatter myself, but I count upon the honesty and equity of Congress.... Mr. Deane ... was ashamed and sorry ... at the conduct of his colleagues with me, of which the blame belongs entirely to Mr. Lee.... Among all these annoyances, the news from America overwhelms me with joy. Brave, brave people![25]

On June 17, 1778, a naval battle left France and England at war with each other and Benjamin Franklin exulting, "All Europe is for us.... Tyranny is so generally established in the rest of the world, that the prospect of an asylum in America for those who love liberty, gives general joy, and our cause is esteemed as the cause of all mankind. . . . Glorious is it for the Americans to be called by Providence to this post of honor."[26]

The onset of open warfare between France and England ended any need for the last shreds of secrecy that still enveloped Roderigue Hortalez et Cie. and the Beaumarchais monopoly. The French government could now feed arms directly to the Americans on its own ships and, whenever possible, eliminate costs of intermediaries. If it needed additional capacity to supplement its navy, it asked for competitive bids by private shipowners. Roderigue Hortalez et Cie. would now have to compete with other shippers for French government contracts. The company was now free to engage in normal commercial trade outside the military sphere, however, and no one in France was more skilled in trade than Beaumarchais. He had learned from the master, Pâris-Duverney.

He now limited his military cargoes to the highest-priced items, such as brass cannon, and he armed his ships with as many guns as they could carry without diminishing their capacity to haul profitably large loads. He decided his ships would be safer traveling in packs, with a powerful ship-of-the-line to protect them. He commissioned an agent to scour French navy yards for a vessel that could serve as both battleship and cargo ship—large enough to carry profitably large loads and enough cannons to protect its own cargo and the rest of the Beaumarchais fleet. His agent located a ship appropriately named the *Hippopotame*—a 900-ton behemoth with fifty cannon that was deteriorating in the harbor at Rochefort, 150 miles north of Bordeaux. Although the French Navy estimated its value at more than 190,000 livres ($760,000 today), by keeping the Beaumarchais and Hortalez names secret, Beaumarchais's agent was able to buy it for 70,000 ($280,000). Cost of repairs raised the total price to about 110,000 livres ($440,000), including appropriate emoluments to overseers at the Rochefort royal arsenal for replacing twenty-six of the oldest cannon with the French Navy's newest twelve-pounders. At the time, a Beaumarchais competitor paid 400,000 livres ($1.6 million) for a much smaller thirty-six-gun frigate.

The port at Rochefort, north of Bordeaux, where Beaumarchais found the
900-ton ship-of-the-line *Hippopotame*, which he renamed the *Fier Roderigue*.
With a 300-man crew and fifty powerful cannons, the ship protected the
playwright's fleet of fifty cargo ships from attack by pirates and privateers.

CABINET DES ESTAMPES, BIBLIOTHÈQUE NATIONALE, PARIS

With a 300-man crew and fifty powerful guns, the *Fier Roderigue*
(Proud Roderigue), as Beaumarchais renamed it, set sail for Chesapeake
Bay with a full cargo of military supplies on board—and an angry minister
of the navy on shore, raging at the director of the royal arsenal for letting
Beaumarchais talk him into giving away the navy's newest cannon. "It is
incredible that you made such a decision," the minister of the navy ranted.
"Make good this mistake if there is still time!"

It was far too late.

In the months that followed, Beaumarchais extricated himself from
debt by ordering his captains to refuse to offload military cargoes in America until substantial quantities of tobacco and other commodities were at
dockside in Francy's legal possession ready to be loaded. For every 100 livres
of military supplies unloaded, the Americans had to load 100 livres of produce to replace the offloaded arms before any more arms were sent ashore.

By then, Francy had discovered—and took advantage of—a curious flaw in the American political system that made each colony independent of the Confederation Congress. As a result, he set up a system of competitive bidding between Virginia, the two Carolinas, and Congress for Beaumarchais cargoes and greatly increased the prices—and profits—Hortalez extracted from each shipment. With the *Fier Roderigue* to protect them, other Beaumarchais ships widened the range of their trading operations to include merchants on the sugar islands. Privateers had increased the risks to cargo ships at sea and sent sugar prices soaring in Europe. Beaumarchais now reaped greater profits trading military supplies to sugar merchants on the islands and letting them try to resell arms to the difficult Americans.

As European demand increased for tobacco, sugar, and other New World commodities, Beaumarchais expanded his fleet to fifty ships and became one of the richest men in France. The protective guns of the powerful *Fier Roderigue* kept losses to a minimum, and to confuse the British, he constantly changed the names of his other ships—even the configurations of their decks. On one crossing, his "navy," as he called his fleet, captured a British ship—the *Marlborough*—and brought her into a French port. A cheering crowd looked on—and mocked the English crew by bursting into the early eighteenth-century French folk song "Malbrough"—a song with a purposely misspelled title (and mispronounced as "Malbrugg") that mocks the battlefield exploits of John Churchill, the Duke of Marlborough, who was obsessed with fighting the French. After Beaumarchais's merchant ship captured the English fighting ship, "Malbrough" became the most popular song in France. Even Marie Antoinette, Louis XVI, and their sycophants joined in the national fun. "Malbrough" remains a part of the central body of children's folk songs in France to this day.

It begins, "Marlborough goes off to war, ha, ha, ha, ha, ha, ha, ha, ha, ha, ha; Marlborough goes off to war, who knows when he'll return . . . ." The song feigns sorrow at its end, revealing that *Monsieur Malbrough est mort* (My Lord Marlborough is dead). Although *mironton* means "funny (laughable) person," it was also selected because of its mellifluous sound, which made for easy repetition in the refrain.

Words and music to the French folk song "Malbrough," composed
in 1709 but made widely popular after Beaumarchais's "navy" captured
the British ship *Marlborough* and sailed her into a French port—
to the cheers, mockery, and singing of the crowd at the pier.

In July 1779, the *Fier Roderigue* was escorting part of the Beaumarchais
"navy" to Granada when it encountered a French war fleet under Admiral
Comte d'Estaing—on his way to confront a British fleet. Seeking every
advantage he could get, he commandeered the *Fier Roderigue* and her sixty
guns. In the battle that followed, the British killed one-third of the *Fier
Roderigue* crew and its captain and left the ship so riddled by cannon shot
that it had to be towed into port in Granada. Although the French won
the battle, the unarmed cargo vessels in the Beaumarchais navy, left un-

protected by the *Fier Roderigue*, fell prey to British raiders, who sank or captured ten of the eleven ships and cost Beaumarchais more than 2 million livres.

"I have only time, Monsieur, to write you that *Le Fier Roderigue* held fast her post in the line of battle and contributed to the success of the King's arms," d'Estaing wrote to Beaumarchais, pledging that "your interests will not suffer.... Brave [Captain] M. de Montaut, unfortunately, was killed. I shall soon send the Minister a statement of the privileges and favors I ask, and I hope you will let me have the necessary information to help me solicit those *your Navy* so justly deserves."[27] Elated by his ship's heroic participation in a French naval victory over the British, the irrepressible Beaumarchais got a loan of 400,000 livres from the French government, acquired four more ships, and by the end of 1779 had restored his huge trading business to levels reached before he lost the *Fier Roderigue*.

By then, too, New York's John Jay had become president of Congress, and, succumbing to Deane's pleas and Francy's implied threats to end Hortalez et Cie. arms shipments, he wrote to Beaumarchais:

> The Congress of the United States, recognizing the great efforts which you have made in their favor, presents you its thanks, and the assurance of its esteem.
>
> It laments the disappointments which you have suffered.... Disastrous circumstances have prevented the execution of its desires; but it will take the promptest measures to acquit itself of the debt which it has contracted towards you. The generous sentiments ... which alone could dictate a conduct such as yours, are the eulogy of your actions and the ornament of your character. While, by your rare talents, you have rendered yourself useful to your prince, you have gained the esteem of this young Republic and merited the applause of the New World.[28]

"I felt my courage revived," Beaumarchais responded after reading Jay's letter. "My pains, my work, and my advances were immense.... Working day and night ... I exhausted myself with fatigue.... I thought that a great people would soon offer a sweet and free retreat to all the persecuted of Europe; that my fatherland would be revenged for the humiliation to which it

President of Congress John Jay was the first American
leader to publicly acknowledge America's debt to
Beaumarchais for supplying the Continental Army
with arms, ammunition, and other essential supplies.

LIBRARY OF CONGRESS

had been subjected by the treaty of 1763 . . . that the sea would become open
to all commercial nations . . . that a new system of politics would open in
Europe."[29]

In February 1778, eighty-four-year-old Voltaire arrived in Paris and sent
word to Beaumarchais that he needed to see him. Although the two had
had an occasional but superficial correspondence, the playwright was both
puzzled and pleased by the legendary philosopher's invitation, hoping it
might relate to Voltaire's position as president of the Académie Française,

the association of so-called French "immortals." Voltaire's visit, however, had nothing to do with the Académie. Apparently sensing his impending death, Voltaire sought to arrange publication of his complete works and insisted, "All my hopes are centered on Beaumarchais."[30] Although almost all his hundreds of formal works—histories, plays, novels, essays, poems—had been published in one form or another here and there, so many governments had banned them that they had yet to be collected and published in a set of complete works in one language, and, indeed, his volumes of letters—especially the revealing correspondence with Frederick the Great—had yet to be published in any language. Although Beaumarchais agreed in principle to publish Voltaire's works, Voltaire died late that spring before the two could arrange a formal method of working together.

Although speculators flocked like vultures with offers to buy Voltaire manuscripts from his heirs, the sheer volume of his works made it unlikely that their publication could generate any profits. And even if a publisher took the risk of publishing them, half the works had been banned in France, thus making their publication in Voltaire's native land all but pointless. French publisher Charles Panckoucke ignored such risks and won the bidding war for Voltaire's manuscripts, but when he realized the volume of material he would have to publish, he concluded that their publication would ruin him financially and offered them to Beaumarchais. Then Catherine the Great of Russia briefly stepped into the picture. Eager to offset the czarist reputation for mindless brutality and present herself as an enlightened monarch, she offered to subsidize their publication. Beaumarchais was incensed and rushed to Versailles to convince Prime Minister Comte Frédéric de Maurepas that Voltaire and his works were an integral part of French heritage. Having flirted on the sly with Voltairian Freemasonry and having read many of Voltaire's works, Maurepas agreed and offered Beaumarchais some discretionary royal funding to publish the works in French, on the condition that he print them outside France.

Now a publisher for the first time in his life, Beaumarchais plunged into his new profession with his customary zeal, confident as always that another fortune awaited him. He paid Panckoucke 160,000 francs for all

Bust of Voltaire by contemporary French
sculptor Jean Antoine Houdon. In February
1778, the eighty-four-year-old Voltaire
asked Beaumarchais to arrange publication
of his complete works.

RÉUNION DES MUSÉES NATIONAUX

of Voltaire's unpublished manuscripts and letters and sent 150,000 livres
to England to buy all of the type, ink, and paper from the estate of John
Baskerville, who had been the world's master producer of quality printing materials before his death in 1775. He arranged with the Margrave of
Baden to lease an unused fort in Kehl, just across the French border in Germany, as his printing plant. After contracting to buy the output of three
paper mills, he set to work studying and learning every aspect of printing
and publishing before hiring a team of workers to begin publishing. Enthralled by Voltaire's writing and wide range of knowledge, Beaumarchais
did much of the editing and transcribing himself, with help from a team of

skilled proofreaders. By the end of 1780, Beaumarchais was ready to issue a prospectus that he sent to potential subscribers across the face of Europe, England, and America. Although he could not advertise in France, he flooded the press of other European countries with so many advertisements and so much publicity that word of his offering reached every potential subscriber in his native land.

When Maurepas died in 1781, the French Catholic Church began a relentless campaign against Beaumarchais, publishing a widely circulated "Denunciation to the Parliament of the Subscription for the Works of Voltaire." Exhilarated by the free publicity the church attacks were generating, Beaumarchais expanded his publishing efforts to include the works of the equally controversial Jean-Jacques Rousseau. By 1783, he completed printing and binding the first Voltaire books. Expecting buyers across the world to snap up copies of the master's works, Beaumarchais published 15,000 complete sets of Voltaire's works in two editions—one deluxe edition of seventy volumes and a less costly edition of ninety-two volumes. He barely managed to sell 2,000 copies. He closed his publishing plant and shipped the tens of thousands of remaining unbound sheets to his home in Paris, where they filled every unused space in his attic, his basement, and under the beds and furnishings of every room.

9

Bright People Are So Stupid

ALTHOUGH LESSER nobles at Versailles still scorned him, Beaumarchais had, in fact, become all but indispensable to the comte de Vergennes and other ministers. Ignoring—and all but mocking—the sneers, stares, and unvented fury of envious sinecures, sieur de Beaumarchais strutted into the palace, along its endless corridors and into private apartments and offices, all but singing as he went, carrying himself like the heir of an old and noble family visiting his castle in the country.

His unorthodox schemes had revitalized French government policies. Bound by conventional thinking and tied to tradition, the high lords of government invariably opposed his schemes when they first heard them, but almost always succumbed to his convincing arguments and, if they succeeded, embraced them as their own. And his schemes almost always succeeded—often in spectacular fashion. Indeed, he had proved himself a policy genius. He had provided the Americans with secret French military aid that had ensured a critical American military victory at Saratoga, revived American morale, and turned the course of the war against the British. By maintaining tight secrecy over the source of the military aid, he had allowed France to stay out of the war long enough for her to rebuild her military to near parity with England. By supporting the Americans with French arms, Beaumarchais had also erased residual American hatred for France from the French and Indian War, and by convincing the French government to be first in recognizing American independence, he had ensured France a major share in the lucrative American trade that had hitherto been England's exclusive preserve.

With these policy triumphs to Beaumarchais's credit, Vergennes and other ministers at Versailles—as well as the king himself—consulted Beaumarchais on a wide range of economic, military, and political policies. "If you will come here, sir, tomorrow, Thursday evening," the comte de Vergennes asked Beaumarchais, "we can have a long interview of the work we commenced last week." With that, Beaumarchais went to Versailles to discuss a problem of international trade that "I have explained in an elementary form, so that when Monsieur le Ministre shows it to the king, his inexperience in such complicated affairs may not prevent him from understanding all its aspects."[1]

In the days that followed, Finance Minister Jacques Necker consulted Beaumarchais on the American tobacco trade and methods of supplying French troops sent to America. Another minister consulted him on financing projected government loans, while the minister of the navy called on him to discuss the financing of ship construction. And Foreign Minister Vergennes—an avid bibliophile—asked him if he could not come up with a scheme to halt the epidemic of theft that was fast emptying the archives of the Bibliothèque du Roi of the most precious, irreplaceable parchment deeds, some dating back centuries. Over the next five years, Beaumarchais invested 100,000 livres (the monetary units "pounds," not "books"), commissioning agents to locate and secretly buy back the documents for the government—and, by threatening to identify those petty noblemen who had "borrowed" the documents, he embarrassed and frightened them into ending their practice of removing materials from the library.

With the onset of war between France and England, Vergennes and the other ministers had little choice but to put military policy in the hands of the military men who would have to direct the war. They continued consulting Beaumarchais on other matters, however, including economic policy—until his ideas crossed an unspecified politico-philosophical line that was too radical for their thinking. After war costs had all but emptied government coffers, he proposed a return to *le plan de Sully*—an economic

The enormous Bibliothèque du Roi, or King's Library, suffered an epidemic of theft until the government commissioned Beaumarchais to recover lost and stolen manuscripts and establish a system of controls that ended the thievery.

RÉUNION DES MUSÉES NATIONAUX

plan the duc de Sully had proposed as director of Protestant king Henry IV's Council of Finance in 1596. Sully infuriated government officials by calling for all officeholders to pay an annual tax to retain their positions—a tax equal to one-sixteenth of the amount they had paid to buy their offices. Beaumarchais's proposal to revive *le plan de Sully* shocked Vergennes and other ministers no less than its proposal by Sully himself had shocked the French aristocracy two centuries earlier. As Sully had done, Beaumarchais outraged the ministry still further by urging restoration of civil liberties to Protestants, which would allow them to buy sinecures and further add to revenues flowing into the national treasury.

Suddenly, the ministers at Versailles concluded that Beaumarchais's motives for supporting American rebels were less attuned to the interests of the French government than the interests of radical social reform espoused by Voltaire, Rousseau, and other philosophes. So instead of replying to his economic proposals, they stopped inviting him to the palace for advice. The ministers no longer needed Beaumarchais, nor did they want to hear what he had to say.

Silas Deane returned to France in June 1780 to pore through receipts and orders placed with Beaumarchais during his years in Paris and to disprove insinuations that he had embezzled French government funds designated for United States military aid. He found that Congress owed Beaumarchais 3.6 million livres. Although Beaumarchais demanded immediate payment, Congress rejected the Deane figures and ignored the Beaumarchais demands.

Although the failure of Congress to repay him distressed Beaumarchais, he refused to "disgrace the greatest act of my life . . . with a vile lawsuit."[2] Deane, however, was appalled, and bitterly denounced members of Congress—even calling the American Revolution an error and advocating reunion with Britain. Accused of treason for his remarks, he remained in exile for most of the remainder of his life—first in Flanders, then in London.[3]

In 1780, French General Jean-Baptiste Donatien de Vimeur comte de Rochambeau sailed to the United States with an army of 5,500 troops. The following year they joined with Washington's Continental Army and a French fleet under Admiral de Grasse to surround a British army under General Lord Cornwallis at Yorktown, Virginia, and force Cornwallis to surrender. It was the last battle of the American Revolution. Two years later, the British recognized American independence, and the war between France and England came to an end—along with Roderigue Hortalez et Cie. In his naive belief that Americans were creating a utopian society, Beaumarchais had shipped more than $210 million (today's dollars) worth of arms, ammunition, and military supplies to the United States *on credit*—including *more than 80 percent* of the Continental Army's entire supply of gunpowder for the war. To his astonishment and deep disappointment, Congress refused to pay a penny of what it owed him.

"A people become sovereign and powerful may be permitted, perhaps, to consider gratitude as a virtue of individuals which is beneath politics," Beaumarchais complained to the president of Congress,

> but nothing can dispense a state from being just, and especially from paying its debts. I dare hope, *Monsieur*, that touched by the importance of the affair and by the force of my reasons, you will be good enough to honor me with . . . the decision of the honorable Congress either to arrange promptly to liquefy my accounts, or else choose arbiters . . . to decide the points debated . . . or else write me candidly that the sovereign states of America, forgetting my past services, refuse me all justice.[4]

Congress responded by naming Arthur Lee, of all people, to review the Beaumarchais accounts, and he concluded that Congress owed Beaumarchais nothing. Indeed, he charged Beaumarchais with owing Congress 1.8 million livres—that is, most of the moneys the French and Spanish kings had given him to start Hortalez et Cie.

With both his arms-trade venture and his Voltaire project at an end, Beaumarchais found himself with time to spare for the first time since the outbreak of the American Revolution, and he returned to his old love—writing. He wrote poetry, of course, and became a prolific composer of popular songs. In addition, as he explained, "I began again to amuse myself with frivolous theatrical plays." In doing so, he revisited his old friend Figaro. Like the nearly fifty-year-old Beaumarchais himself, Figaro had aged somewhat since his exploits as *Le Barbier de Séville*, but his lot had improved. No longer a common barber, he was now steward of the castle of the comte d'Almaviva, whose eyes had been wandering of late, from the face and physique of his aging wife Rosine to his wife's beautiful young maid Suzanne, to whom Figaro was affianced.

P. A. CARON DE BEAUMARCHAIS.

Beaumarchais in his later years, after reaching
the pinnacle of success in the worlds of finance,
international trade, and theater.

As the curtain rises on Figaro's second life onstage, the count has given
Figaro and Suzanne a wedding gift—a large bed, which he has placed in
a suite they are to inhabit in the main part of the castle, between the bed-
rooms of the count and countess. Still set in Spain to shield Beaumarchais
from persecution for mocking French aristocracy, the play opens with Suzanne in a fury over the proposed accommodations.

"If Madame needs help at night," the optimistic Figaro tries to calm
Suzanne, "she has only to ring—and zing!—you'll be in her room in two
seconds. And if Monseigneur needs something at night, he'll ring—and
zing!—I'll be there in three seconds."

"That's wonderful!" Suzanne exclaims. "But when he rings in the morn-

In a scene that satirizes Shakespeare's *Romeo and Juliet*, the comte d'Almaviva, disguised as "Lindor," serenades Rosine beneath her window in act I of Beaumarchais's *Barbier de Séville*.

ing and sends you out on an errand—then zing!—in two seconds he'll be at my door and—zing!—in three he'll be in my . . ."

"What are you saying?"

"I'm saying that the comte d'Almaviva has no intention of sleeping with his own wife. He intends sleeping with yours!"

"So," Figaro now understands, "while I work for his family, he will work to increase mine. What sweet reciprocity! That is too much by half. Now, Figaro, concentrate."[5]

To prepare to exercise his *droit du seigneur*—the questionable right of a nobleman to sleep with a vassal's bride on her wedding night—the count arranges a tryst with Suzanne in the castle garden on the eve of her wedding with Figaro. Suzanne confides in the countess, however, and the two switch clothes, with the countess taking Suzanne's place in the garden. In the dark, the count slips beside the woman he believes to be Suzanne and makes passionate overtures, accompanied by warm and satisfying caresses and kisses—only to have Figaro and the other characters pour into the garden with lanterns to expose the truth. Shamed and humbled, the count returns to his wife's forgiving arms and lets Figaro and Suzanne marry without fear of further harassment, as the curtain falls to general rejoicing onstage—and off. For in outwitting his master—metaphorically overthrowing him—Figaro staged a revolution whose drumbeat resonated far beyond the confines of the French theater—so clearly and menacingly that the king banned its performance.

"It is detestable!" he protested. "It will never be played. . . . The man mocks everything that ought to be respected in government."[6] When Beaumarchais learned of the king's response, Figaro got the best of him and he confided flippantly to his friends, "The king does not want *Le Mariage de Figaro* to be played. Therefore, it shall be played."[7]

The plot itself did not disturb the king as much as Figaro's flippant responses. "Because you are a great lord," Figaro rails at the count, "you think you are a genius. Nobility, wealth, rank, position—it all makes you so proud. And what did you do to earn so many rewards? You took the time to be born—nothing else. Apart from that, you're quite an ordinary man! while I, by God, lost in the faceless crowd, had to apply more knowl-

Figaro literally and figuratively shaves the lecherous Dr.
Bartolo, as the comte d'Almaviva woos Bartolo's ward, the
beautiful Rosine, in Beaumarchais's *Barbier de Séville*.

edge and skills merely to survive than it took to govern the entire Spanish
Empire for the last one hundred years; and you want to duel with me?"[8]

The speech was more than insolent. It bordered on revolution and, indeed, would echo through the streets of Paris for decades thereafter.

Although insolence toward the nobility had cost Beaumarchais his freedom five years earlier, Figaro's words now knew no bounds: "The courts," he cries out at one point, "please the powerful and punish the poor."

"I'm told," Figaro complains later, "that Madrid has established a system of liberty that includes freedom to write what I want. As long as I do not write anything about the government, religion, politics, morality, the aristocracy, the economy, the opera, theater, or anyone's beliefs, I am free to write and publish anything—under the supervision of two or three censors. To profit from such sweet liberties, I shall start a new periodical that will insult no one. I shall call it *The Useless Journal!*"[9]

In comparison to the cheeky remarks in *The Barber of Seville*, the dialogue in *The Marriage of Figaro* was heretical, treasonous. Figaro is merely flippant when he remarks in *Le Barbier* that "the greatest benefit a nobleman can bestow upon me is to leave me alone and do me no harm."[10] In *Le Mariage de Figaro*, Figaro is a revolutionary, demanding top-to-bottom social reform, justice for all, merit rewarded, injustice punished, individual liberties protected. "*Part le sort de la naissance . . . ,*" he sings,

> By the accident of birth
> One is born shepherd, another born king.
> Chance alone has set them apart,
> But their spirits carry no titles or names,
> And death treats them both exactly the same.
> Only Voltaire is immortal;
> Only Voltaire is immortal.[11]

The reference to Voltaire at the end of the play proved particularly galling. Twice imprisoned in the Bastille, Voltaire had spent several decades in exile because of his relentless attacks on royal tyranny, religion, and intolerance.

In contrast to the response of the deeply religious king, his fun-loving queen, Marie Antoinette, found *The Marriage of Figaro* hilarious, as did her playboy brother-in-law and sometimes lover the comte d'Artois, youngest of the king's two younger brothers and the future Charles X. The somber middle brother—the future Louis XVIII—considered the play treasonous, but public pressures—inside and outside the palace—made the

king relent, and orders came from Versailles for the first performance of
Le Mariage de Figaro to be staged at the royal theater. An overflow crowd
of elegantly dressed lords and ladies filled every seat and fell silent as what
appeared to be a character from the play appeared from behind the curtain
center stage. He was, however, a king's messenger: "The king has forbidden
the performance!"

"I really do not know which court intriguers solicited and obtained the
prohibition of the king against acting the piece," said the astonished playwright. "I can only put the script back in my briefcase and wait patiently
until the next opportunity calls on me to bring it out."[12]

After the king's rebellious younger brother the comte d'Artois staged
a private performance of the play at a friend's château, every nobleman of
rank invited Beaumarchais to his château to read excerpts from *Le Mariage*. The longer the king maintained his ban on public performances, the
greater the demand of the nobility for Beaumarchais to read it to them
privately.

Many were French officers who had fought to help Americans win independence from England, thus witnessing and experiencing individual
liberty—and its benefits—for the first time. As the English parliamentarian Edmund Burke put it, "They imbibed a love of freedom nearly incom-
patible with royalty. It seemed a grand stroke . . . [to] humble the pride of a
great and haughty [monarch]."[13]

Figaro invariably evoked gales of laughter from aristocrats in the audience who were convinced he was mocking their rivals, when in fact he was
mocking them. As demand built for an end to the ban, Louis XVI yielded
on condition that censors examine the entire script. After the first censor had examined the play and Beaumarchais had made the appropriate
changes, the king demanded that a second censor examine the play, then
a third, a fourth and even a fifth. The process was on its way to becoming
an endless and impenetrable bureaucratic tangle when Beaumarchais himself met with the censors and lured them into his camp. The fourth censor made no changes, and the fifth actually lauded the play. As in Figaro's
verbal swordplay with the comte d'Almaviva, Beaumarchais had finally

exhausted both the censors and the king—outmaneuvering the latter at every encounter. As d'Almaviva had put it—and as the king himself might well have said—"That good-for-nothing is embarrassing me. Whenever he argues he gets the best of me, pressing in, squeezing and finally cornering me, wrapping me up and tying me in knots."[14]

In March 1784, the king gave his official permission to perform *Le Mariage de Figaro*, but his earlier prohibitions turned what might have been simply another opening of another play into the most extraordinary—indeed, legendary—presentation in French theater history, staged by the most celebrated actors and actresses in France. According to witnesses at the scene, "Even in early morning, all Paris rushed to the Théâtre Français; ladies of the highest rank dined in the actresses' dressing areas to ensure their gaining admission." As the time for the opening curtain drew near, the crowds reached uncontrollable proportions, "doors broke down, iron railings gave way."

It was a historic moment in the French theater.

"When the curtain rose, the finest combination of talent which the Théâtre-Français had ever assembled . . . brought out to best advantage a comedy flashing with *esprit*, shocking some, enchanting others, stirring, inflaming, and electrifying."[15] Citing the denouement, in which a valet and chambermaid outwit their master and strip him of his *droit du seigneur*, the critic declared, "Right here lies the Revolution."[16]

For Beaumarchais, the comte d'Almaviva symbolized the old regime; Figaro, a new society, where all men were entitled to equal dignity, regardless of the social rank in which the accident of birth had placed them. "In this piece," Gudin wrote, "the parterre applauded . . . the courageous man who dared to combat by ridicule the libertinage of the great lords, the ignorance of magistrates, and venality of officers and the unbecoming pleas of lawyers. . . . More than anyone else, Beaumarchais had first-hand knowledge of what he described, for he had been calumniated so outrageously by great lords, and injured by the insolent pleadings of lawyers and *blamé* by bad judges. . . . no author has better understood the human heart or understood the manners of his time."[17]

Le Mariage played an unprecedented sixty-eight consecutive times to sellout crowds, earning nearly 650,000 livres ($2.6 million today), of which nearly 300,000 ($1.2 million) went to the actors and about 42,000 ($168,000) to Beaumarchais—a record in the French theater that would stand up for a century. It met with equal success in theaters across Europe, with the twenty-eight-year-old Wolfgang Amadeus Mozart enthralled by the juxtaposition of drama and comedy—and indeed by the ease with which Beaumarchais had himself woven singing into the dialogue. A year earlier, the composer had met the thirty-four-year-old Venetian librettist Lorenzo da Ponte, and at Mozart's behest, he set to work converting *Le Mariage de Figaro* into an opera. With Mozart insisting that they "present faithfully and in full colors the diverse passions that are aroused," the two men created what they called "a new type of spectacle"—the world's first *commedia per musica*, or musical comedy. For the first time in opera history, music and text were fully integrated rather than standing apart, with the music either a drab ornament for the *recitative* or a separate stand-alone sonata-like interlude without words. Every note, every beat, every word in Mozart's music for *Le Nozze di Figaro* reflected the emotional shades of every breath, syllable, and gesture of the characters.

Written and composed at the end of 1785 and the beginning of 1786, *Le Nozze di Figaro*—with its Italian title and libretto—opened with great fanfare in Vienna on May 1, 1786—and immediately flopped. Although Prague audiences and critics subsequently hailed it as a masterpiece, Italy's operagoers booed it, and Parisians, who embraced the Beaumarchais play with thunderous applause and cheers, sniffed in contempt at the young foreigner Mozart for having dared to stage a musical interpretation of so perfect a French stage production that already had its own music—and to do so in Italian, no less!

The failure of the opera version of *Le Mariage* had little effect on the popularity of spoken presentations. But even as he rode the tide of his greatest literary and stage success, Beaumarchais could not escape the nasty carping of those who so resented his escape from his original social class to fame and fortune. After one critic attacked *Le Mariage* as "a villainous rhapsody" written solely to enrich its author, Beaumarchais immediately proposed using his earnings to found and maintain the Institut de Bienfaisance Maternelle in Lyon to care for impoverished nursing mothers. He turned over all his earnings from *Le Mariage* to the institute in perpetuity, and within six years, the directors of the institute wrote him that his continuing generosity had saved "more than two hundred children who owe their lives to you.... From this feeble stream of money will flow rivers of milk and crowds of vigorous infants."[18] One newspaper published a cartoon with Figaro helping mothers, another with him opening the doors of a debtor's prison.

As he reached the pinnacle of his literary career, however, Beaumarchais's unfortunate inability to ignore criticism brought him face to face with more misfortune. In replying angrily to one newspaper critic, he began his letter, "After having fought lions and tigers to get my comedy onto the stage ..."[19]

The normally benevolent Louis XVI interpreted the reference to "lions and tigers" as meaning the king and the queen, and in an uncharacteristic fit of pique, he ordered the clever playwright's immediate arrest and summary imprisonment—not, however, in a conventional prison like the Bastille. Deciding to outwit the wit, Louis ordered Beaumarchais dragged from his home to the St. Lazare prison for juvenile offenders, where guards threw the fifty-three-year-old playwright across a punishment bench, stripped his bottom bare, and whipped his buttocks before a throng of howling adolescent miscreants.

The press and public also responded with laughter at first—until they learned that the reason for the playwright's humiliating imprisonment had been his comparing the king to a tiger. "Everyone felt in danger," said an aide to the comte de Provence, the king's younger brother, "not only as regarded his liberty, but also as regarded his personal dignity." After four days, mobs demonstrated near the theater and in front of the St. Lazare prison, and the aide warned the comte that "people are inquiring whether anyone can be sure of sleeping tonight in his own bed."[20] On the fifth day, Beaumarchais's imprisonment in a juvenile jail began to embarrass the king almost as much as it had embarrassed the playwright. The king relented and ordered Beaumarchais released, but to the king's astonishment, Beaumarchais refused to leave the prison, issuing instead a memorial demanding to know the specific crime for which he had been arrested and insisting on a full trial. The leaflet denied any connection between the phrase "lions and tigers" and the nation's monarchs. "I took two extremes in the scale of comparison," he explained. "I might have said, 'After having fought with giants.'" He called it "madness" for "any being in France . . . to wish to offend the king," and he thoroughly denied having given "any signs of such madness."[21]

King Louis apparently recognized his own madness and sent aides with an unprecedented, albeit unwritten, apology to Beaumarchais. Eager not to turn the playwright into a martyr, he all but begged Beaumarchais to leave prison, called the detention "shameful," and promised generous compensation. Beaumarchais was wise enough not to trifle any further with the king and left prison.

All the king's ministers attended *Le Mariage* on the evening of Beaumarchais's release from prison, even standing to cheer the performances —and the playwright—at the end of each act and applauding in exaggerated fashion after Figaro tweaked their sensitivities by declaring, "Not being able to degrade intellect, they avenge themselves by persecuting it." The king further rewarded Beaumarchais by sponsoring a performance of *The Barber of Seville* in the theater of the Trianon at Versailles, at which Beaumarchais was guest of honor—with the queen taking the part of Rosine and her brother-in-law the comte d'Artois playing Figaro. Nor was that enough to ease the king's conscience. The king sought to wipe the Beaumarchais slate clean by fully covering all the playwright's losses from the destruction of his fleet and damages to the *Fier Roderigue* when Admiral Comte d'Estaing forced that vessel into battle against the English in the Caribbean. Although the government had offered Beaumarchais a compromise settlement of 1.5 million livres, the king ordered the government to pay the entire Beaumarchais claim of 2.5 million livres. Beaumarchais asked for more, however, reminding the king that he had spent more than 100,000 livres over the previous five years, recovering stolen parchment deeds for the Bibliotheque du Roi at the behest of Vergennes and Maurepas. The king immediately ordered his treasury to reimburse the playwright.

Louis's arbitrary, mean-spirited order to arrest and humiliate Beaumarchais destroyed the public perception of Louis XVI as a wise and benevolent monarch. In a moment of childish outrage he had, for the first time, proved himself a Bourbon—as capable and willing to use his autocratic powers on a whim as his ancestral predecessors. With as little concern as a boy swatting a mosquito, he had all but crushed a man of towering genius in the arts and sciences, the head of one of the nation's richest and most important enterprises, and a man to whom the French Crown had entrusted some of the most important missions in its history. Although the oldest members of the court retained their obsequious reverence for the king, the younger nobility—and the growing French bourgeoisie of well-educated lawyers, doctors, engineers, and other professionals—questioned the legitimacy of his continued powers. Many of them were veterans of the American Revolution and converts to the egalitarian principles that underlay that conflict. They had studied John Locke, Voltaire, Rousseau, and other Age of Enlightenment philosophes, and they knew that the injustices that drew laughter onstage in *Le Mariage de Figaro* were no laughing matter offstage and, indeed, were a danger to them all.

As for Beaumarchais, the humiliating injustice he suffered at St. Lazare proved one injustice too many. Despite the king's abject apologies and compensations, Beaumarchais emerged from St. Lazare a different man—as bitter and angry as ever, but without the defiant laughter. He seemed unable any longer "to laugh at . . . continual misfortune," as Figaro had done in *Le Barbier*, "for fear that I may be obliged to weep." For the first time in his life, Beaumarchais wept at his continual misfortune and, worse, he faced an emotion he had never before encountered: fear. Beaumarchais was afraid.

Without any business affairs to manage or government policies to plan, Beaumarchais pursued his favorite avocation, and wrote the next chapter in the adventures of his alter ego Figaro. In his sequel to *Le Barbier* and *Le Mariage de Figaro*, however, Figaro—like Beaumarchais—had aged. *La Mère coupable* (The Guilty Mother), the third play in the Figaro trilogy, finds the hero both wiser and older—scarred by misfortune and rather sad, without the sparkling wit that had made him so original. Instead of the playful pest and symbol of revolt, Figaro is now a virtual member of the court and trusted counselor to the comte d'Almaviva. The plot revolves around the comte, who has sired an illegitimate daughter, whom he adores—much as Beaumarchais adored his own illegitimate daughter Eugénie. The maudlin complications onstage between the comte, his wife Rosine, and the other characters from *Le Barbier* and *Le Mariage* proved trite, dull, and meaningless—and without the biting humor of Figaro's previous appearances. After fifteen badly attended—and badly acted—performances, *La Mère* closed. Touched nonetheless by the distress he had written into the plot, Beaumarchais decided that, after twelve years together, it was time to marry Marie-Thérèse and "legitimize" their beloved daughter Eugénie.

Beaumarchais's martyrdom raised him to mythic status in France. He could go nowhere without attracting a crowd of admirers. In the months that followed his imprisonment, only his study—and his writing—provided peaceful retreats, and he decided to fulfill a long-standing ambition by composing an opera. After completing the dialogue and song lyrics, he sent his work to his favorite operatic composer, Christoph Willibald Gluck,[22] then in residence at Versailles under the patronage of Queen Marie Antoinette. Gluck rejected the play but referred Beaumarchais to one of his protégés, the Italian composer Antonio Salieri.[23] Beaumarchais sent the play to Salieri, with instructions to "write me music that will be subservient and not dominant, with all its effects made subordinate to my dialogue and drama."[24] Based on a Persian fable of the supernatural, *Tarare* was a melodramatic variation of the Figaro theme: Two warring genii—the genius of Fire and the genius of Nature—create the opera's two primary characters: one of them a prince, destined by birth to become the powerful, despotic king of all Asia; the other, a common soldier named Tarare, who uses his intelligence, courage, and virtue to triumph over evil. He overthrows the king, is himself crowned king, and wins the beautiful leading lady away from the old corrupt monarch.

Thousands lined the avenues leading to the opera in anticipation of opening night. Four hundred troops rushed to the scene and put up barriers to keep the crowd orderly. "Never before did any of our theaters see such a crowd as that which besieged all the avenues of the opera the day of the first presentation of *Tarare*," wrote a journalist in Grimm's *Correspondence*, in June 1787. "Barriers . . . scarcely sufficed to keep it in restraint."[25]

Still called Salieri's, if not Beaumarchais's, "masterpiece," it slipped into the dustbin of operatic archives during the nineteenth century, along with most of the composer's other works,[26] because of music that critics described as "obvious and commonplace." *Tarare* nonetheless contained every theatrical artifice Beaumarchais could devise to please the public— drama, songs, dance, ballet, magnificent scenery, fantasy, philosophy, and even an occasional laugh for comic relief. And, of course, the Figaroan outcry against aristocratic privilege.

Mortel! the cast sings out "majestically," according to Beaumarchais's stage instructions for the climactic closing scene,

> Mortel! qui que tu sois, prince, brahme, ou soldat,
> Homme, ta grandeur sur la terre
> N'appartient point à ton état,
> Elle est toute à ton caractère.[27]

> Mortal man, be you prince, brahmin, or soldier,
> Thy greatness on earth
> Stems not from thy birth
> But from thy character.

It was pure Figaro. Pure Beaumarchais.

Built in 1370 under King Charles V, the Bastille was originally
a fortress guarding the Saint-Antoine gate of eastern Paris.
As Paris expanded in the sixteenth century, modern arms
rendered it obsolete, and Cardinal Richelieu converted it into
a prison, whose fearsome shadow darkened the forbidding
streets of the working-class neighborhood.

Although the public embraced the work, one contemporary critic dissented, calling the music "inferior" and the recitative "almost always insipid and commonplace."[28]

Never content to limit himself to one project at a time, Beaumarchais also sought to revive his spirits by investing his every fantasy into the design of a new home—a retreat for his retirement—where he and his family could live securely in a castlelike dwelling amid gardens unmatched in their beauty even in *Tarare*'s mythological Persia. Always the clever merchant searching for undervalued assets, the playwright bought an acre of vacant land at the gates of the Saint-Antoine working-class slums in eastern Paris, in the very shadow of the forbidding medieval prison—*La Bastille*.

Dissatisfied with what he considered the pedestrian designs of professional architects, Beaumarchais designed and built a structure of his own creation at a cost of 1.7 million francs that surpassed almost every mansion in Paris in elegance and luxury, with the possible exception of the Palais des Tuileries at the Louvre. Napoleon later called it "une folie"—sheer madness. But what madness! A madness that incorporated every element of theatrical magic at Beaumarchais's command. Using tricks of trompe l'oeil perspective, Beaumarchais designed terraced gardens and a winding stream with rowboats that passed beneath a Chinese bridge and seemed to stretch the one-acre rectangle to the horizon, past beds of exotic flowers and shrubs, thick stands of trees, and a rock tunnel that disguised a functioning icehouse. Although fantasy gardens had become the rage of Paris nobility, the Beaumarchais fantasies went beyond any ever before seen. He incorporated a stable for ten horses into an artificial hillside, and on the artificial hilltop above it stood a Greek temple to Bacchus with a surrounding colonnade, topped by a classical dome and a frieze that read, "To Voltaire: He showed the world the errors of its ways." A central carriageway bisected the length of the property, ending in a roundabout at the main entrance of a four-story, castlelike house, where, as in a child's fairy tale, Beaumarchais planned to retire and live happily ever after.

The elaborate garden of the Beaumarchais mansion reflected a growing mania
among eighteenth-century French noblemen for fantasy gardens. A Greek
temple to Bacchus can be seen at upper left; at center is the entrance
to a rock tunnel containing a functioning icehouse.

The front door opened into an enormous, circular salon on the ground
floor, capped by a cupola thirty feet above. Great mahogany panels al-
ternated with grandiose paintings by Joseph Vernet around the central
atrium.[29] Off the main court lay smaller salons, a billiard room with seats
for spectators, and the great man's office. Below ground lay vast kitchens
and wine cellars, while grand staircases led to the upper floors and the
sumptuous apartments he designed for family members and guests. The
house and gardens were so elaborate that, when times permitted, they
would become an all but obligatory destination for visitors to Paris and,
indeed, for many Parisians. Always the showman, Beaumarchais printed
admission tickets, for which he charged nothing and on which he would
often inscribe a few words of original poetry.

Construction on the house began in 1787—just as the French economy began to collapse. The cost of the war with England and the failure of the United States to repay its wartime debts had left the government bankrupt, and in September 1788 the king turned for help to the Estates General, an assembly of noblemen, clergymen, and privileged commoners—professionals, bankers, and bourgeois business and property owners.

In early 1789, after months of useless debates by the Estates General, Versailles announced it would print paper money to pay the Crown's internal debts. The result was economic disaster. Vendors in every industry refused the paper money; textile producers shut their doors and laid off more than 200,000 workers across France—80,000 in Paris alone. The national monopoly of farmers doubled wholesale prices; retail food prices soared. Making matters worse, two successive years of drought and a freak hailstorm in the Paris region decimated crops and produced food shortages that sent prices 60 percent higher. Food riots erupted across France—in the Dauphiné, Provence, Languedoc, Normandy, and Brittany. Mobs of peasants and impoverished workers raided granaries, wheat convoys, and bakeries in every town and city. Mobs swarmed through streets; thieves broke into homes across Paris—including the home of American minister plenipotentiary Thomas Jefferson—to steal anything made of gold or silver to trade for food.

"Paris is in danger of hourly insurrection for the want of bread," Jefferson wrote in haste to Secretary for Foreign Affairs John Jay. "The patience of . . . people . . . is worn thread-bare . . . civil war is much talked about."[30]

Pamphleteers covered Paris walls with leaflets accusing Versailles and the aristocracy of starving the nation. As anarchy spread across Paris, 30,000 troops massed in and around Versailles to protect the king. The rest of the regular army—200,000 men—went on alert in Metz, 180 miles to the east, awaiting the king's order to march into Paris.

Beaumarchais sympathized deeply with the demonstrators, comparing them to the American revolutionaries of the previous decade. As economic distress spread, however, Beaumarchais's unbridled success and his unabashed, conspicuous display of wealth began to alienate those with whom he sympathized. His opulent new house, rising at the edge of the city's poorest neighborhood—in the shadow of the city's cruelest and most despised prison—seemed an "insolent provocation." To counter street-corner provocateurs, he opened the grounds to visitors, letting them come and go as they pleased, and passed out money for food to all the families within a reasonable radius of his house. When an anonymously published pamphlet accused him of having profited from the plight of the American revolutionaries, he fired back indignantly with a letter to the Commune of Paris:

> Since I have been attacked . . . I am going to describe the labor which a
> single man was able to accomplish in that great work. Frenchmen: you who
> pride yourselves to have drawn the desire and ardor of your liberty from
> the example of the Americans, learn that that nation owes me very largely
> her own liberty. . . . I sent at my risks and perils, whatever could be had
> of the best in France, in munitions, arms, clothing, etc., to the insurgents
> who needed everything on credit, at the cost price . . . and that after twelve
> years, I am still not paid. . . . The third of my fortune is in the hands of my
> debtors, and since I have aided the poor . . . four hundred letters at least are
> on my desk from unfortunates, raising their hands to me.[31]

On Sunday, July 12, 1789, thousands of Parisians poured from their churches and milled about the streets and squares, where orators harangued mobs with angry denunciations of priests as purveyors of the king's lies. In the gardens of the Palais Royal, a huge crowd gathered under the plain trees, hypnotized by the resonant voice of Georges-Jacques Danton, an ugly but glib lawyer who thrilled as he watched his words seduce the great mass before him. Suddenly the cry "To arms!" rang out. As some raced for refuge under nearby arcades, the rest of the mob sprang like a great beast of prey, out the gates onto the rue Saint-Honoré, hungering for bread and thirsting for blood. Shots rang out a few streets away near the Tuileries Gardens, where palace guards raked the crowd with fire. By day's end, anarchy raged in the streets. The mob burned and demolished forty-four of the fifty-four hated customs posts that the farm monopoly had built to collect taxes on foodstuffs entering Paris. Brigands took advantage of the surging mob to loot shops and homes in their path. Ordered by officers to fire on the mobs, army regulars—themselves commoners—refused, and when several of their sergeants were jailed for disobedience at the Hôtel des Invalides—the military hospital—the mob and the soldiers smashed through the gates and released them and all other prisoners.

On the morning of July 14, the mob surged through the city, searching for weapons and powder. More than 7,000 stormed the arms depot at the Hôtel des Invalides and seized 30,000 muskets. After finding no powder, they cried out, "À la Bastille," which they knew held a large supply. The mob surged along the rue Saint-Antoine past Beaumarchais's unfinished house to the entrance of the fortress-prison, where the prison governor stepped forward to try to calm the crowd and negotiate with crowd leaders. When part of the mob streamed around him and broke into the inner courtyards, he ordered guards to fire. Ninety-eight besiegers fell dead and seventy-three others lay wounded. After recognizing relatives, friends, and neighbors in the mob, many of members of the French Guard joined the insurrection, turning five cannon around 180 degrees, blasting through the outer walls, and letting the mob surge into the prison. After setting free the only prisoners they could find—four forgers, a libertine, and two madmen—mob leaders massacred prison defenders, then seized the prison governor and dragged him through the streets to the Hôtel de Ville, or city hall, where they hung his torn body from a lamppost and disemboweled him.

As the mob's lust for blood intensified, militiamen joined in the frenzy, roaming the streets in drunken, disorganized bands, looting shops and homes and assaulting anyone who stood in their way or otherwise displeased them. Thousands of brigands, vagabonds, army deserters, and other lawless elements merged with them, donning the red and blue cockades of the revolution and forming a giant, amoeboid mass that oozed

A Paris mob stormed the Bastille on July 14, 1789, and seized the prison
governor. A short time later, they dragged him through the streets
and hanged him from a lamppost near city hall.

RÉUNION DES MUSÉES NATIONAUX

unpredictably in and out of the city's maze of streets and alleyways, its
jelly-like arms extending in one direction before contracting and reemerg-
ing in another. American minister Gouverneur Morris bore witness to its
terrifying appearance outside his club in the Palais Royal:

> After dinner... under the arcade of the Palais Royal waiting for my carriage
> ... the head and body of Mr. de Foulon are introduced in triumph. The
> head on a pike, the body dragged naked on the earth. After, this horrible
> exhibition is carried into the different streets. His crime is to have accepted
> a place in the ministry. This mutilated form of an old man seventy-five is
> shown to Bertier, his son-in-law, the intendant [comptroller] of Paris, and
> afterwards he also is put to death and cut to pieces, the populace carrying
> about the fragments with a savage joy. Gracious God, what a people.[32]

As the American envoy watched, a dragoon passed before him, waving a bloody piece of meat above his head and shouting triumphantly, "Here is Bertier's heart!" Behind him, others, their faces splattered with blood, waved pikes carrying other body parts and marched out through the gates of the Palais Royal onto the rue St. Honoré.

When an aide reported the mob's uprising to King Louis XVI, he seemed perplexed. "Then it is a full-blown riot?" he asked.

"No, sire," his aide replied softly. "It is a full-blown revolution."[33]

10

What Did You Do to Earn So Many Rewards?

THE DAY AFTER the Paris mob stormed the Bastille, Lafayette, the hero of the Battle of Yorktown, took nominal control of the local militia and reestablished a semblance of order. It was difficult. Unlike American militiamen, who had returned to their farms after their revolution, demobilized French troops had nowhere to go after the war with England. France had no frontier wilderness for the disenfranchised to claim, settle, and plant—no forests in which to hunt to sustain themselves and their families. The king, the aristocracy, and the clergy owned all the land, forests, and streams of France, and none but they could hunt, fish, or even set foot on their properties without permission, let alone settle.

As on the previous day, the crowds continued surging through the streets, moving unpredictably in one direction, then another, and eventually tramping over the new Beaumarchais property, where they found little of interest. Laborers were still digging here and there in anticipation of the complex installations. Safely at home in the Hotel de Hollande, Beaumarchais, whose provocative plays and pamphlets had helped incite the uprisings, suddenly awakened to the social ramifications of Figaro's challenge to the comte d'Almaviva:

> Because you are a great lord, you think you are a genius. Nobility, wealth, rank, position—it all makes you so proud. And what did you do to earn so many rewards? You took the time to be born—nothing else. Apart from that, you're quite an ordinary man! while I, by God, lost in the faceless crowd, had to apply . . . knowledge and skills merely to survive.[1]

Across Paris, the "faceless crowd" running riot transformed Figaro's air in *Le Mariage* into a revolutionary march:

> By accident of birth,
> One is born shepherd, another born king.
> Chance alone has set them apart,
> But their spirits carry no titles or names.
> That is why the son of a clod
> Can be worth his weight in gold.[2]

Unprepared for the flames of revolution he had helped ignite, he tried to steer a course of conduct that would tie him to neither the court nor the mob. On July 15, the new mayor of Paris asked him to superintend the demolition of the Bastille, calling on his knowledge of engineering to prevent damage to neighboring houses and keep accumulations of rubble from blocking sewers and drainage ditches. In the months that followed, Beaumarchais assumed authority over what had become a lawless area, wandering the neighborhood to set up food kitchens and sleeping quarters in deserted buildings at his own expense for the poor, homeless, and hungry. Often he saved innocent targets from mob violence.

"On returning to my home, sir," he wrote to the commander of a regiment, "I was happy I could prevent your soldier from setting out in broad day light; he would have been torn to pieces. I gave him an overcoat and hat, which I'd like you to return to me, and I made him take off his gaiters to prevent his being recognized."[3]

Beaumarchais had the foresight to slip away to Switzerland several times and transfer the bulk of his liquid assets to secret accounts he had long earlier established in several Swiss banks.

In the weeks that followed, the king agreed to end thirteen centuries of absolute monarchy in France, with the establishment of a constitutional monarchy under a somewhat representative National Assembly as a national legislature. The king and his ministers would remain the executive branch of government, with the king retaining power of veto over all legislation. With Lafayette in full charge of the National Guard, order returned to the streets of Paris. In Saint-Antoine, the people elected Beaumarchais to the district council, and by early 1791, with the city relatively calm and work on his new house all but completed, he moved into his little palace with his family and sold the Hotel de Hollande. He enrolled Eugénie in a convent school, whose head took full advantage of his frequent visits and renowned generosity to lament the plight of some of the school's other students.

"I send you, Madame, 200 livres for your unfortunate pupil," he responded to the Mother Superior's pleas for one of Eugénie's schoolmates, whose father's financial reverses left her unable to continue at the school. "This is for the year. I will . . . give you three louis, which will make six francs a month (for spending money) for this year, the same as I give my daughter. . . . That she remains in school is all the thanks I ask. Keep the secret for me.'"[4]

With the forbidding Bastille fortress no longer obstructing its view, Beaumarchais's house now looked over a breathtaking panorama of orchards and vineyards to the eastern horizon, where the walls, towers, and spires of the Château de Vincennes soared to the sky. He had grown stout and was so hard of hearing that he used an ear trumpet, but he still enjoyed an audience and gladly welcomed visitors to tour his gardens—often waddling about the gardens with them to explain the relationship of plantings and vistas to stage sets. Evenings saw the most distinguished figures of politics, literature, and the arts gather at his table for food, wine, song, music, and laughter. After dinner, Gudin said, he would often lead his guests into "a great circular salon, partly ornamented with mirrors, partly with landscapes of vast dimensions and . . . seats for an audience." A desk and armchair stood on a dais, where, as in a theater, Beaumarchais read his newest dramas, playing each part with a different inflection and "the pantomime which should characterize him."[5]

His performances so charmed the young Amélie Houret de La Marinière that she all but swooned at the clumsy advances of the fifty-eight-year-old playwright with his ludicrous ear trumpet. Twenty years his junior, she agreed to become his part-time mistress, and his secret visits to her quarters would eventually yield the old playwright some life-saving benefits.

The winter and spring of 1791 saw violence return to the streets of Paris, as the king exercised his veto to block all socially progressive legislation. While gangs roamed the streets attacking homes of aristocrats, hundreds of noblemen fled with their families across French borders to Austrian and Prussian territory. After the king's two brothers fled the nation, the prince de Condé—the king's "Master of the Palace"—fled to Worms to organize an army to return to France and restore the king's absolute powers. With the departure of the nobility, the flow of taxes all but stopped, and the National Assembly ordered all Roman Catholic Church funds turned over to the government instead of Rome. The pope retaliated by severing diplomatic relations and provoking a wave of attacks on churches and church properties in France. Fearing for his daughter's safety, Beaumarchais withdrew Eugénie from the convent school and was so overjoyed at her safe return that he composed a paean to her that became a popular song and won the hearts of Parisian women—along with a slew of unwanted proposals of marriage to Eugénie from Parisian men of all ages.

> Should a handsome bonhomme see stars in your eyes,
> Tell him to speak to your father, so wise;
> He judges with love and knows how to reason
> The man you should marry this beautiful season.
>
> What matters his fortune, position, or name?
> Judge, writer, or soldier are one and the same.
> Spirit and virtue, and talents, my dear,
> Are the only titles with real value here.[6]

Embarrassed by most of the marriage proposals his song provoked, Beaumarchais did receive one he deemed so "serious and honest" that he believed he owed its author a reply:

You have been deceived regarding my daughter. Scarcely fourteen years old, she is far from the time when I will allow her to choose a master.... Perhaps you are quite ignorant of the exact situation. I have only lately taken my daughter from the convent. The joy of her return drew from my indolence a song, which after having been sung at my table, went the rounds. I used the term *bonhomme* in jest of her future home, but it made many persons think that I was already planning her settlement.

But may I be preserved from engaging her before the time when her own heart will give her a consciousness of what it all means, and, Monsieur, this will be an affair of years, not of months.

What the song says jestingly, however, will certainly be my rule to enlighten her young heart. Fortune impresses me less than talents and virtue, because I wish her to be happy....

Beaumarchais[7]

Beaumarchais's joy at his daughter's return was short-lived. The violence racking Paris—and much of France—was taking on a life of its own, erupting randomly, unexpectedly, in any neighborhood, at any time, often with little more provocation than a dispute between a housewife and the baker over the price of a loaf of bread.

"All Paris is up in arms," Gouverneur Morris wrote to George Washington. Morris had replaced Jefferson as American minister plenipotentiary to France and was an eyewitness to much of the violence.

There has been hanged a baker this morning by the populace.... The poor baker was beheaded according to custom and carried in triumph through the streets. He had been all night at work for the purpose of supplying the greatest possible quantity of bread this morning. His wife is said to have died with horror when they presented her husband's head stuck on a pole. ... Paris is perhaps as wicked a spot as exists. Incest, murder, bestiality, fraud, rapine, oppression, baseness, cruelty; and yet this is the city which has stepped forward in the sacred cause of liberty. The pressure of incumbent despotism removed, every bad passion exerts peculiar energy.[8]

In April, the National Guard ignored Lafayette's orders and prevented the king and his family from leaving the Tuileries Palace to attend Easter services. As the Guard watched a mob burn an effigy of the pope at the nearby Palais Royal, Lafayette resigned his command, and the National Assembly elevated a savage, power-hungry attorney Maximilien Robespierre to the post of public prosecutor, then the most powerful government office in France. On June 20, the king and queen and their children fled Paris, hoping to reach the eastern frontier and a safe haven in Austrian territory. Troops caught their carriage the next day and returned the royal family to the Tuileries Palace in Paris, where they imprisoned them in their quarters.

Although troops kept some parts of Paris relatively calm, two of the poorest, most heavily populated areas festered with misery: Montmartre, to the north, where 20,000 emaciated unemployed peasants had migrated from the drought-stricken countryside to seek nonexistent manufacturing jobs they imagined they would find in the city. The second social sore stretched across the eastern industrial suburb of Faubourg Saint-Antoine, where Beaumarchais now lived and where hunger and despair gripped 50,000 unemployed workers and other "heroes of the Bastille." With the drought extending into its third year, millers had little wheat to make flour, and bread prices climbed 60 percent.

In the midst of bread shortages, malcontents rained leaflets across the city to inflame public passions with descriptions of the king, queen, and aristocrats gorging themselves on exotic foods and wines while the people starved. The king had lost all power to rule, and the National Assembly had fallen under the control of Robespierre and his band of political *enragés*, a double entendre in French that can mean either "enraged men" or "madmen." On August 1, Robespierre addressed the nation, declaring the French people "indivisible" and effectively rendering any dissenters guilty of treason if they threatened that "indivisibility."

Acting on Robespierre's principle, his *enragés* forced the assembly to ignore the new constitution and usurp the powers of a supreme governing council—a politburo that revoked the king's authority, abolished aristocracy, dissolved the Roman Catholic Church, and expelled members who opposed its decrees. To reduce the staggering national debt, the assembly ordered all religious artifacts in church and cathedral treasuries seized and melted into gold and silver bullion, destroying centuries of religious artworks. It then nationalized the lands of the king, the church, and all émigré noblemen (i.e., those who had fled the country), and it eliminated private property rights, giving every citizen the right to hunt, fish, and trespass on anyone's property. The new laws provoked immediate, widespread class warfare, with workers surging through city streets and alleyways, stripping every unguarded mansion of its treasures and slaughtering their owners, servants, and anyone else they found who could not identify himself or herself as a bona fide revolutionary. Outside the cities, peasant mobs burned and looted stately homes, châteaus, and castles, destroying a millennium of French art.

Added to the savagery of class warfare were the brutalities of religious conflict, with more than half the priests in France refusing to abjure their faith and take secular vows to the state. Parishioners split accordingly —often into armed camps in the same city neighborhood or village, with *refusés* attacking *jureurs* (those who swore allegiance to the state) as religious heretics, while *jureurs* attacked *refusés* for political heresy and treason.

With mobs slaughtering women and children as well as men, Beaumarchais grew frantic. The individual liberties that Figaro had embraced on theater stages had produced nothing but anarchy in real life on Paris streets. Afraid for his family's safety, he sent his wife and daughter and his sisters to the English Channel port city of Le Havre, where violence had not yet erupted and where, if necessary, they could escape quickly by boat to England.

"His house was at the entrance of that terrible faubourg, like the Palace of Portici at the foot of Vesuvius," explained his friend Gudin. "The eruption of the volcano was as yet only at rare intervals . . . [but] with the lava always boiling, it was inevitable that it would overflow and engulf the house."[9]

Although Beaumarchais had promised to follow his wife and daughter to Le Havre, he became entangled in a plot too complex for even him to

Maximilien Robespierre, a lawyer who led the
extremists in the French National Assembly and
Convention and initiated the Terror, which sent tens
of thousands of innocents to the guillotine.

RÉUNION DES MUSÉES NATIONAUX

have written for Figaro—or for even the clever Figaro to have untangled.
Two years earlier, the Austrians had crushed a rebellion in Belgium and
seized 200,000 muskets, of which it had sold 52,345 to a Dutch merchant,
who stored them in a warehouse in the small Dutch seaport of Terweren,
Zeeland. Knowing that Beaumarchais had supplied American forces with
arms and ammunition, the merchant suggested that he buy them for the
French army. It would be a scandal, the merchant warned, if the French
playwright refused such an opportunity to serve his country.

Sixty years old and growing more deaf by the day, Beaumarchais had
sought only to escape turmoil by retiring to the peace of his gardens at
Saint-Antoine, but he knew that immediate arrest awaited anyone per-

ceived as an enemy of the state, with entire families often left to rot in dungeons for the perceived misdeed of a single family member. "Regardless of his decision, he faced danger," Gudin explained. "They would have made it a crime on his part to have refused to procure the muskets. . . . He had only a choice of dangers. He decided to expose himself to the danger of being useful to his country."[10]

Beaumarchais reported the offer to the minister of war, who arranged for a bank to transfer 500,000 francs to the playwright to purchase the guns, but insisted that Beaumarchais post a personal bond of 750,000 francs, refundable at the time he delivered the muskets to the French military. Beaumarchais did as he was told, then sent an agent to Holland to consummate the purchase.

With the French economy in shambles and millions facing famine, the National Assembly acted to prevent mass uprisings and the spread of anarchy. On January 1, 1792, it proclaimed the beginning of the "Era of Liberty" by requiring everyone in France to carry a passport when traveling anywhere within the country—even down the street from one's home. Assembly leaders channeled the resulting popular furor by accusing Europe's monarchies of creating the famine in France and declaring "war as indispensable to the revolution." Calling for worldwide revolution, they pledged, "We will not be satisfied until all Europe is afire. . . . All Europe, including Moscow, will become Gallicized, Jacobinized, communized."[11]

On April 28, 1792, the French government sent its armies pouring across northern, eastern, and southwestern borders to pillage rich agricultural lands in neighboring countries. Austria, Prussia, Denmark, Poland, and Spain declared war against France, but Holland desperately sought to remain neutral. To avoid antagonizing either side, the Dutch government created an impenetrable tangle of red tape that produced indefinite delays for Beaumarchais's agent as he tried to purchase the arms. Beaumarchais tried asking the French minister of war for help but never could find one. As each new political faction seized power in the tumultuous National Assembly, a new minister of war appeared—only to disappear the following day when his government fell, forcing Beaumarchais to return and retell his story of the guns in Holland to new functionaries and apply for new import permits.

As Beaumarchais stumbled down War Department corridors in Paris, the French army's advance into Austria and Prussian territory came to a halt, and without a fresh supply of arms and ammunition, French troops were unable to prevent Austrian and Prussian armies from counterattacking. French troops and civilians alike grew enraged over the failure of the French government to supply the army with enough weapons. As the first enemy troops poured across the eastern French border, an enterprising bureaucrat in the War Department finally issued Beaumarchais a passport to go to Holland to fetch the muskets, but it was too late.

Mobs blocked the streets, crying "Treason! Treason!" over the War Department's failure to supply troops with arms. Radical revolutionaries seized control of the National Assembly and created a Criminal Tribunal to try everyone suspected of treason. Twenty-nine moderates in the assembly protested, and Robespierre sent a mob of thugs to surround the hall. They broke through the doors, sliced off the head of one of the recalcitrant assemblymen, and dragged the twenty-eight others off to prison.

In the days that followed, the Criminal Tribunal immediately ordered 3,000 "suspects" arrested and imprisoned for antirevolutionary activities, while the assembly ordered the removal or destruction of all statues of kings, queens, and other aristocrats in Paris. It banned the use of aristocratic terms such as *Monsieur* (my sire) and *Madame* (my lady) in favor of *citoyen* and *citoyenne*—"citizen" and "citizeness." With the end of aristocracy came a ban on the use of the prefix "de," signifying manorial rights, and Pierre-Augustin Caron de Beaumarchais now became Citoyen Caron, with the same surname he had worked so hard to discard on his climb to fame and fortune.

"What is to become of us, my dear?" he lamented to his wife. "Now, we are to lose all our dignities. What ruin! . . . what destruction! . . . The Revolution has had a great influence . . . but it must be confessed that, in trying to straighten our tree, we have made it bend in the opposite direction."[12]

A member of the invading mob waves the head of a victim at the president of the French National Assembly. The mob went on to drag twenty-eight assemblymen to prison, then slaughter 600 of the king's guards and 200 servants at the Tuileries Palace.

With Austrian and Prussian troops advancing toward Paris, Paris mobs and militiamen searched the city for rifles and muskets. Aware of Beaumarchais's connection to the Holland guns deal, some mob leaders suggested that Beaumarchais had stored the guns in his house. As 30,000 rioters edged ever closer to his property, rumors multiplied and spread that Beaumarchais's stone castle also held boundless stores of wheat and foodstuffs, as well as arms . . . and coins . . . and silver . . . and gold ingots. . . . "Il est riche!" went the cry—"He is rich!" As the mob grew, Beaumarchais decided to go to the gates to address it, but Gudin restrained him, arguing that someone would almost certainly assassinate him if he appeared. Beaumarchais returned to his bedroom, donned one of his many disguises, and fled by a side entrance.

After he left, servants followed his parting instructions to open all gates and doors to prevent needless destruction and give the mob open access to his property. As the invaders surged into the gardens, the sheer magnificence of the landscape startled and enthralled them—many stopped in their tracks to gasp at its beauty. With most of the invaders slowing to a walk, only a handful actually approached the door of the playwright's home and almost obsequiously asked permission to search for foodstuffs and weapons.

"Whatever the reason," Gudin recalled, "someone proposed to swear that they would destroy nothing. The crowd swore, and . . . after searching everywhere, the only arms that mob leaders found were Beaumarchais's hunting rifle and sword, which they left untouched. . . . Truth here resembles fable." Gudin called the mob's behavior "the fruit of the benefits which he had lavished on the poor of his neighborhood. If he had not been loved, if he had not been dear to his domestics, all his goods would have been pillaged."[13]

Although all was intact when he returned home, Beaumarchais felt violated, and, as after his humiliating imprisonment in juvenile prison after the opening of *Le Mariage*, he could no longer find it in his soul "to laugh at everything" as Figaro had done. Beaumarchais could only weep. The aristocracy had violated him early in his life for rising above his station to champion commoner rights; now the commoners whose rights he had championed had violated him, and he realized that commoners were as capable of injustice, cruelty, and arrogance as the aristocrats they despised —no better, no worse. Power rendered them all the same.

"What an incredible series of events!" Figaro cried out in despair. "How did it happen to me? I have seen everything, done everything, worn out everything. At last my illusion is shattered and I am wholly disabused . . . *désabusé . . . désabusé . . . désabusé*."[14]

On the August 23, 1792, Gudin awoke to find armed sentinels at the doors of the Beaumarchais mansion and beneath the windows. "I hastened to my friend's apartment and found him surrounded by sinister men searching his papers and putting his effects under seal. . . . When they were through they took him with them, and I was left alone in that vast palace, guarded by *sans culottes* whose aspect made me doubt whether they were there to conserve the property or to pillage."[15]

His captors took Beaumarchais to police court, where he learned he had been "denounced" by an unknown enemy for having concealed the Dutch muskets at an undisclosed location—a crime punishable by death on the guillotine. Too deaf to understand the charges, he called up every bit of Figaro's guile trying to understand his accusers. With no idea of what his accusers had said, he defended himself with such incongruous arguments that the court began to laugh at his nonsensical responses. Convinced that Beaumarchais, like Figaro, was mocking them, the court sent him off to prison to await a verdict in a common cell with a score of other *nobles misérables*. A week later, a guard opened the cell gate and called his name. "Your denouncer has been declared culpable. You are free to go."[16]

Unbeknownst to Beaumarchais, his young sometimes-mistress—Amélie Houret de La Marinière—was a regular guest in the public prosecutor's bed and had pleaded successfully for the playwright's release.

On the day of Beaumarchais's release, the Prussians laid siege to Verdun, 140 miles east of Paris. Convinced that every aristocrat was ready to welcome the foreign invaders, a mob broke into the prisons of Paris and massacred 3,000 prisoners, including those in the cell Beaumarchais had abandoned two days earlier. On September 21, 1792, the radical National Convention replaced the National Assembly and declared "royalty abolished in France."

With his release, however, Beaumarchais came under increased government pressure to consummate the purchase of the muskets in Holland, and until he fulfilled the commission, he remained under suspicion of obstructing the flow of arms to the French army—in effect, treason.

Again, though, he needed a passport and waited interminably to see the new minister of war—only to learn that the minister had left town. Tired and disheveled, he stumbled to the office of the minister of foreign affairs. A caricature of his former self and of the dashing Figaro, he appeared with his ear trumpet, ill-kempt and unshaven, cackling incoherently, terror-stricken by the fate that might await him and his family if he failed in his mission. The minister had no idea what Beaumarchais was saying and ordered an aide to lead the old man to the street.

Exhausted and confused, Beaumarchais—like King Lear on the heath—roamed the narrow streets of Paris at random, turning here, there, anywhere—often crying out in a rant, "*Fi*-garo! *Fi*-garo!"

With echoes of bloodthirsty mobs resounding in every alley, he gasped for breath as he shuffled through the maze of dark passageways, in the grip of terror, dodging shadows of real and imaginary enemies until he found his own door. It was long after midnight. A week later, a mob massacred fifty-three aristocrats being transferred from Versailles to a Paris prison. Convinced the mob was on its way to seize him, Beaumarchais fled during the night into the nearby countryside, where he darted aimlessly down country lanes and across muddy fields and finally collapsed at the door of a farmhouse, all but insane from fear and fatigue. With little sympathy for city folk, the farmer and his wife sent the disheveled playwright to their barn for the night. Fearing assassination on the open road to Paris the next day, Beaumarchais traveled the narrow pathways across fields and forests to reach the edge of the city, where he shuddered among the echoes of the mob's chants for blood:

> Oui, ça ira, ça ira, ça ira!
> Les aristos à la lanterne,
> Oui, ça ira, ça ira, ça ira!
> Les aristos, on les pendra![17]

Beaumarchais darted from corner to corner, along the darkest, narrowest alleys he could find, hugging walls as tightly as possible until he found his wall—the wall that surrounded his house. He sneaked into the garden, then into the house, where his friend Gudin awaited to embrace him and help restore his sanity.

After Beaumarchais recovered from his ordeal in the wilderness, he spent two weeks pestering members of the Executive Committee, pleading obsequiously for a passport to go to Holland to secure the muskets for the army of the Revolution. Danton, at last, grew convinced of the playwright's sincerity and talked committee members into signing an official appointment for Beaumarchais to go to Holland as a secret government agent.

Knowing the Dutch opposed the sale of the muskets to France, Beaumarchais went to London and talked an English merchant into a scheme to convince the Dutch government he was buying the muskets for their ally Britain instead of the French government. The merchant advanced Beaumarchais enough funds for a deposit and signed a contract of intent to purchase, and Beaumarchais set off for Holland to retrieve the muskets. Once he was in Holland, however, Dutch authorities saw through the ruse, and when he returned to London, authorities arrested and imprisoned him, charging him with fraud.

On January 15, 1793, the National Convention convicted King Louis XVI by a vote of 707 to 0 of conspiring to deprive the public of its liberties. Two days later, the Convention voted 361 to 360 to execute the king. To ensure the vote for execution, Robespierre imprisoned enough dissidents to ensure the monarch's death—including America's Tom Paine. With the crowd chanting madly, *Ça ira, ça ira . . .* , a wooden cart took King Louis XVI to the Place de la Révolution (now Place de la Concorde) on the morning of January 21, and, at 10:22, the executioner released the guillotine blade that sliced off the royal head. The executioner reached into the basket and held the lifeless trophy above his own head to display it to the roaring crowd as royal blood dripped down his hand, wrist, arm, and grinning face.

The beheading of the king outraged the civilized world but only excited the lust for blood among leaders of the French Revolution. Under orders

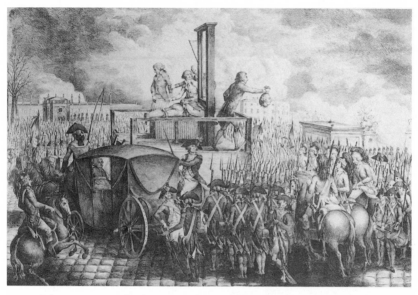

The executioner displays King Louis XVI's head from the scaffolding
of the guillotine on the place de la Révolution, now the place
de la Concorde, on January 21, 1793.

RÉUNION DES MUSÉES NATIONAUX

from Danton to end the royal line, a gang of thugs burst into Queen Marie
Antoinette's prison cell a few months after her husband's murder and tore
her shrieking eight-year-old son—now the boy-king Louis XVII—from
her arms. It was the last time his mother or anyone else other than his
abductors would ever see him alive or dead. No trace of his body or documentary evidence regarding his fate has ever been found. An empty tomb
awaits him still in the burial ground of French royals at St. Denis, outside
Paris.

The monarchs of Europe acted in concert at the murder of one of their
own. Britain and Holland declared war and joined the coalition against
France, then Russia joined. The British government agreed to buy the
52,345 guns that Beaumarchais was to have bought in Holland and released
Beaumarchais from his London prison to return to Paris. Accusations that
he had negotiated the British arms purchase preceded him to Paris, however, and, with the guillotine awaiting the entire family of anyone who

failed the French Revolution, the Executive Committee gave him what it called a simple way to prove his patriotism. It ordered him to return to Holland, outbid the British, and bring the guns to France.

Beaumarchais went to Amsterdam, where officials refused to reopen the bidding. He then went to Hamburg, then Basel, trying to find intermediaries to act as agents in reopening the bidding. It proved an endless journey. To skirt various Dutch, Belgian, and German battlegrounds, he had to take circuitous routes through Germany and Switzerland, applying for and waiting an eternity for passports in every duchy and principality along the way. Months passed, and in January 1794 the Executive Committee determined that Beaumarchais had stayed out of the country too long and declared him an émigré and seized his home. Madame Beaumarchais protested, presenting documentary evidence of his having left the country on an official mission. She succeeded in recovering possession of her husband's home, but after another six months without a word from her husband, government agents sealed his house, seized his bank accounts and other assets, and took his wife, daughter, and two sisters off to prison to await their inevitable encounters with the guillotine as the family of an émigré.

By the end of July 1794, Robespierre's paranoia had become too ghastly for even his most loyal supporters. After accusing members of the Convention of plotting against him, he ordered the arrest and execution of every deputy—the entire Convention. It was one demand too many. By then the number of women and children left widowed and orphaned by the guillotine had reached staggering proportions, and the adoring mob that had raised Robespierre to power suddenly turned against him, marching to the Convention and crying, *À bas Robespierre*—"Down with Robespierre."

Convention delegates demanded that he name those in the hall he suspected of treason. He refused, and the once-timid delegates joined arms and staged a coup d'état, abolishing the Executive Committee and ordering the arrest of Robespierre and his immediate confederates. That evening, July 23, 1794, a pistol shot blew off half his jaw; some said he had attempted suicide, but a guard claimed that he had shot Robespierre trying to escape. The source of the shot was immaterial. With his head swathed in blood-soaked bandages, Robespierre lay in agony for but one night; the guillotine put him out of his misery the following day—along with nineteen of his closest political allies, including his brother. While a mob watched in silent disbelief, seventy-one more Robespierristes followed him to the same fate the following day in a bloody finale to the Terror.

The final toll of the Terror would remain unmatched in the civilized world until the twentieth century. In only two years, the French government sent 1 million of its citizens—men, women, and children—to prison. In a nation of 26 million souls, 200,000 are known to have died; untold thousands of others—many simply nameless, homeless, jobless peasants and workers—were summarily killed without knowing why and dumped into mass graves. Inspired by the American Revolution against tyranny, the French Revolution had simply replaced monarchic tyranny with mob tyranny. Only about 2 percent of those condemned to die on the guillotine were, in fact, aristocrats.

After Robespierre's death, moderates moved into seats of powers and began releasing hundreds of thousands of imprisoned "suspects," including political prisoners, aristocrats, and other alleged enemies of the state. Police released the Beaumarchais women on August 8—with all charges against them expunged. In an ironic aftermath, however, Madame de Beaumarchais immediately divorced her beloved husband to conform with a new law that forced wives of émigrés to divorce their husbands or suffer the penalty of death in lieu of their husbands. "Your decrees," shouted an indignant Madame de Beaumarchais to the court, "force me to demand a divorce. I obey, although my husband, charged with a commission, is not an émigré and never had the thought. I attest to it, and I know his heart. He will justify himself of this accusation as he has all the rest, and I shall have the satisfaction of marrying him a second time."[18]

Early on October 4, 1784, a British frigate arrived in Terweren, Holland, to take possession of the 52,345 guns Beaumarchais had sought to purchase, and as the ship disappeared over the horizon it carried with it all Beaumarchais's hopes of recovering his French citizenship and his once-enormous fortune. He had spent most of the 500,000 francs in government funds to try to purchase the guns, and he now stood to forfeit the 750,000-franc personal bond he had given the government to ensure his delivering the muskets to the French army. All but certain to face charges of treason if he returned to France, Beaumarchais had no choice but remain an émigré—perhaps for the rest of his life. But unlike most French émigrés, he was a French spy and risked arrest everywhere in Europe except the Free City of Hamburg, where it now appeared he would have to remain indefinitely.

11

Tout finit par des chansons /
Everything Ends in Song

BEAUMARCHAIS SPENT a total of two years in Hamburg—exiled from his native France and, sadly, from most of the many French émigrés in Hamburg. As they had when he first set foot in the palace of Versailles as a clockmaker's son, exiled courtiers in Hamburg refused to include commoners in their elegant soirées, where they mingled with such notables as the comte d'Artois—the future Charles V. All but friendless and unable to tap his own financial resources in Switzerland, Beaumarchais faced poverty and hunger for the first time since his adventure as a runaway adolescent rebelling against his demanding father. He grew depressed and believed he was fast approaching his end. To anyone who would listen, he denied being an émigré: "After serving the cause of liberty in America," he cried out, "I have served the true interests of France with all my powers and without personal ambition. I shall prove that I am still serving her—even though I am the butt of persecution that is both stupid politically and nefarious. It is absurd to believe that a man who had dedicated himself to the restoration of the Rights of Man in America would be reluctant to put the same principles into practice in France."[1]

He spent much of his time writing letters to old friends and a few essays—*memorials*—addressing what he considered critical issues. One of the most critical had been America's debt to him for the arms, ammunition, and goods he shipped to them at the beginning of the Revolutionary War. In 1793, Congress asked U.S. Secretary of Treasury Alexander Hamilton to review the documents related to the Beaumarchais claim.

Hamilton concluded that the American government owed Beaumarchais 2.28 million francs. But in 1794, Gouverneur Morris, the United States minister plenipotentiary to France, laid eyes on the receipt Beaumarchais had signed for the 1-million-livre loan as seed money from the French government to start his company Roderigue Hortalez. Reiterating the arguments of Franklin and Arthur Lee, Morris insisted the money had been an outright gift of the French government, for which Congress owed nothing. "We owe nothing, and will pay nothing."[2]

The decision stunned Beaumarchais. Injustice at the hands of those he had believed to be just! He expected injustice from the despots who ruled France, but not from "the brave people" in the land of liberty, as he called the Americans. Rejected by the land of his birth, he now faced rejection by the land of his fantasies. It was all too much.

"Americans!" he appealed to the people of the United States in a final *cri de coeur* on April 10, 1795. "I have served you with indefatigable zeal and I have received . . . only bitterness as a reward. . . . I die your creditor. Allow me therefore, now that I am dying, to bequeath to you my daughter, that you may endow her with a portion of what you owe me. . . . Adopt her as a worthy child of the state."[3]

As calm returned to Paris, one, then two, then more theater companies reopened with presentations of one sort or another. A revival of *Tarare* at the Opéra de Paris not only drew a standing-room-only audience and thunderous cheers, it revived popular sentiment for Beaumarchais. In October 1795, a new government—The Directory—seized power, crushed the remnants of radical revolution, and, by the end of the year, agreed to an armistice to end the war in Europe. In April 1796, it permitted Beaumarchais to return to France.

Old, deaf, his fortune depleted, he returned to find a derelict, uninhabitable structure where his palatial mansion had stood. Broken walls surrounded what had been his magnificent gardens—now a tangled jungle, crawling with rats, cats, and wild dogs. The glorious scenario of eternal

The crumbling wall around Beaumarchais's home in
eastern Paris, near the ruins of the Bastille prison, at the end
of the French Revolution. Beaumarchais rebuilt the structure
and gardens to their former glory and lived there until his
death in 1799. The French government bought the estate in
1818 and leveled it to permit street modernization.
The boulevard Beaumarchais now spans the property,
leading to the place de la Bastille.

AUTHOR'S COLLECTION

gaiety he had so carefully created had vanished. The echoes of barbarism
—cries for blood and shrieks of agony—replaced the spirit of song, love,
laughter, and dance that had once resounded in his heart. And the terror
—the ever-present terror . . .

Gathering up the vestiges of Figaro's resilient spirit, Beaumarchais
created a quick plot for ensuring his family's safety. His first step was to
bless Eugénie's marriage to a young officer who had protected her and her
mother from revolutionaries. Beaumarchais found André Delarue "a good
young man who persisted in wishing to marry her when it was thought I
possessed nothing; she, her mother, and I considered we ought to reward

this generous attachment. Five days after my arrival I made him this hand-some present."[4]

Beaumarchais then remarried his own wife and took the entire family to his wife's family home in Orléans while workmen began repairing the mansion near the spot where the Bastille had stood. Although deeply in debt to the government, he lived as quietly and unobtrusively as possible in Orléans, drawing little attention to himself as he slipped in and out of the city on the road to Basel, Switzerland, and the bank where he had wisely stored some gold and silver specie before the revolution. Little by little, trip after trip, often in disguise, he retrieved enough gold coins to pay for the restoration of his house in Paris and ensure his own and his family's safety and security in the immediate future. He took Marie-Thérèse with him on one trip and Eugénie on another, to open a secret account for each of them and transfer enough cash to ensure them a modicum of comfort after his death.

In May 1797, the entire Beaumarchais family returned to their mansion in Paris—only to find the capital in the grips of a wave of poverty that left thousands sleeping on the streets. The Directory raised taxes of the rich, imposing a new property tax based on the number of doors and windows in each house. The Beaumarchais mansion had 200 windows, and Beau-marchais had to make a hurried trip back to Basel to recover enough money to pay his taxes. He made frequent appeals to the government for a review of his debts from the mission to Holland to buy muskets. After two years, a special commission ruled on January 8, 1798, that because of the con-tinual turnover in key ministerial posts, the French government itself was responsible for the failure of the Beaumarchais mission. After a complex accounting, it found that rather than his owing the state any money, the state owed Beaumarchais nearly 1 million francs. Although high taxes and runaway inflation would reduce the purchasing power of this and other funds in his control, Beaumarchais would be able to live the rest of his life in relative comfort.

Despite the injustices he had suffered, Beaumarchais retained his benev-olent instincts. He wrote to "My brother, my friend, my Gudin," who was living in poverty in the country outside Paris and arranged for his longtime friend to come and live in the mansion. He even sent financial help to Mme. Goëzman, the judge's wife who had demanded bribes during the La Blache trial and would have seen Beaumarchais jailed for life at the time. The guillotine had claimed her husband during the revolution and left her destitute. Without a thought of vengeance, Beaumarchais arranged for her to find adequate lodging and board for at least a year. Like the comte d'Almaviva, Beaumarchais recognized that "anger is good for nothing."[5]

As some of the old Beaumarchais spirit flickered back to life, some song, laughter, and gaiety—albeit subdued—echoed through the house again. Although he could hear little through his ear trumpet, Marie-Thérèse followed the tempo with her hands, and he sang with fervor, seizing every last minute of life with rediscovered joy. He revived his beloved Figaro, revitalizing *La Mère coupable*—the third play in the Figaro trilogy, which had proved a failure at the Théâtre du Marais in 1792. Convinced that the mediocrity of the players was at least partly responsible, he asked the Théâtre Français to stage it. After the darkness of revolution, French audiences needed some light-hearted optimism, and critics gave *La Mère* good reviews. Although it eventually disappeared from the repertoire of the French theater, it revived Beaumarchais's celebrity for a moment. Although he couldn't hear a word they said, crowds of admirers surrounded him whenever he appeared outside his home, and French notables vied with each other to invite him to dine—among them French Foreign Minister Talleyrand and even the celebrated General Napoléon Bonaparte. "I shall be glad to meet the author of *Le Mére coupable*," declared the military leader.[6]

Not long after his and Figaro's triumph with *La Mére*, Beaumarchais sat with family and friends at the bedside of his last surviving sister as she lay dying. True to family tradition, she began to sing softly, a lovely folk song with comical last lines in each verse. She died much as she had lived, with the entire family in song, albeit subdued. A year later, on the night of May 17, 1799, Beaumarchais said good night to his family and friends and climbed the stairs to his room to go to sleep. He and Figaro died peacefully during the night—without either having the final word.

12

All of Which Proves That a Son of a Clod
Can Be Worth His Weight in Gold

AS MIGHT BE expected, Beaumarchais wrote his own epitaph, insisting that he lived his life with "gaiety and *bonhommie*":

> I have had enemies without number. . . . It was natural enough. I played every instrument, but was not a musician. I invented good machines, but was no engineer. I composed verses and songs, but was no poet. I wrote some pieces for the stage, but people said, "He is not an author. . . . He is the son of a watchmaker."
>
> I raised the art of printing in France by my superb editions of Voltaire, but I was not a printer. Unable to find lawyers to defend me, I wrote memorials, but people said, "These are not the work of a lawyer, and he cannot be allowed to prove he is in the right without a lawyer."
>
> I advised ministers on great issues of financial reform, but people said, "This man is not a financier." I traded in the four quarters of the globe, but I was not a merchant. I had forty ships at sea but was not a shipowner.
>
> Weary of seeing our uniform habitations and our gardens without poetry, I built a house which is spoken of, but I did not belong to architecture or the arts.
>
> And of all Frenchmen, I am the one who did the most for the liberty of America, the begetter of our own liberty . . . for I was the only person who dared to form the plan and commence its execution, in spite of England, Spain, and even France. But I was not a minister.
>
> What was I then?

I was nothing but myself, and myself I have remained, free in the midst
of fetters . . . happy in my home, having never belonged to any coterie . . .
having never paid court to any one, and yet repelled by all.[1]

His family buried Beaumarchais amid a shady cluster of trees in the magnificent gardens of his home. Like his birth, his death came in the same
year as George Washington's. With the family's cash resources all but gone,
Marie-Thérèse took in lodgers to maintain herself and property. In 1818, the
state reconfigured the approaches to the city and bought the Beaumarchais
house and property for 500,000 francs. After transferring Beaumarchais's
remains to a proper cemetery—he now lies in the Père Lachaise—it razed
the house and gardens, paved over the entire property, and turned it into
a major roadway. The boulevard Beaumarchais now covers most of what
had been one of the most beautiful estates in Paris. Beaumarchais's only
known surviving descendant was his daughter Eugénie, who gave birth
to two boys and a girl by her husband André-Toussaint Delarue. Having
served as an aide to General Lafayette in 1789, Delarue went on to become a colonel in the National Guard and eventually a brigade marshal.
Of his two sons, the older entered the army, rising to the post of brigade
marshal, and the younger went into the government's finance ministry.
Beaumarchais descendants still survive.

Le Barbier de Seville and *Le Mariage de Figaro* remain two of the greatest plays in the history of French theater. Some critics insist they are *the*
greatest. For whatever reasons, Mozart's *Le Nozze di Figaro* did not evoke
universal enthusiasm until after the final defeat and fall of Napoléon in
1815, when it went on to become one of the world's most popular operas.
Gioacchino Rossini had been but four years old when *Le Nozze di Figaro*
debuted in Vienna. By 1815, when *Le Nozze* finally caused a stir in the

opera world, Rossini was twenty-three and had already composed more than a dozen operas, including the extraordinarily popular *Tancredi* and *L'Italiana in Algeri*. Drawing from the success of *Le Nozze*, Rossini decided to adapt Beaumarchais's other great play, *Le Barbier*, and, with librettist Cesare Sterbini and the patronage of Rome's Teatro Argentina opera company, Rossini created the great opera *Il Barbiere di Siviglia*.

Il Barbiere opened on February 20, 1816, with Figaro's guitar out of tune as he sang beneath Rosina's window. As the singer desperately tried tuning his instrument, a string snapped, his voice cracked, the audience hissed, a cat ran across the stage, the audiences in the balconies mewed, and, as the curtain fell on the first act, the crowd booed Rossini out of the theater. Then, in a startling and inexplicable turnabout on the second night, a new audience cheered the performances and hailed *Il Barbiere* as a masterpiece. In the weeks that followed, audiences across Europe agreed—as did an American audience when an English translation opened in New York in May 1819. Legend has it that when Rossini visited Beethoven in Vienna in 1822 and asked the aging master for guidance in furthering his musical career, Beethoven replied, "Compose another *Barbiere di Siviglia*." There was, however, only one Barber of Seville, only one Figaro, only one Beaumarchais.

Pierre Augustin Caron de Beaumarchais wrote five full-length plays, several one-act plays or *parades*, and one opera (all listed in the appendix). A prolific poet and composer, he often combined his poetry and music to create popular songs and songs that turned his plays into precursors of modern musical comedies.

Beaumarchais wrote scores of poems, and composed an equally large number of songs for which he wrote the lyrics. Nearly forty are in print and included in *Oeuvres complètes de Beaumarchais*, listed in the bibliography. Among his most charming and best loved were his *seguedillas*, based on the music of a Spanish dance, for which poems of either four or seven verses were written. Here is an example, with too many French puns for any but those at ease in French to understand thoroughly, but the sounds of the words and the meter make them delightful to read aloud, and an inadequate translation alongside provides the broad meanings, if not the beauty, of the poem.

Je veux ici mettre au grand jour
Le train don't l'Amour tracasse la vie;
C'est comme une cavalerie
Don't l'ordre et la marche varie;
[Refrain]
    Quand la tête trotte, trotte, trotte, bientôt
    La queue est au galop.

D'une mantille, deux beaux yeux
Ont lancé des feux sur une victime:
Le coeur s'embrase, l'on s'anime;
Mais n'oubliez pas la maxime
[Refrain]

L'on va, l'on vient, matin et soir
On voudrait se voir; On donne parole.
Tout en empêche, on se désole;
L'un est furieux, l'autre est folle
[Refrain]

Enfin on goûte au rendez-vous
Les biens les plus doux,
Mais on se dépêche:
L'un est épuisé, l'autre est fraiche;
Car, au Prado, sur l'herbe sèche,
Quand l'amoureux trotte, trotte, trotte,
Bientôt, la belle est au galop.

On peut tirer un sens moral
Du chant trivial
D'une séguedille;
Retenez ma leçon gentille:
Trop souvent auprès d'une fille
Quand la tête trotte, trotte, trotte, bientôt
La bourse est au galop.
—P.-A. C. de B.

I want to shine some light on the ways
Love can ruin one's happiest days.
Like wild horses in full disarray,
Each out of step, going every which way.
[Refrain]
    When the horse in front slows down to stop,
        The one at the rear charges by at a quick clip-clop.

From behind a *mantilla*, two beautiful eyes
Target a victim with lances of fire.
His heart goes aflutter; a-bump with desire,
But never forget the old maxim, sire:
[Refrain]

Time flies in the morning and all afternoon.
"We must see each other; Let's do it quite soon."
"I'm sorry I'm busy . . . maybe in June."
He's furious with her; she's as mad as a loon.
But when the horse in the front slows . . . [Refrain]

At last they arrange a sweet rendezvous
To savor the splendors of love evermore.
But in the mad rush for pleasures galore,
He lies exhausted while she yearns for more.
The grass is so soft, her desires implore,
When a lover is tired and ready to stop,
She'll run to another at a quick clip-clop.

There's a moral to learn
From this trivial tale
From an old seguedilla
With a lesson so stale:
Beware of women you meet on the trail,
Whose soft words entrance and urge you to stop.
She'll run with your money at a quick clip-clop.
—H. G. de U.

Coda

Of all the roles that Beaumarchais created on- and offstage, he named Roderigue Hortalez and "the honorable part which I had in the liberty of America" as "the greatest act of my life . . . the glory of my entire life."[2] Although some historians rank him as "the most underrated French hero of the American Revolution,"[3] Congress, to its disgrace, refused to pay him a penny for the arms he shipped to America. When he died, the nation whose liberty he saved owed him at least 2.28 million francs—$8.5 million in today's dollars, but worth far more in terms of purchasing power in 1799. In the years before and after his death, five American Founding Fathers—John Jay, Thomas Jefferson, James Madison, James Monroe, and Alexander Hamilton—pleaded with Congress to square accounts with Beaumarchais and, after he died, with his estate. In 1816, the duc de Richelieu supported the Beaumarchais claim with an eloquent letter to Congress—that went unnoticed. "The Claims of the Heirs of Beaumarchais" appeared on the agenda of each session of Congress without any consideration. In 1822, Beaumarchais's daughter Eugénie Delarue, by then forty-five years old, again pleaded with America's lawmakers to settle the case.

"As a reward for the devotion of Beaumarchais to your cause, shall his daughter be deprived of her fortune, and finish her life in vain and cruel expectation?" she wrote. "Till the last minute of his life, he begged you to decide upon his claim. . . . Such were the last wishes of his heart in the long pursuit of his just claims."[4] Congress ignored her request and left her letter unacknowledged. The rest of America did much the same. While the nation renamed hundreds of cities, towns, villages, lakes, rivers, mountains, and institutions to honor other Founding Fathers, it failed to name a single town in America or even raise a monument to commemorate the French spy who saved the American Revolution during its early years, when Washington's patriots faced British armies alone, without adequate military supplies. Not a stone bears his name; no portrait hangs in the National Portrait Gallery or any other American museum that honors the nation's patriots. He lies in Paris, forgotten by all but devotees of eighteenth-century French theater.

In 1835, the U.S. government was about to make a claim of its own against France, but realized it would have little chance of obtaining a hearing as long as the Beaumarchais case remained open. Congress offered the Beaumarchais heirs an 800,000-franc, take-it-or-leave-it settlement—about $3 million in today's dollars, or about 35 percent of what the government owed Beaumarchais for America's liberty and independence. Exhausted by the long process and weary of hollow American proclamations of "justice for all," the Beaumarchais family accepted the settlement.

. . . which proves that the son of a clod can be worth his weight in gold.

—FIGARO[5]

Fin

Full-Length Plays (in chronological order)

Eugénie, a drama in five acts

Les deux amis, ou Le Négociant de Lyon (The Two Friends, or, The Merchant of Lyon), a drama in five acts

Le Barbier de Séville, ou La Précaution inutile (The Barber of Seville, or, The Useless Precaution), a comedy in four acts

La folle journée, ou Le Mariage de Figaro (A Crazy Day, or, The Marriage of Figaro), a comedy in five acts

L'autre Tartuffe, ou La Mère coupable (The Other Tartuffe, or, The Guilty Mother), a drama in five acts

Opera

Tarare (Tarare), an opera in five acts

One-Act Plays (*Parades*)

Colin et Colette

Les Bottes de sept lieues (The Seven-League Boots)

Les Députés de la halle et du Gros-Caillou (The Delegates of the Market and of [the community of] Gros-Caillou)

Léandre, marchand d'agnus, médecin et bouquetière (Leander, the Vendor of Herbs, Medicines, and Flowers)

Jean Bête à le foire (John the Beast at the Market) [Note: The word *bête* can also mean "stupid" and is used as a pun in the title, which can be translated "Stupid John at the Market."]

Oeil pour oeil, dent pour dent (An Eye for an Eye, a Tooth for a Tooth)

NOTES

The epigraph to this book is from act 1, scene 6, *Le Barbier de Séville, ou La Précaution Inutile*, in Beaumarchais, *Oeuvres complètes de Beaumarchais* (Geneva, Switzerland: Éditions Famot, 1976), 52. Hereafter cited as *Oeuvres*. Unless otherwise noted, all translations from French works are my own.

1. We Must Help the Americans

1. Douglas Southall Freeman, *George Washington: A Biography*, 6 vols. (New York: Charles Scribner's Sons, 1954), 4:198, citing Reed Papers, New-York Historical Society.

2. Colonel Joseph Reed to George Washington, December 22, 1776, W. W. Abbott et al., eds., *The Papers of George Washington, Revolutionary War Series, June 1775–January 1779*, 18 vols. to date (Charlottesville: University of Virginia Press, 1984–present), 7:414–17. Hereafter cited as *PGW Rev.*

3. Henri Doniol, *Histoire de la participation de la France à l'établissement des États-Unis d'Amérique*, 5 vols., quarto (Paris: Imprimerie Nationale, 1886), 1:616.

4. Freeman, *Washington*, 4:194n.

5. GW to Lund Washington, September 30, 1776, *PGW Rev.* 6:82–87.

6. John Durand, ed., *Documents of the American Revolution* (New York: Henry Holt and Company, 1889), 22–23.

7. Louis de Loménie, *Beaumarchais and His Times: Sketches of French Society in the Eighteenth Century from Unpublished Documents*, trans. Henry S. Edwards (New York: Harper & Brothers, 1857), 266.

8. Doniol, *Histoire de la participation de la France*, 1:402–3.

9. *Journal et Mémoires du Marquis d'Argenson* (Paris: Ratheray, 1859), 1:325–26, 371–72; 4:131.

10. Jacques Brosse, ed., *Mémoires du Duc de Choiseul* (Paris: Mercure de France, 1987), 192–93.

11. Ibid., 198.

12. Ibid., 63.

13. Dinwiddie to GW, March 14, 1754, in W.W. Abbott and Dorothy Twohig, eds., *The Papers of George Washington, Colonial Series, 1748–August 1755*, 10 vols. (Charlottesville: University Press of Virginia, 1983–95), 1:75.

14. Donald Jackson and Dorothy Twohig, eds., *The Diaries of George Washington*, 6 vols. (Charlottesville: University Press of Virginia, 1976–79), 1:195.

15. Robert Douthat Meade, *Patrick Henry: Patriot in the Making* (Philadelphia and New York: J. B. Lippincott, 1957), 171.

16. Richard B. Morris, ed., *Encyclopedia of American History* (New York: Harper & Brothers, 1953), 74–75.

17. Edward S. Corwin, *French Policy and the American Alliance of 1778* (Princeton, N.J.: Princeton University Press, 1916; reprinted Gloucester, Mass.: Peter Smith, 1969), 42.

18. Frederich Kapp, *The Life of John Kalb, Major-General in the Revolutionary Army* (New York: Henry Holt and Company, 1884), 47.

19. Doniol, *Histoire de la participation de la France*, 1:84.

20. Ibid.

2. Gold by God! The Fuel of Life!

1. Georges Lemaitre, *Beaumarchais* (New York: Alfred A. Knopf, 1949), 8.

2. Loménie, *Beaumarchais and His Times*, 46.

3. Ibid., 49–51.

4. Ibid., 51.

5. Elizabeth S. Kite, *Beaumarchais and the War of American Independence* (Boston: Richard G. Badger, The Badger Press, 1918, 2 vols.), 1:51–52.

6. *Sieur Caron Fils* à *l'auteur du "Mercure," 15 novembre 1753*, in *Oeuvres*, 733–34.

7. Loménie, *Beaumarchais and His Times*, 54.

8. July 31, 1754, in ibid., 55.

9. Letter to *Mercure*, June 16, 1755, in Loménie, *Beaumarchais and His Times*, 54.

10. From a song entitled *Romance*, in *Oeuvres*, 813.

11. Loménie, *Beaumarchais and His Times*, 59n.

12. Jean-Jacques Rousseau, *The Basic Political Writings: Discourse on the Sciences and Arts, Discourse on the Origin of Inequality, Discourse on Political Economy, On the Social Contract*, trans. and ed. Donald A. Cress (Indianapolis: Hackett, 1987), 60.

13. Ibid., 141.

14. Unlike the piano, harp pedals raise the pitch of strings by semitones and whole tones. Until about 1720, harp strings were tuned diatonically. The introduction of the first pedal mechanism allowed the harpist to play sharps and flats. Beaumarchais's contribution marked one step in the instrument's gradual, century-long evolution into the modern double-action harp with seven pedals.

15. Refrain from *La gallerie des femmes du siècle passé*, in *Oeuvres*, 817.

16. Kite, *Beaumarchais and the War of American Independence*, 1:62–63.

17. Ibid.

18. Paul-Philippe Gudin de la Brenellerie, *Histoire de Beaumarchais: Mémoires iné-*

dits publiés sur les manuscrits originaux (Paris: Librairie Plon, 1888), cited in Loménie, *Beaumarchais and His Times*, 67.

19. Ibid., 68.

20. Ibid., 68–69.

21. Ibid.

22. Ibid., 69–70.

23. Kite, *Beaumarchais and the War of American Independence*, 1:78.

3. Last Night Poor, Wealthy Today!

1. Loménie, *Beaumarchais and His Times*, 78.

2. Ibid.

3. Kite, *Beaumarchais and the War of American Independence*, 1:83.

4. Ibid., 1:91.

5. Beaumarchais to André-Charles Caron, undated, in Loménie, *Beaumarchais and His Times*, 94ff.

6. Ibid.

7. Ibid.

8. Ibid.; emphasis in original.

9. Beaumarchais to André-Charles Caron, 1764, in Loménie, *Beaumarchais and His Times*, 104.

10. Caron de Beaumarchais to Geneviève Madeleine de Beaumarchais, formerly Lévêque, *née* Watebled, July 15, 1769, in Loménie, *Beaumarchais and His Times*, 133–34.

11. Cynthia Cox, *The Real Figaro: The Extraordinary Career of Caron de Beaumarchais* (New York: Coward-McCann, 1963), 38, 39.

12. Loménie, *Beaumarchais and His Times*, 171.

13. Ibid., 136.

14. *Boston Gazette*, March 12, 1770.

15. Charles F. Adams, ed., *The Works of John Adams, Second President of the United States: With a Life of the Author*, 10 vols. (Boston: Little, Brown & Company, 1850–56), 1:349–50.

16. Beaumarchais, *Le Barbier de Séville*, act 1, scene 2, in *Oeuvres*, 148.

17. Caron de Beaumarchais to Gudin de La Brenellerie, February 1773, in Loménie, *Beaumarchais and His Times*, 165–66.

18. Kite, *Beaumarchais and the War of American Independence*, 1:188–89.

19. Ibid.

20. Ibid., 1:172.

21. De la Vrillière to Sartines, March 1773, in Loménie, *Beaumarchais and His Times*, 166.

4. So You Mistreat Some Poor Devil...
Till He Trembles in Disgrace!

1. Caron de Beaumarchais to Sartine, March 11, 1773, in Kite, *Beaumarchais and the War of American Independence*, 1:197–98.

2. Constant to Beaumarchais, in Loménie, *Beaumarchais and His Times*, 170.

3. Beaumarchais to Constant, in ibid., 171.

4. Beaumarchais to Mme. d'Étioles, March 4, 1773, in ibid., 170–71.

5. Beaumarchais, *Le Barbier de Séville*, act 5, scene 2, in *Oeuvres*, 223.

6. Beaumarchais to the duc de la Vrillière, March 21, 1773, Loménie, *Beaumarchais and His Times*, 169.

7. Kite, *Beaumarchais and the War of American Independence*, 1:211.

8. *Oeuvres*, 351.

9. Ibid., 387.

10. Ibid.

11. Ibid., 365–66.

12. Ibid., 367–72.

13. Loménie, *Beaumarchais and His Times*, 194.

14. Ibid.

15. Loménie, *Beaumarchais and His Times*, 198–99.

16. Kite, *Beaumarchais and the War of American Independence*, 1:242.

17. Ibid.

18. Ibid., 1:243.

19. Ibid., 1:243–44.

20. Ibid., 1:244.

21. Ibid., 1:246.

22. Ibid., 1:198. In fact, Jeanne Bécu was the illegitimate daughter of a domestic of the treasurer of the province of Lorraine. Sent to a convent for her education, she followed her mother into domestic service, but at seventeen left the convent to work as a sales girl in an elegant shop for high-fashion women's clothes on the rue Saint-Honore in Paris. She caught the eye of a playboy and patron of the arts from Toulouse, Jean-Baptiste du Barry, who was known as Le Roué (a rake) and, not surprisingly, took her as his mistress. After teaching her basics of art, music, and literature, he presented her to the Maréchal Richelieu, a great nephew of the cardinal, and he, in turn, arranged for Louis XV's chief valet to present her to the king.

23. Lemaitre, *Beaumarchais*, 137.

24. Loménie, *Beaumarchais and His Times*, 210.

25. Kite, *Beaumarchais and the War of American Independence*, 1:255.

5. I'm the Busiest, Cleverest Fellow I Know

1. Loménie, *Beaumarchais and His Times*, 214.

2. Ibid., 215.

3. Ibid., 217–222.

4. Ibid.

5. Refrain from *Robin*, in *Oeuvres*, 816.

6. Bazile, *Le Barbier de Séville*, act 2, scene 8, in *Oeuvres*, 156.

7. Loménie, *Beaumarchais and His Times*, 252.

8. Kite, 1:292–93.

9. Figaro, *Le Barbier de Séville*, act 1, scene 2, in *Oeuvres*, 149.

10. M. de Flassan, *Histoire générale et raisonnée de la diplomatie française depuis la fondation de la monarchie jusqu'à la fin du règne de Louis XVI*, 7 vols. (Paris, 1809), 5:454.

11. Loménie, *Beaumarchais and His Times*, 233–34.

12. Kite, *Beaumarchais and the War of American Independence*, 1:38.

13. GW to John Hancock, August 4, 1775, *PGW Rev.* 1:223–39.

14. Doniol, *Histoire de la participation de la France*, 1:84.

15. Ibid., 232.

16. Doniol, *Histoire de la participation de la France*, 1:377.

17. Loménie, *Beaumarchais and His Times*, 226.

18. Ibid., 231; Frederic Gaillardet, *Mémoires sur la chevalière d'Eon : La Verité sur les mystères de sa vie* (Paris: E. Dentu, 1866), 257ff.

19. Ibid., 236.

20. Kite, *Beaumarchais and the War of American Independence*, 2:25.

21. Ibid., 238.

22. Ibid., 242–43.

23. Loménie, *Beaumarchais and His Times*, 243.

24. D'Eon died in 1810; a post-mortem examination stated, "I certify by the present that I have examined and dissected the body of the Chevalier d'Eon . . . and that I found the male organs of generation perfectly formed in every respect. May 23, 1810. Thos. Copeland, surgeon." Cited in Loménie, *Beaumarchais and His Times*, 225n.

6. Plotting and Pocketing

1. Burton J. Hendrick, *The Lees of Virginia: Biography of a Family* (Boston: Little Brown, 1935), 229.

2. Ibid., 231.

3. Loménie, *Beaumarchais and His Times*, 266.

4. Doniol, *Histoire de la participation de la France*, 1:407.

5. Morris, *Encyclopedia*, 88.

6. Doniol, *Histoire de la participation de la France*, 1:368–69.

7. GW to the Cherokee Indians, October 1757, GWP, C01.5:27–28.

8. Edmund Burke, *First Speech on the Conciliation with America and American Taxation before Parliament*, April 19, 1774.

9. From "A Friend to America" to GW, November 20, 1775, PGW Rev. 2:404–5.

10. John Dickinson was a Congressman from Pennsylvania, Benjamin Harrison from Virginia, John Jay from New York, and Thomas Johnson from Maryland.

11. Doniol, *Histoire de la participation de la France*, 1:267, 289–90. For the entire text, see ibid., 267, 287–92.

12. Durand, *Documents*, 59–73.

13. Doniol, *Histoire de la participation de la France*, 1:243–49.

14. Ibid.

15. Ibid.

16. Loménie, *Beaumarchais and His Times*, 273.

17. Doniol, *Histoire de la participation de la France*, 1:240–48.

7. I Wish to Serve Your Country as if It Were My Own

1. Francis Wharton, *The Revolutionary Diplomatic Correspondence of the United States, Edited under Direction of Congress, with preliminary index, and notes historical and legal*, 6 vols. (Washington, D.C.: Government Printing Office, 1889), 1:367.

2. Doniol, *Histoire de la participation de la France*, 1:240–48.

3. Durand, *Documents*, 90.

4. Ibid., 2:98.

5. Kite, *Beaumarchais and the War of American Independence*, 2:100.

6. Ibid.; *PGW Rev.*, 7:414–17, Colonel Joseph Reed to George Washington, December 22, 1776.

7. Wharton, *Revolutionary Diplomatic Correspondence*, 2:97.

8. Ibid., 2:78.

9. Ibid., 78–79.

10. Kite, *Beaumarchais and the War of American Independence*, 2:84–85.

11. Ibid., 86–87.

12. Loménie, *Beaumarchais and His Times*, 279.

13. Ibid., 295.

14. Ibid.

15. Deane to Beaumarchais, July 20, 1776, Wharton, *Revolutionary Diplomatic Correspondence*, 2:102.

16. Durand, *Documents*, 97.

17. Deane to Beaumarchais, July 24, 1776, Wharton, *Revolutionary Diplomatic Correspondence*, 2:105.

18. Wharton, *Revolutionary Diplomatic Correspondence*, 2:129–31.

19. Ibid., 2:201–2.

20. Beaumarchais to Vergennes, October 14, 1776, Kite, *Beaumarchais and the War of American Independence*, 2:112–13.

21. Beaumarchais to Vergennes, September 21, 1776, Doniol, *Histoire de la participation de la France*, 1:519–20.

22. Loménie, *Beaumarchais and His Times*, 291.

8. Figaro Here, Figaro There . . .

1. Loménie, *Beaumarchais and His Times*, 292–93.

2. Beaumarchais to Vergennes, February 3, 1777, Doniol, *Histoire de la participation de la France*, 2:359–60.

3. Ibid., 293, 293n.

4. Brian N. Morton and Donald C. Spinelli, *Beaumarchais and the American Revolution* (Lanham, Md.: Lexington Books, 2003), 120.

5. GW to John Augustine Washington, November 6–19, 1776, *PGW Rev.* 7:102–5.

6. Colonel Joseph Reed to George Washington, December 22, 1776, in ibid., 7:414–17.

7. Wharton, *Revolutionary Diplomatic Correspondence*, 2:248–51.

8. Kite, *Beaumarchais and the War of American Independence*, 2:124.

9. Ibid., 111 (citing *Correspondence and Public Papers of John Jay*, 1890, p. 97).

· 10. Ibid., 110.

11. Ibid.

12. Lemaitre, *Beaumarchais*, 230–31.

13. Ibid., 139.

14. Ibid., 140–41.

15. Ibid. 141.

16. Kite, *Beaumarchais and the War of American Independence*, 2:162.

17. Ibid., 167.

18. Ibid., 147–48.

19. Kite, *Beaumarchais and the War of American Independence*, 2:156.

20. Ibid., 188–89.

21. Vergennes to the President of Congress, March 25, 1778, Wharton, *Revolutionary Diplomatic Correspondence*, 2:519.

22. Kite, *Beaumarchais and the War of American Independence*, 2:191.

23. Ibid., 2:186–93.

24. William Carmichael to Beaumarchais, September 3, 1778, Kite, 2:196–97.

25. Beaumarchais to Francy, December 20, 1777, Loménie, *Beaumarchais and His Times*, 298–302.

26. Franklin and Deane to Committee of Secret Correspondence, March 12, 1777, Wharton, *Revolutionary Diplomatic Correspondence*, 2:283–90.

27. Lemaitre, *Beaumarchais*, 252.

28. John Jay to Beaumarchais, Durand, *Documents*, 134.

29. *Mémoire justificative à la cour de Londres*, 1779, in *Oeuvres*, 582–92.

30. Loménie, *Beaumarchais and His Times*, 353.

9. Bright People Are So Stupid

1. Kite, *Beaumarchais and the War of American Independence*, 2:246.

2. Ibid., 203.

3. In 1789, Deane boarded a ship bound for the United States, but died under mysterious circumstances before the ship left port. An 1846 congressional audit of his affairs found him not only innocent of embezzlement but due a considerable sum from the government.

4. Kite, *Beaumarchais and the War of American Independence*, 2:203.

5. *La Folle Journée ou Le Mariage de Figaro*, act 1, scene 1, in *Oeuvres*, 189–90.

6. Lemaitre, *Beaumarchais*, 274.

7. Ibid., 275.

8. *Le Mariage de Figaro*, act 5, scene 3, in *Oeuvres*, 223.

9. Ibid.

10. *Le Barbier de Séville*, act 1, scene 2, in *Oeuvres*, 149.

11. *Le Mariage de Figaro*, act 5, scene 19, in *Oeuvres*, 230.

12. Loménie, *Beaumarchais and His Times*, 278.

13. Edmund Burke, *Reflections on the Revolution in France* (1790), in *The Collected Works of the Right Honourable Edmund Burke* (London: C. Rivington, 1801).

14. *Le Mariage de Figaro*, act 3, scene 8, in *Oeuvres*, 210.

15. Loménie, *Beaumarchais and His Times*, 381.

16. Kite, *Beaumarchais and the War of American Independence*, 2:220.

17. Ibid., 223.

18. Beaumarchais "aux auteurs du Journal de Paris," August 12, 1784, in *Oeuvres*, 770–71.

19. Loménie, *Beaumarchais and His Times*, 386.

20. Ibid., 387.

21. Ibid., 388.

22. Born in Vienna, Christoph Willibald Gluck (1714–1787) composed more than one hundred operas, eleven symphonies, and other works.

23. Born in Verona, Antonio Salieri (1750–1825) composed forty operas.

24. Loménie, *Beaumarchais and His Times*, 408.

25. Ibid., 407.

26. James Anderson, *The Harper Dictionary of Opera and Operetta* (New York: HarperCollins, 1989), 561.

27. *Tarare*, act 4, scene 10, in *Oeuvres*, 264.

28. Loménie, *Beaumarchais and His Times*, 408.

29. Joseph Vernet (1714–1789) admired the works of Poussin and Lorraine and produced a variety of paintings that include sweeping landscapes with equally sweeping views of Rome and Naples.

30. Jefferson to Jay, September 23, 1789, in Unger, *Lafayette*, 248.

31. Kite, *Beaumarchais and the War of American Independence*, 2:243–45.

32. Beatrix Cary Davenport, ed., *A Diary of the French Revolution by Gouverneur Morris (1752–1816), Minister to France during the Terror*, 2 vols. (Boston: Houghton Mifflin, 1939), 1:158–59.

33. Brand Whitlock, *La Fayette* (New York: D. Appleton, 1929, 2 vols.), 1:329.

10. What Did You Do to Earn So Many Rewards?

1. *Le Mariage de Figaro*, act 5, scene 3, in *Oeuvres*, 223.

2. Figaro, *Le Mariage de Figaro*, act 5, scene 19, in *Oeuvres*, 230.

3. Loménie, *Beaumarchais and His Times*, 414.

4. Kite, 2:248–49.

5. Ibid., 240–41.

6. Ibid., 250.

7. Ibid., 251.

8. Davenport, 1:252.

9. Kite, *Beaumarchais and the War of American Independence*, 2:252.

10. Loménie, *Beaumarchais and His Times*, 422.

11. Harlow G. Unger, *Lafayette* (Hoboken, N.J.: John Wiley & Sons, 2002), 293.

12. Loménie, *Beaumarchais and His Times*, 417–18.

13. Kite, *Beaumarchais and the War of American Independence*, 2:255–56.

14. *Le Mariage de Figaro*, act 5, scene 3, in *Oeuvres*, 224.

15. Kite, *Beaumarchais and the War of American Independence*, 2:256–57. (*Sans culottes*: French Revolution radicals, noted for wearing long pants of coarse homespun instead of the knee-breeches and hose that aristocrats and their servants wore.)

16. Ibid., 2:257.

17. Arguably, the lyrics can be translated as follows: "All will be well when we hang the 'aristos' [slang for 'aristocrats'] from the lampposts; all will be well when we hang them all." A street singer is said to have written the words to *Ça ira* in the spring of 1790 to the music of a then popular dance. Originally meant as a patriotic tribute to

constitutional rule, revolutionaries perverted it into a terrifying chant that became more popular than *La Marseillaise* and, in fact, was played before the curtains rose in all theaters until Napoleon came to power.

18. Kite, *Beaumarchais and the War of American Independence*, 2:264.

11. *Tout finit par des chansons* / Everything Ends in Song

1. Lemaitre, *Beaumarchais*, 331–32.
2. Ibid., 205.
3. Kite, *Beaumarchais and the War of American Independence*, 2:263.
4. Loménie, *Beaumarchais and His Times*, 441.
5. *Le Mariage de Figaro*, act 3, scene 4, in *Oeuvres*, 208.
6. Loménie, *Beaumarchais and His Times*, 448.

12. All of Which Proves That a Son of a Clod Can Be Worth His Weight in Gold

1. Loménie, *Beaumarchais and His Times*, 456–57.
2. Kite, *Beaumarchais and the War of American Independence*, 2:246.
3. *American Heritage*, May–June 2000.
4. Durand, *Documents*, 267–72.
5. Figaro, *Le Mariage de Figaro*, act 5, scene 19, in *Oeuvres*, 230.

BIBLIOGRAPHY

Abbott, W. W., and Dorothy Twohig, eds. *The Papers of George Washington, Colonial Series, 1748–August 1755.* 10 vols. Charlottesville: University Press of Virginia, 1983–95.

Abbott, W. W., Dorothy Twohig, Philander D. Chase, and Theodore J. Crackel, eds. *The Papers of George Washington, Revolutionary War Series, June 1775–January 1779.* 18 vols. Charlottesville: University of Virginia Press, 1984–.

Alden, John R. *A History of the American Revolution.* New York: Alfred A. Knopf, 1969.

Argenson. *Journal et mémoires du marquis d'Argenson.* Paris: Ratheray, 1859.

Beaumarchais. *Oeuvres complètes de Beaumarchais.* Geneva, Switzerland: Éditions Famot, 1976.

Bobrick, Benson. *Angel in the Whirlwind: The Triumph of the American Revolution.* New York: Simon & Schuster, 1997.

Bodin, Soulange. *La Diplomacie de Louis XV et le Pacte de Famille.* Paris, 1894.

Brosse, Jacques, ed. *Mémoires du duc de Choiseul.* Paris: Mercure de France, 1987.

Burke, Edmund. *The Collected Works of the Right Honourable Edmund Burke.* London: C. Rivington, 1801.

———. *Speeches and Letters on American Affairs.* London: Everyman's Library, 1942.

Corwin, Edward S. *French Policy and the American Alliance of 1778.* Princeton, N.J.: Princeton University Press, 1916; reprint, Gloucester, Mass.: Peter Smith, 1969.

Cox, Cynthia. *The Real Figaro: The Extraordinary Career of Caron de Beaumarchais.* New York: Coward-McCann, 1963.

Doniol, Henri. *Histoire de la participation de la France à l'établissement des États-Unis d'Amérique.* 5 vols., quarto. Paris: Imprimerie Nationale, 1886.

Durand, John, ed., *Documents of the American Revolution.* New York: Henry Holt and Company, 1889.

Fierro, Albert. *Dictionnaire du Paris disparu.* Paris: Editions Parigramme; reprint, CPL, 1998.

Flassan, M. de. *Histoire générale et raisonée de la diplomatie française depuis la fondation de la monarchie jusqu'à la fin du règne de Louis XVI.* 7 vols. Paris, 1811.

Freeman, Douglas Southall. *George Washington: A Biography.* 6 vols. New York: Charles Scribner's Sons, 1954.

Gaillardet, Frederic. *Memoires sur la chevaliere d'Eon: La Verité sur les mysteres de sa vie d'apres des document authentiques.* Paris: E. Dentu, Librairie-Editeur, 1866.

Hendrick, Burton J. *The Lees of Virginia: Biography of a Family.* Boston: Little, Brown, 1935.

Jackson, Donald, and Dorothy Twohig, eds. *The Diaries of George Washington.* 6 vols. Charlottesville: University Press of Virginia, 1976–79.

Kapp, Frederich. *The Life of John Kalb, Major-General in the Revolutionary Army.* New York: Henry Holt and Company, 1884.

Kite, Elizabeth S. *Beaumarchais and the War of American Independence.* 2 vols. Boston: Richard G. Badger, The Badger Press, 1918.

Lancaster, Bruce. *From Lexington to Liberty: The Story of the American Revolution.* Garden City, N.Y.: Doubleday, 1955.

Lemaitre, Georges. *Beaumarchais.* New York: Alfred A. Knopf, 1949.

Lintilhac, Eugène. *Beaumarchais et ses oeuvres.* Paris, 1887.

Loménie, Louis de. *Beaumarchais et son temps: Études sur la société en France au XVIIIe siècle.* 2 vols. Paris: Michel Lévy frères, 1856.

———. *Beaumarchais and His Times: Sketches of French Society in the Eighteenth Century from Unpublished Documents.* Trans. Henry S. Edwards. New York: Harper & Brothers, 1857.

Matthews, Brander, ed., *The Chief European Dramatists: Twenty-One Plays from the Drama of Greece, Rome, Spain, France, Italy, Germany, Denmark, and Norway from 500 B.C. to 1879 A.D.* Boston: Houghton Mifflin, 1916.

Meade, Robert Douthat. *Patrick Henry: Patriot in the Making.* Philadelphia and New York: J. B. Lippincott, 1957.

Métra, François, et al. *Correspondance secrète, politique et littéraire.* 18 vols. London, 1787–90.

Morris, Gouverneur. *A Diary of the French Revolution by Gouverneur Morris (1752–1816), Minister to France during the Terror,* ed. Beatrix Cary Davenport. 2 vols. Boston: Houghton Mifflin, 1939.

Morris, Richard B., ed. *Encyclopedia of American History.* New York: Harper & Brothers, 1953.

Morton, Brian N., and Donald C. Spinelli. *Beaumarchais and the American Revolution.* Lanham, Md.: Lexington Books, 2003.

Racine, *Phaedra,* trans. Robert Lowell; Beaumarchais, *Figaro's Marriage,* trans. Jacques Barzun. New York: Farrar, Strauss and Cudahy, 1961.

Tulard, Jean, Jean-François Fayard, and Alfred Fierro. *Histoire et dictionnaire de la Révolution Française, 1789–1799.* Paris: Robert Laffont, 1987.

Unger, Harlow Giles. *The French War against America: How a Trusted Ally Be-*

trayed Washington and the Founding Fathers. Hoboken, N.J.: John Wiley & Sons, 2005.

———. *Lafayette.* Hoboken, N.J.: John Wiley & Sons, 2002.

———. *The Unexpected George Washington: His Private Life.* Hoboken, N.J.: John Wiley & Sons, 2006.

Wharton, Francis. *The Revolutionary Diplomatic Correspondence of the United States, Edited under Direction of Congress, with preliminary index, and notes historical and legal. Published in conformity with Act of Congress of August 13, 1888.* 6 vols. Washington, D.C.: Government Printing Office, 1889.

Whitlock, Brand. *La Fayette.* 2 vols. New York: D. Appleton, 1929.

Reference Works

Anderson, James. *The Harper Dictionary of Opera and Operetta.* New York: HarperCollins, 1989.

Bartlett, John, and Justin Kaplan, eds. *Familiar Quotations.* 16th ed. Boston: Little, Brown, 1992.

Boatner, Mark May, III. *Encyclopedia of the American Revolution.* New York: David McKay, 1966.

Morris, Richard B., ed. *Encyclopedia of American History.* New York: Harper & Brothers, 1953.

Le Petit Robert des Noms Propres. Paris: Dictionnaires Le Robert, 1994.

INDEX

Library of Congress Cataloging-in-Publication Data

Unger, Harlow G., 1931–

Improbable patriot : the secret history of Monsieur
de Beaumarchais, the French playwright who saved the
American Revolution / Harlow Giles Unger.

   p. cm.

Includes bibliographical references and index.

ISBN 978-1-58465-925-9 (cloth : alk. paper)

ISBN 978-1-61168-216-8 (e-book)

1. Beaumarchais, Pierre Augustin Caron de, 1732–1799.

2. Dramatists, French — 18th century — Biography.

3. Diplomats — France — Biography.   4. France —
History — 18th century.   5. United States — History —
Revolution, 1775–1783 — Participation, French.   I. Title.

PQ1956.U54   2011

842'.5 — dc22

[B]

2011014242